BOOK SYNOPSIS

This leadership manual ministers deliverance and healing to past, present, and emerging leaders, while providing wisdom and tools, for maintaining and sustaining as a healthy leader that effectively revolutionize current and further generations. This leadership manual takes the leader on a transforming spiritual journey that:

- Examines the characteristics of wounded versus healthy leaders.
- Explores the impact wounded and healthy leaders have on those they lead, the ministry, the body of Christ, and the world at large.
- Provides deliverance and healing tools that allows you to break free of demonic strongholds, cleanse from the enemy's unhealthiness, while being equipped to bringing sustaining deliverance and healing to others.
- Brings deliverance and healing to wounded leaders and those wounded by leaders.
- Provides tools for restoration and balance in ministry, as the leader is transformed and SHIFTED into a new revived stature of wellness in God.
- Equips leaders with wisdom and tools needed to deal with and bypass woundness.
- Provides revelation of how to seek God in preaching biblical truth, repentance, conviction, and holiness without compromising, belittling, abusing, or further breeding anti-church and anti-Christ mentalities into people and society.
- Imparts revelation concerning the need for counselors and counseling centers in ministries, while releasing tools needed to further equip believers to live a healthy life.
- Provides revelation on the importance of creating and living through a God ordained vision plan for the leader's life and ministry; provides examples for writing vision plans for one's personal life, family, ministry, respite, healing, restoration when wounded or deliverance from sin and character flaws, etc.
- Strengthens the leaders revelation and relationship with God, where they do not just experience him, but live in him.

The Leader will be empowered, transform, and equipped by adding this manual to their arsenal. It is a weapon that sets leaders free, and annihilates the enemy's plan to bring reproach upon the church and God, where people rebel against the church, God, and eternal life with him.

Healing The Wounded Leader
TaquettaBaker@Kingdomshifters.com
(Website) Kingdomshifters.com
Connect with Taquetta via Facebook or YouTube

Copyright 2017 – Kingdom Shifters Ministries

All rights reserved. This book is protected by the copyright laws of the United States of America. This book may not be reprinted for commercial gain or profit. The use of occasional page copying for personal or group study is permitted and encouraged. Permission will be granted upon request.

Taquetta's Bio

Taquetta Baker is the founder of Kingdom Shifters Ministries (KSM). She has authored fourteen books and two decree CD's. Taquetta has a Master's Degree in Community Counseling with an emphasis on Marriage, Children and Family Counseling, a Bachelor's Degree in Psychology and Associates Degree in Business Administration. In addition, Taquetta has a Therapon Belief Therapist Certification from Therapon Institute and has 22 years of professional and Christian Counseling experience.

Taquetta is also gifted at empowering and assisting people with launching ministries, businesses and books and provides mentoring, counseling and vision casting through Kingdom Shifters Kingdom Wellness Program. Taquetta serves on the Board of Directors for New Day Community Ministries, Inc. of Muncie, IN. In October 2008, Taquetta graduated from the Eagles Dance Institute under Dr. Pamela Hardy and received her license in the area of liturgical dance. Before launching into her own ministry, Taquetta served at her previous church for 12 years. She was a prophet, pioneer and leader of Shekinah Expressions Dance Ministry, teacher, member of the presbytery board, and overseer of the Altar Workers Ministry. Taquetta receives mentoring and ministry covering from Bishop Jackie Green, Founder of JGM-National PrayerLife Institute (Phoenix, AZ), and was ordained as an Apostle on June 7, 2014.

Taquetta flows through the wells of warfare and worship and mantles an apostolic mandate of judging and establishing God's kingdom in people, ministries, communities, and regions. Taquetta travels in foreign missions and throughout the United States. She has mentored and established dance, altar workers, deliverance, and prophetic ministries. Taquetta ministers in the areas of fine arts, all manners of prayer, fivefold ministry, deliverance, healing, miracles, atmospheric worship, and empowers and train people in their destiny and life's vision.

Connect with Taquetta and KSM at kingdomshifters.com or via Facebook. For more information regarding Bishop Jackie Green at Jgmenternational.org.

Forward
BY: Bishop Dr. Jackie L. Green
Founder & Overseer of JGM Enternational, Redlands, CA

I WAS DEEPLY HONORED TO BE ASKED TO WRITE A FORWARD FOR <u>**'HEALING THE WOUNDED LEADER.**</u>

I WAS TRULY AMAZED AT THE WISDOM THAT FLOWS FROM APOSTLE TAQUETTA BAKER AND THE DEPTH OF EXPERIENCE SHE BRINGS TO THE BODY OF CHRIST. I MUST SAY THE BOOK IS RICH WITH HEALING STRATEGIES FROM THE THRONEROOM OF GOD.

I PARTICULARLY WAS MINISTERED TO IN THE SECTION BELOW:

"The dysfunctional functioning leader can operate in woundedness for years with minimal to no consequences. This is mainly because the dysfunctional functioning leader often has people around them that mask their wounds. Often such leaders have "fixers" around them that help them conceal sin issues and wounds. At times, the fixer is their spouse, children, close confidant, armor bearers, team members, and even overseers. Moreover, the higher the platform, the less likely that wounded leader will adhere to truth about the dysfunction they operate in, and their need for help. "

I believe God is going to use this book to heal the "dysfunctional functioning leaders" all across America, and even in the government and Hollywood today in our nation.

The book addresses some tough issues of Kingdom advancement and what it will look like to uproot the world systems and usher in the Kingdom of God.

The author says: *"God does not want the world's seven idolatrous mountains. He wants to either destroy them or establish his kingdom in their midst so souls can be drawn out of those areas to his light and salvation. I WILL SAY IT AGAIN! God does not want any idolatrous systems. He does not want Hollywood. He does not want the demonic market place. He either wants demolish it or establish his kingdom within it, so he can draw souls to eternal life with him. Truth is, many Christians do not want to demolish Hollywood, because they want fame and fortune. "*

This book could be considered a "textbook for leading a healthy and whole Christian life." This book exalts Jesus Christ and honors the Holy Spirit which is where our true healing will come. Finally, this book will bring balance to the healing process for the wounded leader, wounded church, wounded rich and famous, and the wounded family and our wounded government (those in high places) and our troubled society. There is a generation that will live and recover, even the generations yet unborn, that will be healed and set free because of the boldness, clarity, experience, training in counseling, discernment and love of God that propelled the finishing of this excellent work!

Forward
Written By: Nina Cook
Elder & Rising Leader at Kingdom Shifters Ministries, Muncie, IN

This manual on healing the wounded leader is a vast, massive treasure chest of much needed revelation, wisdom, and life experience that will impart, plant, and produce life changing practices into the lives of many. The value and the wealth is so rich in each chapter, because it is not just good information, it gives step by step instructionst on how to apply, and walk out the different processes of healing, deliverance, and transformation that you may undergo as a leader. The tangibility of each personal experience that is shared reaches into your life and snatches you up to a new level of breakthrough in the situations and circumstances that you may be in because of the victory the author shares through her own experiences as a leader. It is a source of elevation. The more she shares and the more the manual unveils, the more you feel the elevation, uplifting, and empowering that is pouring from it. It makes the very demanding, and immense, yet, rewarding call to leadership seem possible to bare, and be excellent in the power of Jesus, and the exertion of his word in your life. It is a restorer of hope and faith within itself, and a source of healing even as you read it.

This manual will literally carry you to the next level as a leader as you engage in all that is revealed, and allow God to work in your life. As a rising leader I am immensely appreciative of a manual like this, because it will save me so much heartache and pain, and rescue me from making many mistakes that can be avoided because of the wisdom that is revealed here. It is one of a kind, because not many are concerned about the well- being of the leaders, and who is feeding the body of Christ, and being exemplified as examples of Christ. This gives me a true depiction of the heart, character, and nature of what Godly leaders should look like. While also giving me a roadmap for many of the challenges that are inevitable in the life of a leader. It gives me direction for how to take care of myself as a leader so that I can remain healthy in the totality of my life, and as I impact and influence the lives of those whom God sends to my care. It teaches what a healthy leader looks like, and how to walk with God in relationship as he processes me through seasons where healing, rest, deliverance, and restoration is needed, all from the perspective of abiding and living inside of God.

There is a depiction of leaders that is constantly displayed in and out of the church where the leader is seen as always being strong, perfect, and always giving, giving, and giving and not receiving. And as a growing leader I have been plagued and influenced by these same mindsets. I thought that it was important for me to be perfect, know everything and be able to answer all questions even my own, and always be the giver. But, through the revelation in this manual I have learned that being a leader is about through my relationship and sold out lifestyle to God, flowing through Jesus in me to help guide, counsel, cover, and etc. those who he entrusts me with. It has taken a load of lies and false burdens off of me, whew! Being a leader is about being trusted with the lives of others, because my life is solely and purely rooted in dying to myself so that God's will is done in the lives of those that I touch. And since dying is not easy, there will be times where wounds and hurts will inflict my life. But, this manual teaches me that it is ok to be hurt and it is ok to be wounded because this is evidence of the call, but do not stay there, as this is evidence of dropping and aborting the call; Being diverted by the wounds rather than learning and being further positioned in the fulfilling of destiny due to the wounds. Jesus' continual wounds and eventual death on the cross further aligned him in the fulfilling of his God ordained purpose and destiny, but he did not stay there, he rose and completed the work. As a rising leader I have received a resurrection impartation, that whatever wounds and hurts I undergo as a leader I have the wisdom, lessons, revelation, and power to keep rising over and over and over and over again and complete the work granted to me as God's chosen leader, HEALED and whole.

TABLE OF CONTENTS

Forward:	Jackie Green & Nina Cook
Dedication:	Page 1
Chapter 1:	Introduction To The Wounded Spirit 2
Chapter 2:	Reasons Leaders Are Unhealed 5
Chapter 3:	Characteristics Of The Wounded Leader 11
Chapter 4:	Spiritual Cleansing: Maintaining Deliverance & Healing 16
Chapter 5:	The People's Choice 28
Chapter 6:	The Dysfunctional Functioning Leader 33
Chapter 7:	Challenging Oppressions That Inflict Wounds 38
Chapter 8:	When God Requires You To Minister Wounded 67
Chapter 9:	Abiding In Christ Decree 77
Chapter 10:	Dismantling Wounds of Betrayal 80
Chapter 11:	Moses! The Deliverer Needed Deliverance 90
Chapter 12:	Sampson! The Immature Careless Leader 92
Chapter 13:	Deliverance From The Fixer Spirit 96
Chapter 14:	Discerning Unhealed Areas of Testimonies 101
Chapter 15:	Embracing Process As Lifestyle 109
Chapter 16:	Restoring Counseling In The Body Of Christ 113
Chapter 17:	Counseling Versus Mentoring 118
Chapter 18:	Characteristics Of A Healthy Leader 124
Chapter 19:	Leader! Be Thou Made Whole 132
Chapter 20:	Reviving The Wounded Leader 136
Chapter 21:	Balance Respite For The Leader 140
Chapter 22:	Suggestions For Taking Time To Rest 149
Chapter 23:	Balancing Family And Ministry 153
Chapter 24:	Dealing With Sin Struggles As They Surface 156
Chapter 25:	Dealing With Wounds As They Surface 158
Chapter 26:	Writing Successful Vision Plan 163
Chapter 27:	Vision Plan For The Wounded Leader 172
Chapter 28:	Prayer For Breaking Religious Fears & Control 179
Chapter 29:	Deliverance From The False Gospel 185
Chapter 30:	Leaving & Cleaving Ministries 187
Chapter 31:	Deliverance From The Wounded Leaders 199
Chapter 32:	Restoring Relationships After Deliverance 206
Chapter 33:	Healthy Relationship Nuggets 208
Chapter 34:	The Art Of Accountability 215
Chapter 35:	Wise Preaching 219
Chapter 36:	The Leader's Remnant 229
Chapter 37:	Understanding Platforms 239
Chapter 38:	Healing The Rich & Famous 251

DEDICATION

This manual is dedicated to
- Wounded leaders who were wounded by other wounded leaders.
- Believers who have been wounded and abused by leaders.
- Good Leaders who are experiencing warfare, persecution, and betrayal, because of the impact wounded and false leaders have had on the lives of people, ministries, the body of Christ, and the world.
- Leaders who are striving to be, and desire to be healthy Godly leaders.
- Leaders who desire wisdom and tools for being healthy Godly leaders.

On behalf of every leader that has ever hurt you, abused you, taken advantage of you, not discerned who you are in God, stifled who you are in God, disappointed you, failed you, betrayed you, I would like to stand as a proxy leader and apologize. I see your pain and I am sooooooooo sooooo sorry. I see that your pain, rebellion, and anti-Christ mentality is not all your fault. That some of it was bred in you by religion, unhealthy and false leaders, error in applying God's word, error in preaching styles and delivery, religious abuse disguised as God's word, prophecy, wrath, and judgement. I repent for every wrong doing conducted against you by leaders and the church. I ask that you to humbly forgive us as leaders, for not being the example of God we should have been and should be, and even for not being quickly repentive of our error that caused you pain. I ask that you resist being like us, and allow God to heal you. Do not breed what we put in you. Forgive us and use this manual to let God heal you, heal your calling, and equip you to being a healthy leader that is a true example of God's glory.

I decree that as you take your pain to God and choose to forgive, that deliverance and healing will be your portion in Jesus name. I decree as you use this manual to allow God to further process you to wholeness, that each page will equip you with supernatural power to preach biblical truth without abusing people, and that you draw souls to true converted salvation, deliverance and healing, proclaim the gospel of Jesus boldly fam signs and wounders following, while tangibly establishing God's name, identity, will, plan, and kingdom in the earth.

Go forth and know that God has chosen you, and is with you. His presense will be evident as you are transformed into a trailblazing, curse breaking, demon busting, healthy leader. SHIFT!

INTRODUCTION: THE WOUNDED SPIRIT

Chapter 1

Proverbs 18:14 *The spirit of a man will sustain his infirmity; but a wounded spirit who can bear?*

The Amplified Bible reads: *The strong spirit of a man sustains him in bodily pain or trouble, but a weak and broken spirit who can raise up or bear?*

The Message Bible states: *A healthy spirit conquers adversity, but what can you do when the spirit is crushed?*

When a wound occurs, there is an actual tear, puncture, strike, damage or trauma to the impacted area. When our spirit is wounded it's literally *"smitten, afflicted(troubled, grievous, in pain), it is broken (ruptured, fractured), stricken, injured, damaged (Strong's Concordance)."*

When a leader has a wounded spirit and does not seek healing, he or she is putting the burden of their woundedness upon those they oversee. The leader is expecting the people to bear the pain, hurt, strongholds, sins, offenses, and consequences of them being unhealed.

As leaders our wounds can come from different places. We can have
- Unresolved issues from the past
- Challenges, struggles and wounds due to experiences, strongholds, and trial in our personal lives
- Woundedness by those we are called to continually minister to and heal

This is all compact by the wounds that we encounter from warfare due to being the leader and vision carrier of the ministry, and from walking in destiny and in obedience with God.

The body of Christ has given the mindset that leaders are to sacrifice their own healing for the sake of God, the ministry, and the people. Yet this is not biblical and definitely has caused a great falling away in the body of Christ.

Ecclesiastes 3:3 contends that there is *"A time to kill, and a time to heal; a time to break down, and a time to build up."*

<u>Heal</u> is *raphah* in the Hebrew and means:
1. to mend (by stitching), i.e.
2. (figuratively) to cure, to (cause to) heal

3. to be healed by or likened unto a physician
4. to repair, thoroughly, make whole, make healthful

Jesus' main purpose for coming as the Messiah was to deliver, heal, cure, mend our relationship with God, and restore eternal life. He came for all people, including leaders. Being leaders does not exempt us from needing deliverance, healing, empowerment, and continual communing and refreshing with the Lord.

> *Proverbs 11:25 says:* *The liberal soul shall be made fat: and he that watereth shall be watered also himself.*

> *Matthew 10:8 commands:* *Heal the sick, cleanse the lepers, raise the dead, cast out devils: freely ye have received, freely give.*

- How can you give something you have not received?
- How can you heal when you are unhealed?
- How can you deliver when you are not delivered?
- How can you refresh and encourage when you are not replenished and empowered?
- How can you save when you as a leader are not truly converted into and operating in the fullness of salvation yourself?

Many leaders are trying to give something they do not have and wonder why people remain bound, in cycles, up one day and down the next. These dynamics are not because God's gospel does not work. They are because we are reaping what we are sowing. Many are reaping the reality of what we are truly imparting into people.

The *liberal soul* is healed and liberated unto salvation and this is evident by the prosperity of God's peace, power, wellness and balance that is upon them.

And as the *liberal soul* gives out in watering others, he or she also receives watering. Sometimes this can automatically happen, and then other times, we must position ourselves to be watered.

Jesus often positioned himself to be healed and refreshed. He did not automatically expect the ministry he did to heal and restore him. All throughout his walk, we see him stealing away to have personal time of prayer, communion, and counsel with God. He adequately stewarded the mantle of salvation upon his life by taking time away to make sure he was in right standings with the Lord. And through this posture, he was automatically watered and refreshed. In *Mark 6:30-32*, we find Jesus encouraging the apostles to steal away and rest.

> *Mark 6:30-32 reads:* *And the apostles gathered themselves together unto Jesus, and told him all things, both what they had done, and what they had taught. And he said unto them, Come ye yourselves apart into a desert place, and rest a while: for there were many*

coming and going, and they had no leisure so much as to eat. And they departed into a desert place by ship privately.

Jesus was telling them to take time for themselves. That there is always much ministry to do – much comings and goings - but they needed time to reflect, refresh, and heal.

Many leaders are disciplined in prayer and bible study time. But much of this time is consumed with praying for others and studying for ministry. There then is the assumption that this is time away with Jesus. But really this is works. Time away with Jesus is intimate time with him regarding you and him. Jesus told the apostles *"now you yourself come."* When leaders have healed everyone else, they themselves must come and be healed before the Lord.

One of the greatest gifts that Jesus gave aside from eternal life was his Holy Spirit as a counselor. There are times where leaders can be so clogged and burdened with other peoples' issues and ministry trials and responsibilities, that they cannot hear God for themselves. This is where we need to seek counsel of the Holy Spirit through spirit filled, educated counselors, that can help bring direction and healing to us.

The challenge here is leaders often seek other leaders who are also wounded and burned out, so they do not get the adequate guidance, support, attention, and accountability that they need to sustain in a process of deliverance and healing. And until we see counseling as a necessary gift in the body of Christ, we will continue to have falling wounded leaders and sheep, and a great drawing away, as people seek other alternatives to be delivered, healed, and guided in their destiny.

REASONS LEADERS ARE UNHEALED

Chapter 2

Unresolved Past Issues - Many leaders have unhealed wounds and issues from their past. These issues accompanied with ministry challenges and burdens, cause wounds in their soul, heart, mind, and spirit. A lack of time dedicated to focused healing confound these factors.

Lack of Genuine Family and Personal Support - Many leaders do not have the support of their biological families. These relationships are often sacrificed for the sake of being obedient to doing the work of the Lord. Many leaders incur wounding from words and deeds induced by family members who ridicule the leader's walk and ministry. Many family members are jealous, lack knowledge and revelation of the person's destiny, and speak curses against the leader and his or her ministry. These actions challenge the personal changes God has made in the leader's life, as family members are angry that the leader chooses God's plan over family traditions and cultural mindsets that are more so strongholds, false honor and obligation, than the will of God for the family line. Many leaders resort to cultivating a family within the community of their ministry to compensate for the lack of support from their natural family. Yet often times, the spiritual families are focused more on being close to the leader rather than having and being able to govern genuine relationships and fellowships with the leader. These relationships help fulfill some of the void, but lack true solace of a loving down hearted family. The leader in turn spends a lot of his or her time experiencing loneliness even though he or she is constantly around and giving of himself or herself to people.

Church Hurts – Many leaders experience woundedness in the church. They experience:
- Jealousy, woundedness, sexual abuse, verbal and physical abuse from the church.
- Many are used for their giftings, but are rarely prayed for, empowered, instructed, trained, promoted, or equipped to walk in their personal calling and destiny.
- Some are outcast and pushed out the church, or made to feel like they do not belong or are unwanted.
- Many are angry for having to attend services and events that produce little to no fruit, and do not spiritually feed and equip them. Yet, if they do not attend, they are viewed as rebellious, irresponsible, immature, and not serious about the things of God. These events are designed for them to prove their anointing and display that they are serious about walking in the giftings and callings on their lives. Leaders view many of these services and events as religious acts more so than moves of God; they attend out of obligation and false loyalty, but are resentful that they have to attend to prove themselves.
- Many are corrected, rebuked, and told what they are not, rather than empowered in who they are. Once released from this mindset, some rebel against

constructive criticism, chasening, and biblical standards. They view this as religious, and a part of the law rather than a balanced part of our walk with God.

The leader eventually leaves the church to start their own ministry or SHIFT to another ministry, but never addresses unresolved hurts, resentment, bitterness, abuse, envy, anger, low self-worth, and unforgiveness from previous ministries. Leaders commence to spewing out their woundedness, as they go forth in their own ministry or assist with other ministries. They will make a lot of negative comments about church and religion. These comments will appear as if they are kingdom minded, spiritually enlightened, and are above church and religion, but really they are rooted in pride and judgement due to church woundedness.

Kingdom Heirs - Many leaders are kingdom heirs of their family line. This means they have been chosen to break curses and to defy and dismantle the culture strongholds and traditions that keep the family bound by familiar spirits and cycles; such that the blessings and works of the cross can adequately govern the family line. Many do not know this about themselves so they spend a lot of time battling familiar spirits and culture strongholds through conflicts with family members, but also within the community and region to which they minister. This warfare can be weighing and wounding, especially when the person has not grasped their full identity and purpose, as it relates to combating these strongholds.

Many kingdom heirs have been assigned by God to take the place of the monarchy within their family line that keeps the family bound to demonic and culture struggles and bondages. The devil knows this so he tries to expel the kingdom heir from the family line altogether through conflict, abuse, rejection, etc. Or the devil causes hardship, drama, and/or chaos, where the kingdom heir does not value their family line, dread being birthed into it or do not even know his or her lineage.

Often their is no peace or resolving of issues, because the kingdom heir's very presence, successes, uniqueness, and anointing, challenges the familiar spirits and cultural strongholds in the family. Just them being in the midst causes these spirits and customs to conflict with them. Many kingdom heirs stop going around their family because of this, and understandably so. But that does not change the fact that the person is a kingdom heir and has been ordained to transform that lineage into the light of God. The assignment is still theirs to bear, and they have been given the responsibility to intercede, war, and stand in proxy for that family with their very life. Their very life becomes the watchman and gatekeeper of that lineage, and because of the choices they make, the lineage is restored in the blessings, fruit, and plan of the Lord.

When we accompany being a kingdom heir with being a leader in ministry, we have a powerhouse leader, but also one who will experience a lot of hardship and wounding. Especially if they are not aware of their purpose in their family and is only focused on their purpose in ministry. The enemy uses their ignorance to wreak havoc in their lives and make them wish they were not chosen. Yet, their love for God makes them stay saved and in God's will, even though they wish they were living another life.

Examples of kingdom heirs in the bible:
- Joseph knew his purpose as a kingdom heir and restored prosperity and the blessings God to his family lineage and to the nation of Israel.
- Moses did not know his purpose as a kingdom heir and struggled in his identity as the deliverer of the Israelites. He was angry about being a Hebrew, and about being raised as an orphan in Pharoah's house. He did not understand the purpose of all this and lived in inadequacy about who he was called and destined to be.
- Jehoash was saved by an aunt from his grandma, Athaliah, who killed all her grandchildren who were heirs to the family lineage, so that she could become king. Jehoash was hidden until he was old enough to reign as king. He was seven years old when he liberated and restored the lineage of David as governing rulership over Israel.

Initially Broken - Many start their ministry in brokenness and have been given the mindset that they can heal as they heal others. Yet many are not sufficiently converted unto salvation and wellness, where they can sustain in imparting into others from a broken place.

False Loyalties and Obligation - Many feel like they cannot take a break; that the ministry and people cannot operate without them.

Pride and Idolatry - They have become the vision carriers of the people and ministry rather than operating through the strength and spirit of God.

Unrealistically Self-Sacrificing - Many tend to put the wellness of the people and ministry above their own.

Obedient & Sacrificing But Not Sold Out - Some leaders are unhealed because there soul is not mature enough to handle the level of sacrifice and obedience that is necessary to carry the vision that God has called them to. Though they are obedient and sacrificing, the emotional turmoil that comes with not truly being sold out causes wounds in their soul. These wounds are created through murmur, complaining, and dreading one's spiritual walk. These places need to be healed as otherwise there is a bleeding that occurs upon those they are leading and sacrificing for.

Broken Identity - By the time many leaders have reached a position or platform where their purpose can really make an impact, they have experienced brokenness in their identity that has caused woundedness in some way. The challenge to have to prove you are called, prove you are worthy to walk in your calling, battle your way to ministry status against the very people that should be helping you mature and grow in the Lord, can really breed confusion and hurt in a person. Also the need to be validated and valued due to a broken identity from childhood, teenage and young adult experiences, are confounded when compacted by ostracism from the church.

Many leaders renew personal identity through their positions within the church and their opportunities to do ministry. Their identity then is rooted in pleasing others and gaining the praises of others, than being stabilized in the identity of the Lord. Many fluctuate in how they demonstrate their woundedness because they feel healed and thrive when people are receiving and paying attention to them, and are a wreck and suicidal when they are not being validated. Sometimes these leaders operate in control and manipulation in effort to make people receive them. Some of them become more worldly and flashy in appearance in effort to draw attention to themselves. Yet, the word and anointing on their lives is not able to sustain the platform and position they have achieved. We then begin to see their wounds, but make excuses for them, because we like them – their style and uniqueness. We keep feeding their wounds by validating who they are rather than whose they are. We have done these leaders an injustice by not helping them to heal and really walk in the identity and destiny of God for their lives.

Sin - Sin is a death wound. It is a fatal wound upon the soul and life of a person. The entire reason Jesus died and rose again was to take away death caused by sin and to return us to eternal life. Anytime we engage in sin, we have incurred a wound that must be healed. ***Isaiah 53:5 contends:*** *But he was wounded for our transgressions, he was bruised for our iniquities: the chastisement of our peace was upon him; and with his stripes we are healed.* Many leaders are wounded due to unrepentant sin, or wounds due to sin. We must have a heart to repent quickly, and to pursue healing of the sins we commit.

Denial - Many leaders think they are healed when really they are bleeding all over the place. They mistake their anointing, power gifts, and success as indicators for healthiness. This is a false deception that causes many leaders to fall from platform statuses and positions; fall into sin, into hardship, and idolatry.

Lukewarm - Some have lost sight of the true gospel where deliverance, healing, and salvation are pivotal qualities of being converted.

Exchanged God's Plan for Man's Plan - Many have altered the original vision with man made provision and works, and now they have to continue implementing those things to keep the vision and their lifestyle afloat.

Imbalance of Home and Ministry - Many leaders incur wounds because they do not have adequate help in carrying the vision of the ministry. This causes them to be spread too thin between church and home life. Since they cannot possibly fill every void of the ministry, the enemy uses this to inflict warfare and challenges. Since they are not engaged enough in their home life, division and drama often occurs between the leader and their spouse, children, immediate and extended family. Wounds occur as word curses are spoken, and conflicts manifest and linger due to the leader feeling like they have to choose between ministry and family, or in their mind, God and family. The leader makes vows to do better, but the demand of an over extended ministry causes them to break those vows. Spouses, kids, and the leader are all wounded. Many spouses and children form a rebellion and hatred towards God, the church, and ministry, due to living under the government of this painful truth. Leaders incur the guilt and burden of this, which causes more wounding as they fluctuate from resenting ministry and resenting family. Both are a thorn in their side and a wound in their soul. The inability to acquire a middle ground of compromise and a healthy balance confounds the wounds.

Imbalance of Releasing the Vision - Many have a huge vision, but lack balance in pacing themselves to efficiently bring it to pass. Impatience, a need for success, and a lack of pacing oneself, creates an urgent microwave mentality. In this instance, leaders tend to be more focused on success than whether they have maintained their salvation, or the conviction of the Holy Spirit. Many do not realize they are unhealed as the grace movement has replaced the self-examination, true repentance, and being sufficient role models for the word they preach and the God they serve.

Busyness/Not Making or Taking Time - Leaders say they do not have time to heal or deal with personal pains and challenges. Personal wellness should be a part of their daily, weekly and yearly regimen and lifestyle. You cannot make time for something you do not value. Leaders must value personal healing as much as they do the people and the ministry. You cannot sufficiently carry a vision half whole.

Inadequate Accountability - Many leaders tend to be unaccountable to other unhealed leaders who do not have the anointing and lifestyle to hold them accountable. Many leaders are accountable to imbalanced leaders who are too busy to adequately hold them to standard and walk with them in destiny. The covering tends to be in name only rather than deed.

The mindset of covering in the body of Christ has become about having someone say they are over our ministry rather than someone who truly has the vision for the vision carriers' life and calling, and being able to intercede, birth, and carry their life and calling in the spirit. Many overseers are in name only and only come around to do damage control and clean up messes. Since they have not adequately journeyed in destiny with the leader, they cannot provide an adequate vision plan to help restore that leader to wholeness. Since the overseer has not consistently encouraged or empowered a lifestyle of wholeness, that leader has become used to operating unhealed. Instability, sin, and woundedness becomes their lifestyle and even their way of drawing souls to God. Many wounded leaders use their wounds and character flaws as evangelism tactics, rather than ministering the true gospel of Jesus Christ.

Betrayal - Though we as leaders should expect betrayal since Jesus experienced it, it does not make enduring it any less painful. The key is going through the experience of betrayal. Many leaders get stuck inside the trauma and woundedness of the experience. And even after it is over, their soul, heart, and spirit is stuck in the pain of what happened. This is indeed understandable, because betrayal is a vicious murderous experience. You can never really prepare for it, even if you know who will betray you. Betrayal comes for your identity, worth, position, authority, and destiny. Betrayal is usually done by someone who clearly knows who you are, your value, and your purpose, but is willing to sacrifice it for personal gain. Being appalled at this fact confounds the woundedness of betrayal. Leaders however, cannot remain stuck inside betrayal, as the venom of it will cause you to operate in it. Fear of being betrayed again will spiral you into handling the ministry and people inappropriately, where you begin to become your own destiny killer. You begin to kill your own work through the pains of your woundedness. It is essential that leaders take time to be healed from betrayal. Go through the experience, then go through healing, so the woundedness can be your testimony rather than your Judas.

Warfare and Challenges from Being Vision Carriers - 1Peter 3:14* and *Matthew 5:10, These scriptures reveal that we will suffer and be persecuted for the gospel's sake. We need times of healing and refreshing from the trials of ministry.

Lack of Vision for Sustaining Wellness and Wholeness - Leaders have been groomed by religion that sold out means to literally kill yourself for the gospel sake. Seasons of rest and consecration for personal healing are seen as selfish or unbiblical. Most fasts and consecrations are conducted for spiritual and ministerial reasons, where they are more about the people and the ministry, than the leaders' own personal deliverance and healing. It is essential that leaders acquire a vision that respite is essential. They must set aside time in their weekly and monthly schedules to rest and refresh, while also taking seasons for personal consecration for receiving adequate deliverance and healing.

CHARACTERISTICS OF A WOUNDED LEADER

Chapter 3

Lets take a moment to explore the characteristics of a wounded leader. Please know that this is a small list that is intended to provoke enlightenment in further discerning and examining yourself and other leaders in your sphere that may need deliverance and healing.

Wounded Leaders:

- Have a need to control everything and/or have their hand in everything to avoid being disappointed.

- Use their platform, position, relationships and interactions to make offensive, hurtful, pet peeving, ridiculing type comments, that are rooted in their hurts about life, ministry, God and people.

- Superficial and surface; lack pure transparency where the wellness of salvation is clear and visible.

- Make excuses for their sins and wounds. Blame others for their actions or do not take responsibility for their actions. Play the grace card rather than seeking God for deliverance and healing.

- View all churches and religion as ungodly even though there are many churches who are of God, and despite religion and religious acts being two very different contextual matters. Make a lot of negative comments about the church and religion, but is really wounded due to past unresolved issues related to ministry experiences. Will appear as if they have gained spiritual insight beyond religion and the church, but much of their comments are to belittle, ridicule and lash out at the church for how they have been treated. There will be a division mindset in relations to them and people who attend organized religion or who still deem organized religion very beneficial and a necessary part of the body of Christ.

- Misrepresent or misuse the scriptures to justify his or her sins and wounds.

- Make others feel guilty or fearful for questioning their sins and/or wounds.

- Will lie or release false prophecy to cover sins and wounds.

- Cry and manifest their hurts and pains while ministering to the wounds of others. However, when not ministering, they are often emotionless, unfeeling, insensitive, hard, stony, rigid, emotionally and physically guarded with the people and things of God. Most often such leaders are protecting themselves because they have wounds, and fear being further wounded.

When the wounded leader is crying while ministering, we often assume this the compassion of Jesus Christ, but there is a difference. A compassionate person is moved to manifest the heart of God that breeds change and transformation. A wounded person is moved to manifest their pain that incites your pain. You are emotionally drawn into them based on experience, but the deliverance and healing is not there to birth forth transformation. This is the reason you will feel good for the moment, and then be dealing with that pain, and even more pain a few days later. You have just received an impartation of woundedness into your woundedness as commonality of experiences cannot heal you.

Woundedness and Burnout
Burn out is when a leader needs a time of rest and consecration, but refuses to take it due to false or delusional obligations and loyalties to God and the people; Often there is a fear associated with the false obligations and loyalties, such as fear that someone will take their position while they are resting.

When a leader is burned out they flow through the wells of bitterness, anger, verbal aggression, intimidation and control. This is because:
- They are extremely tired and drained physically, emotionally and spiritually.
- They are operating on fumes and have nothing to give.
- Tiredness causes them to be easily angered and frustrated even by minor things.
- They are irritable, negative, skeptical, and pessimistic.
- They lack temperance, and patience, while being overly critical and insensitive in their leading style.
- They feel justified in their actions as they have taken on a disposition that they have to do everything themselves, because nothing gets done properly without them.

It is important for leaders to recognize the signs of burnout and take time to refresh and restore themselves as when they do not acknowledge this, burnout can result in wounding others while further wounding themselves.

Burnout can cause unhealthy, emotional and abrupt decision making that can wound and even abort the vision of the ministry. When leaders are not willing to take time to refresh and be delivered and healed, they have become an idol to the people and the vision. They carry the burden of the people and ministry rather operating through the spirit and strength of God.

Discerning Burnout: Lets conduct a burnout check as this is essential for knowing when respite, deliverance and healing is needed.

- *Stress* - feeling strained, weighted, burdened by life and one's responsibilities; experiencing a physical pressure or pull, while having to exert force or energy to engage in the day and to complete tasks.
- *Exhaustion* - feeling tired all the time. The tiredness can be felt in your body, mind and emotions. Experiencing restlessness and thought racing while trying to sleep; attempting oversleep in effort to compensate for tiredness, yet increase sleep does not break the exhaustion.
- *Dissatisfied With Life* - Wearied while displaying impatience and dissatisfaction even with things that should bring joy and pleasure. Difficult to enjoy things due to exhaustion and weariness.
- *Emotional Imbalance* - Easily irritated, frustrated, and angered. Feel a lack of self-worth or unappreciated. Experience loneliness, emptiness, resentment, and as if you have to do everything even though help is available to you. Experience double mindedness, pessimism, and is plagued with negative thoughts about life, people, and responsibilities. There is a heaviness upon the heart and body in the form of depression and grief. There can be crying for no reason or a feeling of wanting to cry but the tears do not flow.
- **False Obligation and Loyalty** - There is a sense of false obligation and loyalty to complete tasks and take on tasks that are not of immediate important. There is a false obligation and loyalty to follow through with duties even when others are offering assistance or when others recognize you need rest. This is pride at work.
- *Lack of Motivation* - Do not desire to engage in day to day activities. Difficulty getting out of bed, progressing forward with the day. There can also be a dragging through the day accompanied by enthusiasm, ability to encourage self or be encouraged. At times there will be surge of strength exerted by will power, but then this strength will be zapped by the reality of burnout.
- *Distraction* - Difficulty concentrating, focusing, remembering things, problem solving, making important decisions, leading others, while being easily distracted by plaguing negative thoughts, weariness, and the fact of being exhausted and not having anything to give.
- *Lack of Self Care* - Stop eating right, exercising, praying, spending time with God, studying your bible, equipping self in one's gifting and calling, vacationing, taking weekly personal days, spending time with family and friends, grooming self to one's taste and standards.
- *Unhealthy Coping Mechanisms* - Resort to drinking, drugs, smoking, overeating, under eating, poor eating habits, self-medicating by taking sleeping pills or pills for energy, inordinate sex acts, engaging in risky or unhealthy behaviors and activities.
- *Relationship and Family Issues* - Exhibiting poor coping, conflict resolution, communication, anger management, relational, and social skills. Difficulty receiving and giving constructive criticism; easily

offended, while harboring unforgiveness, bitterness, retaliation and resentment.
- ***Unhealthy Boundaries*** - Not being discerning in one's relationships and interactions. Becoming more than God is requiring to those in need or those you counsel, mentor or shepherd. Engaging in unhealthy emotional ties. Have a need to fix, rescue, or Lord over a person or task. Becoming sexually attracted, sexually engaging, and/or getting personal or emotional needs met in relationships and interactions that are not with a person that is your wife or husband.
- ***Moral Discrepancies*** - Exhibiting behaviors that is out of your character and standards, and is definitely not the character or nature of God. (e.g. yelling at people, being combative, disruptive, yielding to sin, risking public reproach, ministering through issues and through personal perceptions while causing harm or challenges for others).
- ***Poor Performance Level*** - Feel as if you are giving your all, but work ethic is not up to par; duties and responsibilities consume your mind and thoughts, but you really are not getting much accomplished due to sluggardness and burnout. There is a downgrade to your performance compared to when you are refreshed and balanced in your day to day activities. Even if a goal is achieved, you recognize that it was not your best and/or that it took more energy, focus, work ethic and time than necessary.
- **Health Problems** - Experience stress related health problems (e.g. headaches, stomach aches, ulcers, digestive issues, respiratory infections, depression, anxiety, heart issues, addictions).

Woundedness & Instability

When a leader is wounded, instability will be evident in their words, thought processing, emotions and actions. The bible called this double-mindedness. Depending on the symptoms, the counseling arena calls this bipolar disorder, major depression or schizophrenia. Usually, but not always the case, a wounded leader that is unstable, is battling internal warfare with themselves, their generations, and/or sometimes with God. Though they can be battling demonic oppression, often a wounded leader will contend it is the enemy battling them or they are experiencing warfare for the ministry and the people. And though there internal war is affecting the ministry and people, it is usually there own battle due to unsealed wounds.

Many unstable leaders have the potential to kill those they oversee spiritually and physically. Due to there attacks manifesting without warning. When dealing with an unstable leader, you will feel guarded when interacting with them, because you never know when they will attack. The instability causes them to be carriers of the destiny killing spirit, as they strike hard and keen, and it is usually against the mantle and calling on your life. Saul is a perfect example of a wounded leader.

> ***1Samuel 18:10-11 reads:*** *And it came to pass on the morrow, that the evil spirit from God came upon Saul, and he prophesied in the midst of the house: and David played with his hand, as at other times: and there was a javelin in Saul's hand. And Saul cast the javelin; for he said, I will smite David even to the wall with it. And David avoided out of his presence twice.*

Even though an evil spirit came upon Saul, he was prophesying. Prophesying should have been a good thing, but though his gift was manifesting, along with it came a murdering spirit. One prophesy was flowing out his mouth, while another one was flowing out of his heart as he was prophesying. In his heart he said *"I am going to nail David to the wall."*

Many times when our leaders are unstable, we make excuses for their actions. We are either operating in false compassion, delusion, bewitchment, or we are so captivated by the gift. We do not see the wounded unstable leader that is blessing us with one gift, while killing us with another gift.

David was playing the harp - operating in his gift like he normally would in effort to bring peace to Saul. The scripture said that David had done this often times before when Saul was tormented by the evil spirit, therefore this was a common occurrence. Yet the very leader David was trying to soothe, was trying to kill him. Many times, we are trying to soothe our unstable wounded leader with our gifts, services and loyalty, when they need deliverance, healing and transformation. Our wounded leaders may not have javelins, but their woundedness can be a javelin, or an open door to the enemy coming in and stabbing you. When the wounded leader ministers, he or she is exposing you through their impartation. They cannot adequately seal what they put in you, or cover you while you receive and walk in what was imparted. Also, if they are not in a place of processing, they have given you a part of their brokenness through that impartation.

Wounded leaders are also very insecure. They hide their insecurity with pride, false sense of self, stealing God's glory, and stealing the spoils of war that really are a reproach and sin against God. Many take credit for the things God and people perform, or refuse to award or accolade anyone who they fear will receive more glory and praise than them.

SPIRITUAL CLEANSING!

MAINTAINING DELIVERANCE & HEALING

Chapter 4

This chapter will not only discuss the spirits you will be overthrowing, but will provide tools and strategies for sustaining your freedom, while learning to live a lifestyle of wellness with God. This chapter will provide you with knowledge of some of the strategies and tools that will be listed throughout this manual. You will be fully armored to break the power and stronghold of the devil, as your revelation and arsenal becomes empowered with truth and weaponry to dismantle, seize, and invalidate the enemy. SHIFT!

> *Matthew 10:8 Heal the sick, cleanse the lepers, raise the dead, cast out devils: freely ye have received, freely give.*

Leprosy in the Greek is *leora* and means:
1. scaliness, i.e leprosy
2. the most offensive, annoying, dangerous, cutaneous disease
3. the virus of which generally pervades the whole body, common in Egypt and the East

Cleanse is *katharizo* in the Greek and means:
1. make clean, cleanse
    a) from physical stains and dirt
        - utensils, food
        - a leper, to cleanse by curing
        - to remove by cleansing
    b) in a moral sense
        - to free from defilement of sin and from faults
        - to purify from wickedness
        - to free from guilt of sin, to purify
        - to consecrate by cleansing or purifying
        - to consecrate, dedicate
2. to pronounce clean in a levitical sense

Leprosy is an infectious disease that causes disfiguring sores, nerve damage, and progressive debilitation. In the bible, lepers, or those infected with leprosy, were outcasts because of fear and necessity. Leprosy has the potential to spread from person to person. If lepers were not isolated, then they were a threat to society, due to contaminating others with leprosy.

Lepers are also isolated due to how others react to them. The manner in which the disease physically alters a person, the fear others had regarding how lepers looked, and fear of contracting what they had, were factors in them being in isolation.

> ***Leviticus 13:45-46*** *And the leper in whom the plague is, his clothes shall be rent, and his head bare, and he shall put a covering upon his upper lip, and shall cry, Unclean, unclean. All the days wherein the plague shall be in him he shall be defiled; he is unclean: he shall dwell alone; without the camp shall his habitation be.*

> ***Numbers 5:1-3*** *And the LORD spake unto Moses, saying, Command the children of Israel, that they put out of the camp every leper, and every one that hath an issue, and whosoever is defiled by the dead: Both male and female shall ye put out, without the camp shall ye put them; that they defile not their camps, in the midst whereof I dwell.*

Though the bible does not exactly speaks this truth, however, the revelation is clear that the people viewed leprosy as God's wrath and judgment on a person's life due to sin. God may not have caused people to have leprosy, yet, the manner to which leprosy would affect our lives is the same way sin affects our lives. Lets take a moment to explore the comparison:

- Sin causes us to be unclean, impure, unhealthy.
- Our sin contaminates and influences others; it pollutes society and the world at large.
- We think people cannot see our sins, but sins can be seen in our presentation, disposition, personality, clothing, conversation, perceptions, communication, interactions, relationships, how we handle situations, and how we live our lives (Out of our heart flow the issues of life ***Proverbs 4:23***).
- Sin outcasts us from God's presence and his plan for our lives.
- Sin defames God and tarnishes his reputation, especially when we are living a life of sin, but contend we serve God.

When we consider the concept of cleansing the lepers or shall we say, cleansing sins, it is important to cleanse the infection and cleanse what is causing the infection.

> ***Matthew 8:1-4*** *When he was come down from the mountain, great multitudes followed him. And, behold, there came a leper and worshipped him, saying, Lord, if thou wilt, thou canst make me clean. And Jesus put forth his hand, and touched him, saying, I will; be thou clean. And immediately his leprosy was cleansed. And Jesus saith unto him, See thou tell no man; but go thy way, shew thyself to the priest, and offer the gift that Moses commanded, for a testimony unto them.*

A lot of times, we want to use will power to stop sinning. When using will power we are operating through a well of self-control. You are striving to control your impulses and choices. But if you could not keep yourself from engaging in the sin, how can you stop yourself from never doing it again? We need Holy Ghost power!

> ***Ephesians 3:16*** *He would grant you, according to the riches of His glory, to be strengthened with power through His Spirit in the inner man.*

God's Holy Ghost power empowers us to grow strong, so we can withstand against sins and worldliness.

> ***The Amplified Bible*** *May He grant you out of the rich treasury of His glory to be strengthened and reinforced with mighty power in the inner man by the [Holy] Spirit [Himself indwelling your innermost being and personality].*

Even if you use your own will to stop sinning, you are still unclean if you do not allow God's Holy Ghost power to cleanse you from sin.

In ***Matthew 8:1-4***, Jesus laid hands on the lepers and they were made clean. This is miraculously awesome and is a form of deliverance and healing that many of us have experienced when encountering Jesus. Even with this miraculous cleansing, the leper still had to make a lifestyle change to remain clean.
- He could not return to the leper camp as he would risk being contaminated again.
- If his leprosy was a sin issue, then he had to reframe from that sin to maintain his deliverance and healing.
- Even as the leper's community had changed, his relationships and interactions had to be changed.

The leper's identity and lifestyle had to change to maintain his healing. Such a change requires a processing to wholeness. This requires relationship with God beyond just the initial encounter of deliverance and healing. We have to journey with him in a lifestyle change, learn his plan for us for maintaining healing, and walk that plan out in our daily lifestyle.

This brings us to this scripture:

> ***Isaiah 64:6*** *But we are all as an unclean thing, and all our righteousnesses are as filthy rags; and we all do fade as a leaf; and our iniquities, like the wind, have taken us away.*

<u>Unclean</u> is *tame* in the Hebrew and means:
1. to be unclean, become unclean, become impure, regard as unclean
2. to be or become unclean, to defile oneself, be defiled
   - sexually
   - religiously
   - ceremonially
   - by idolatry
3. to profane (God's name)

<u>Filth</u> is *ed* in the Hebrew and means:
1. to set a period, the menstrual flux, soiling, filthy
2. menstruation
   - a filthy rag, stained garment
   - figuratively of best deeds of guilty people

> ***The Amplified Bible*** *For we have all become like one who is unclean [ceremonially, like a leper], and all our righteousness (our best deeds of rightness and justice) is like filthy rags or a polluted garment; we all fade like a leaf, and our iniquities, like the wind, take us away [far from God's favor, hurrying us toward destruction].*

Even our righteousness needs cleaning in God's eyes. Just like we cleanse our physical body, we have to cleanse our hearts, minds, thoughts, emotions, loins, foundation, and the inner man of things lodged in our flesh. When we cleanse our physical bodies we are detailed in making sure we clean every part of our bodies. We even purchase the correct hygienic products to assist us with cleaning our bodies, while making sure we remain clean. And if a product does not work, we do not keep using it. We will try different products until we find out what products work best in keeping our bodies clean, vibrant, and fresh.

We need this same standard for our spiritual lives. And because our righteousness is filthy, we should be cleaning our soul, hearts, minds, and our inner man daily just like we do our physical bodies. For even when we think we are clean, to God we have things that we need to be cleansed from.

Lets explore the Holy Spirit equipping you with healing techniques you can use to bring cleansing to your life:

- ***Infilling of the Holy Spirit*** (***Acts 1-2, Acts 13:22*** *And the disciples were continually filled with joy and with the Holy Spirit*). All of us receive the Holy Spirit upon us when we accept Jesus as our personal savior. When I speak of infilling, I am referencing speaking in tongues where God's voice and power speaks through you and empowers you. When God's power flows through you, his voice equips you with greater heavenly sound and power to annihilate the enemy. There are somethings the enemy will not respond to in your voice, but he will if you speak in tongues. If you do not speak in tongues, begin to study the purpose of doing so, while asking the Holy Spirit to manifest his voice through you. If you do speak in tongues, practice praying in your prayer language for at least 30 to 60 minutes a day. I encourage people to speak in tongues the entire time they are in the shower or while they are driving to work. This is the perfect time, because you are generally alone, and can focus on allowing the Holy Spirit to empower you. You do not have to know what you are saying or even have a prayer focus. The more you speak in tongues, the more you will know what you are saying, and the more the Holy Spirit will guide you in knowing what to pray for, against, and how to use your prayer language to cleanse yourself of the filth of the enemy.

- *Spirit of Lord* – Empowers you with the wisdom, revelation, knowledge, counsel, understanding, and guidance needed to handle your daily affairs and journey in a destiny lifestyle with the Lord. (*Isaiah 11:2 And the spirit of the LORD shall rest upon him, the spirit of wisdom and understanding, the spirit of counsel and might, the spirit of knowledge and of the fear of the LORD*). Declare continually that you are consumed in the spirit of wisdom, revelation, understanding, etc. Refuse to accept and cleanse all confusion, ignorance, foolery, witchcraft, bewitchment, mind control, mind blinding/binding, lack of knowing, lack of guidance, etc. Assert your right to have the spirit of the Lord teach you all things (*John 14:26 But the Comforter, which is the Holy Ghost, whom the Father will send in my name, he shall teach you all things, and bring all things to your remembrance, whatsoever I have said unto you*).

- *Blood of Jesus* – Purges, purifies, redeems, reconciles, sanctifies, sanitizes, forgives, heals, and frees you from death (*Ephesians 1:7 whom we have redemption through his blood, the forgiveness of sins, according to the riches of his grace*). We hear a lot about pleading the blood, but the blood is an application. Jesus applied his blood to our sins and sicknesses, and through his perfected blood, we were redeemed, and made whole. You can apply the blood of Jesus to your soul, heart, mind, thoughts, personality, character, identity, righteousness, body, and command redemption, life, and wholeness to come. You can soak yourself in the blood until you see breakthrough in these areas, or as a daily application of being cleansed and free in God.

- *Binding, Loosing & Casting Out Devils* – Delivers you from demons, and strongholds (*Matthew 16:19 And I will give unto thee the keys of the kingdom of heaven: and whatsoever thou shalt bind on earth shall be bound in heaven: and whatsoever thou shalt loose on earth shall be loosed in heaven*). Bind means "*to knit, chain, tie, and to fasten, put under subjection, to forbid, prohibit, declare to be illicit.*" Loose means to "*loosen, cast off, break (up), destroy, dissolve, (un-)loose, melt, put off, to declare unlawful, to overthrow.*" You possess the power to bind up demons and demonic kingdoms, forbid them to remain in you and others. You can bind yourself, others, your ministry, your atmosphere, land and region to God and his kingdom. You can also loose yourself from demonic powers, and forbid and overthrow their working in your life, lives of others, your ministry, your atmosphere, land, and region.

- *Casting Out Devils* – Deliverance ministry is a part of our right and health as believers of Jesus Christ. It is our daily manna and authority to be free of demons and their demonic stronghold. Jesus has given us power over all the power of the enemy. Cast out means to "*eject with violence, drive (out), expel, leave, pluck (pull, take, thrust) out, put forth (out), send away.*" We can cast the devil out of

our lives and be free of his demonic fruit, filth, oppression, depression and possession.
- o *Matthew 10:8 Heal the sick, cleanse the lepers, raise the dead, cast out devils: freely ye have received, freely give.*
- o *Luke 10:19 Behold, I give unto you power to tread on serpents and scorpions, and over all the power of the enemy: and nothing shall by any means hurt you.*
- o *Luke 11:20 But if I with the finger of God cast out devils, no doubt the kingdom of God is come upon you.*

It is important to assert power and authority over the enemy because he is always trying to claim rights to us and what belongs to us. The devil is not passive and is always seeking to possess, devour, and destroy what is ours. We must be offensive and aggressive in letting him know that he cannot have our lives, families, ministries, atmosphere, land, regions, nations.

- *Fruit of God* – Fills, restores, produces, reproduces (*Galatians 5:22-23 But the fruit of the Spirit is love, joy, peace, long suffering, gentleness, goodness, faith, Meekness, temperance: against such there is no law*). Cleanse yourself of all defiled, demonic, and unhealthy fruit that does not represent the character and nature of God, while filling yourself up in all of the fruit that represents his character and nature.

- *Breaking Curses* – Provides personal, generational, regional, cultural freedom from negative words spoken over you, sent to you, or curses implemented due to personal and generational sins (*Galatians 3:13 Christ hath redeemed us from the curse of the law, being made a curse for us: for it is written, Cursed is every one that hangeth on a tree*).
  - o Repent for personal, generational, regional and cultural strongholds.
  - o Loose the blood of Jesus to cleanse the curse and all filth associated with it.
  - o Bind and cast out any spirits operating with the curse.
  - o Declare your freedom through Jesus Christ (*2Corinthians 3:17 Now the Lord is that Spirit: and where the Spirit of the Lord is, there is liberty*).
  - o Fill yourself back up with the fruit of God.

- *Word of God* – Discerns, divides what is of God and what is not of God, cuts out, does surgery, instills God's truth, will, and plan (*Hebrews 4:12 For the word of God is quick, and powerful, and sharper than any two-edged sword, piercing even to the dividing asunder of soul and spirit, and of the joints and marrow, and is a discerner of the thoughts and intents of the heart*).
  - o Use the word of God to divide what is of God in your life from what is not of him.
  - o Use the word of God to extract what is not of God from your soul, heart, mind, body, and spirit.
  - o Use the word of God to overthrow every lie that the enemy uses to keep you bound to demons.

- o Use the word of God to cut out any word, character trait, hurt, pain, and flaw that keeps you bound to demons.
- o Spend time studying, meditating on, and soaking yourself in the word of God. Allow God's word to go inside of you (heart, mind, soul, identity), and cleanse everything that is contrary to the word of God for your life. Study and meditate on God's word and be refilled in his truth concerning your identity, purpose, destiny, and who he is as your daddy God.

- *Fire of God* – Burns out, fuses, refines, purges, purifies, consumes, and test (***Malachi 3:2-3*** *But who may abide the day of his coming? and who shall stand when he appeareth? for he is like a refiner's fire, and like fullers' soap: And he shall sit as a refiner and purifier of silver: and he shall purify the sons of Levi, and purge them as gold and silver, that they may offer unto the Lord an offering in righteousness*). Sometimes you will cast out demons, but their deposits and attributes are still lodged in you. Use the fire of God to purge and burn out these demonic deposits. You can also purify and refine yourself with the fire of God. Demons hate the fire of God and the blood of Jesus. Fire is judgment to demons. You can use the fire of God to torment demons and send them fleeing from your life, blood line, ministry, land, atmosphere, and region. (***Revelations 20:10*** *And the devil that deceived them was cast into the lake of fire and brimstone, where the beast and the false prophet are, and shall be tormented day and night for ever and ever*).

- **Fullers' Soap** – Is a washing by trampling, treading, stamping, scrubbing. It is liken to trampling or scrubbing something hard until it is clean. (***Malachi 3:2-3*** *But who may abide the day of his coming? and who shall stand when he appeareth? for he is like a refiner's fire, and like fullers' soap: And he shall sit as a refiner and purifier of silver: and he shall purify the sons of Levi, and purge them as gold and silver, that they may offer unto the Lord an offering in righteousness*). When there are things in you that require deep cleansing, use the fuller soap of God to scrub and trample them out.

- *Power of God* – Delivers, overthrows demonic powers and governments, releases the virtue and government of God, releases miracles, signs, and wonders (***Acts 1:8*** *But ye shall receive power, after that the Holy Ghost is come upon you: and ye shall be witnesses unto me both in Jerusalem, and in all Judaea, and in Samaria, and unto the uttermost part of the earth*). Use the power of God to annihilate the powers of the enemy (***Luke 10:19*** *Behold, I give unto you power to tread on serpents and scorpions, and over all the power of the enemy: and nothing shall by any means hurt you*). Study the power of God as you will find that you have the ability to recreate and create body parts, birth forth things that you need, bring excellency to your heart, mind and soul, release virtue into your life, annihilate the power of the enemy, such that it brings deliverance and healing.

- *Glory of God* – Whatever we need and desire from God is inside his glory. The Glory refreshes, fills, refills, fulfills, creates, recreates, revives, renews, makes whole, establishes the presence of God, draws us into intimacy and relationship with God, while instilling God's character, nature, truth, knowledge, revelation, and pleasures forevermore (***Psalms 16:11*** *Thou wilt shew me the path of life: in thy presence is fulness of joy; at thy right hand there are pleasures for evermore*). You should be living inside the presence of God. This is where your direction of life is revealed. As you walk in alignment with God, continual fulness of joy and pleasures of God should be evident in your life. If you live in the glory of God, you should be living a fulfilled life no matter what trials and tribulations may occur. Ask God for revelation on how to build a relationship with him where you abide in his presence. Use his presence to refresh, fulfill, and fill you. Continually cultivate your life and atmosphere in his presence so you can be a true glory carrier (***John 15:4*** *Abide in me, and I in you. As the branch cannot bear fruit of itself, except it abide in the vine; no more can ye, except ye abide in me*).

- ***Rivers of Living Water*** – Stirs, replenishes, breeds life, vitality, beauty, youthfulness, creativity, strength, efficiency, and releases what is inside of you to whatever you are sending it to (***John. 7:38*** *He that believeth on me, as the scripture hath said, out of his belly shall flow rivers of living water*). It is important to spend time cleansing and stir the rivers that are inside of you, such that the wells that you flow out of, are pure as whatever is in you will be released to those you minister too.

- ***Pluck Out*** – Roots out, pulls down, destroys, and throws down (***Jeremiah 1:10*** *See, I have this day set thee over the nations and over the kingdoms, to root out, and to pull down, and to destroy, and to throw down, to build, and to plant*). Some spirits and demonic attributes are imbedded in your foundation and need to be uprooted.
  - You can pluck out demons.
  - You can command demons and strongholds that are lodged deep within you to come up out of you by the root. That root can even be generational, so keep that in mind, or it can be a root in you that has been there for years.
  - You may have to cut the root in pieces then pull them out. You may have to pull down something such as pulling down strongholds, imaginations, and prideful spirits that have exalted themselves above God and may have even exalted themselves as idols in your life.

  You cannot be nice to demons and with wickedness. Your mission has to be to destroy them just like they want to destroy you. The devil understands he is in a fight and will throw you around like you are a piece of paper. You have to enter your fight with him, and be willing to toss him and trample on him as if your life depends on it – because it does. Use the power and authority of God to uproot, pull down, destroy and throw down.

- ***Hammer Down*** – Walls, barricades, barriers, hindrances, and blockages, have to be hammered down (***Jeremiah 23:29*** *Is not my word like as a fire? saith the LORD; and like a hammer that breaketh the rock in pieces?*) Sometimes these fortifications are made by us, sometimes the words and ideologies of others cause these walls and barriers, and sometimes they are made by the devil. Either way they need to come down. Use the hammer of God to break down walls and barriers that have been erected to hinder your breakthrough.

- ***Run Through Troops*** – Blast through groups of troops that keep you bound or that may be blocking your breakthrough (***Psalm 18:30*** *For by thee I have run through a troop; and by my God have I leaped over a wall*). If you read ***Psalm 18:30-51***, you will discern that it is the power of God that enables you to do this. When you find yourself in tough life situations, ganged up on by demons or you come up against a stronghold that does not want to budge in your life, ask God to empower you to run through troops. Then as you pray and deal with these situations in your natural life, use your faith, power and authority to blast through these bondages.

- ***Resist the Devil*** – Stand against, oppose, withstand, set against the devil and all that concerns him (***James 4:7*** *Submit yourselves therefore to God. Resist the devil, and he will flee from you*). Before demons and filth will leave you, you have to fall out of agreement with it. The devil and his filth cannot stay if there is nothing in you wanting him to remain. You have to break every covenant with it, divorce it, hate it, dread it being in you, and resist it from being a part of your life. Spend time breaking covenants with the devil, sin, pleasures of sin, mindsets, errors, and anything that keeps you in relationship with the enemy and his filthiness.

- ***Breaking Soulties*** – Soulties can be Godly or ungodly in nature. Just how generational curses are passed down, soulties are transferred from you and the other person and vice versa. Soulties can be formed through close friendships and interactions, covenants, vows, commitments, promises, physical intimacy, and etc. You can also have a soultie by having an unhealthy attachment to something or someone that has taken the place of God in your life or that has become an addiction in your life. Your soul, heart, mind, and body can be intertwined, bound, knitted, or in covenant with that person, place or thing. In addition you exchange parts of yourself with the person you are in a soultie with. Parts of their personality, soul, heart, thoughts, mindsets, character, nature, and other deposits, infuse you and begin to influence and live in you and vice versa. Also, whomever they have had relationship with and have not cleansed themselves of, is being passed on to you and vice versa.

  Godly Soultie – Soulties can be Godly and healthy. They possess the fruit and nature of God and empower your life, ministry, purpose and destiny. A healthy soultie has God's character, nature, fruit, will, and plan for our lives, as we can be tied to good things but they may not necessarily be God's design.

1Samuel 18:1 *And it came to pass, when he had made an end of speaking unto Saul, that the soul of Jonathan was knit with the soul of David, and Jonathan loved him as his own soul.*

Ecclesiastes 4:9-12 The Amplified Bible *Two are better than one, because they have a good [more satisfying] reward for their labor; For if they fall, the one will lift up his fellow. But woe to him who is alone when he falls and has not another to lift him up! Again, if two lie down together, then they have warmth; but how can one be warm alone? And though a man might prevail against him who is alone, two will withstand him. A threefold cord is not quickly broken.*

Matthew 18:19 *Again I say unto you, That if two of you shall agree on earth as touching any thing that they shall ask, it shall be done for them of my Father which is in heaven.*

Marriage Soultie – When we get married, our lives are knitted in covenant without our spouse and we become one with them. There is no longer I, or two people. The two become one when married. You are of your spouse and your spouse is of you.

Genesis 2:24 *Therefore shall a man leave his father and his mother, and shall cleave unto his wife: and they shall be one flesh.*

Matthew 19:5 *And said, For this cause shall a man leave father and mother, and shall cleave to his wife: and they twain shall be one flesh?*

Ungodly Soultie – An ungodly soultie is any knitting of ourselves with a person, place, or thing that is not of God or that is not God's will and plan for our lives. God will not have you bond to sin, idolatry, unhealthiness, unfruitfulness, or bondage. He will not have you engage or remain in a relationship that is transgression against his word, will and plan for your life. God will not have you tie to something that is going to deplete you rather than build you in him and in your identity, purpose and destiny.

Corinthians 6:16 *What? know ye not that he which is joined to an harlot is one body? for two, saith he, shall be one flesh.*

Genesis 34:1-3 *And Dinah the daughter of Leah, which she bare unto Jacob went out to seethe daughters of the land. And when Shechem the son of Hamor the Hivite, prince of the country, saw her, he took her, and lay with her, and defiled her. And his soul clave unto Dinah the daughter of Jacob, and he loved the damsel, and spake kindly unto the damsel. Verse 8 And Hamor communed with them, saying the soul of my son Shechem longeth for your daughter: I pray you give her him to wife. Sexual involvement can form such entangling tentacles of soul ties that it is extremely hard to break off the relationship.*

> ***Proverbs* 5:20-24** *And why wilt thou, my son, be ravished with a strange woman, and embrace the bosom of a stranger? For the ways of man are before the eyes of the Lord, and he pondereth all his goings. His own iniquities shall take the wicked himself, and he shall be holden with the cords of his sins. He shall die without instruction; and in the greatness of his folly he shall go astray.*
>
> ***Psalms* 1:1** *Blessed is the man that walketh not in the counsel of the ungodly, nor standeth in the way of sinners, nor sitteth in the seat of the scornful*
>
> ***2Corinthians* 6:14-18** *Be ye not unequally yoked together with unbelievers: for what fellowship hath righteousness with unrighteousness? and what communion hath light with darkness? And what concord hath Christ with Belial? or what part hath he that believeth with an infidel? And what agreement hath the temple of God with idols? for ye are the temple of the living God; as God hath said, I will dwell in them, and walk in them; and I will be their God, and they shall be my people. Wherefore come out from among them, and be ye separate, saith the Lord, and touch not the unclean thing; and I will receive you, And will be a Father unto you, and ye shall be my sons and daughters, saith the Lord Almighty.*

Soultie with a Place – You can be tied to a place, and it can become a high place in your life, where you do not want to leave it or cannot leave it. You can be tied to a place where God has brought you out, but the tie keeps pulling you back in. Spiritually you are free, but your soul is bound to it. Lot's wife had a soultie with Sodom and Gomorrah. God was destroying the city because of the perversion, idolatry, lewdness, and lawlessness. God only allowed so many to live and allowed them time to get out of the city before he destroyed it. As they were walking out, Lot's wife looked back and turned into a pillar of salt.

> ***Genesis* 19:23-26** *Then the Lord rained upon Sodom and upon Gomorrah brimstone and fire from the Lord out of heaven; And he overthrew those cities, and all the plain, and all the inhabitants of the cities, and that which grew upon the ground. But his wife looked back from behind him, and she became a pillar of salt.*

Even though God had graced Lot's wife with deliverance, her eyes and heart had regard for what she was leaving behind. Because her soul was still knitted to Sodom and Gomorrah, God caused her to perish with it. Being tied to something that God is freeing you from will deplete your life and even bring destruction upon you.

Agreement with God's will for the relationship along with healthiness is important in a Godly Soultie.

Amos 3:3 Can two walk together, except they be agreed?

The Message Bible Do two people walk hand in hand if they aren't going to the same place?

When the agreement is unhealthy, it makes for an ungodly soultie. Also regardless to whether you agree or not, if a soultie is formed, it has to be broken in order for you to be free of whatever was knitted and transferred through that tie. This is vital, as rape, incest, abuse, mind control, religious sects, erred beliefs, etc. are ties that form without our agreement, out of ignorance, fear, or lack of knowledge, depending on the circumstance. When they are not broken, whatever the offender deposited lives in us. Some people result in manifesting traits of their offender, while others live in the false identity of what was deposited. Also when you get divorced, it is best to break soulties with your ex spouse. Many people have a difficult time moving forward because there souls are still tied to their ex spouse. The covenant of marriage must be repented for and broken in the spirit realm, and soulties must be cleansed and broken so you can be free from all that was deposited and shared while married. It is important to break and cleanse soul ties. This can be done by

- Spending time before the Lord identifying every ungodly soultie you have in your life.
- Confessing and repenting for your role in the soul tie, even if it was just giving into the lies and false identity of your offender.
- Forgiving the person you had a soultie with and forgiving yourself for engaging in the soul tie.
- Breaking and removing the soultie. Be sure to call out every person's name you have a soul tie with; go through these steps, and break and remove each tie.
- Using the blood of Jesus and the fire of God, cleanse yourself of all ungodly deposits, and command any parts of your soul, heart, mind and identity to be restored back to you.
- Occasionally spend time cleansing out any unhealthiness in your Godly soultie relationships, and any deposits that may have come from misunderstanding, miscommunication, taking one another for granted, being more to one another than God was saying, or becoming lax, fleshy or imbalanced in your interactions.

THE PEOPLE'S CHOICE

Chapter 5

Some wounded leaders start off healthy and good. They end up wounded and rebellious, because they were chosen to be an idol, rather than chosen in the reality and nature of who God created and destined them to be. We as the people set them up to become wounded.

Saul was the people's choice leader of his day. He was the people's desire. Often when people choose a leader they are seeking someone that they can identity with, look up to, are the potential and idolization of them, and of who they have decided they should be by comparing themselves to someone else. The leader people choose is often who they wish they could be, and want to experience and partake of, but do not want to invest in the work to become. The challenge with this is God is not trying to make us more human or to be the potential of ourselves. God created us in the reality of ourselves - spiritual beings that are like him - the image of him that he created.

> *Genesis 1:28 So God created man in his own image, in the image of God created he him; male and female created he them.*

> *1Samuel 8:1-10 And it came to pass, when Samuel was old, that he made his sons judges over Israel. Now the name of his firstborn was Joel; and the name of his second, Abiah: they were judges in Beersheba. And his sons walked not in his ways, but turned aside after lucre, and took bribes, and perverted judgment. Then all the elders of Israel gathered themselves together, and came to Samuel unto Ramah, And said unto him, Behold, thou art old, and thy sons walk not in thy ways: now make us a king to judge us like all the nations.*

> *But the thing displeased Samuel, when they said, Give us a king to judge us. And Samuel prayed unto the Lord. And the Lord said unto Samuel, Hearken unto the voice of the people in all that they say unto thee: for they have not rejected thee, but they have rejected me, that I should not reign over them. According to all the works which they have done since the day that I brought them up out of Egypt even unto this day, wherewith they have forsaken me, and served other gods, so do they also unto thee. Now therefore hearken unto their voice: howbeit yet protest solemnly unto them, and shew them the manner of the king that shall reign over them. And Samuel told all the words of the Lord unto the people that asked of him a king.*

Sidebar Prayer: Heal the wounded leader Jesus, while delivering the people from idolatry, potentiality, laziness, and wanting to see and experience, but not be who you called them to be. SHIFT!

When the people said, "*now make us a king to judge us like all the nations,*" they were rejecting the judgement, government, and ruling of God for man's kingdom. They were looking for an easy way around the standards God had set for their lives. They did not use their hands, and make an idol king like the Israelites did in Moses' day, when they made the golden calf (*See Exodus 32*). But, they had created their image in their ideologies, and were demanding that Prophet Samuel manifest what they created.

We see this a lot today. People following leaders whose kingdom allows them to live contrary to the standards of God. Because of the anointing, gifts, and calling on that leader's life, the people will contend that God chose the leader for them. ***Sidebar Wisdom:*** God may very well give you a leader, but that does not mean he chose the leader for you. You wanted potential relationship with him instead of reality, so he gave it to you. My God! God will keep trying to draw us into him, but after a while, after we keep seeking the type of God we want instead of who he really is, he will release his hand and let us have what we want. We like this chosen leader aka idol god because it allows us to sin, do us, and to settle for less than who we really are to be, while still operating in a form of religious practices. We appear saved, feel saved, and even believe we are saved, because our leader is now our measuring rod, and we have finally met the standard. We can feel good about who we are and demand that everyone else accept us too. We are a false image of ourselves and do not know it. We are being led by our own will and desires made flesh for us, rather than the true and living God. Shaking my head!

Okay back to the story! Saul actually had a great destiny aligned for him.

> ***1Samuel 9:1-2*** *Now there was a man of Benjamin, whose name was Kish, the son of Abiel, the son of Zeror, the son of Bechorath, the son of Aphiah, a Benjamite, a mighty man of power. And he had a son, whose name was Saul, a choice young man, and a goodly: and there was not among the children of Israel a goodlier person than he: from his shoulders and upward he was higher than any of the people.*
>
> ***The Amplified Bible*** *THERE WAS a man of Benjamin whose name was Kish son of Abiel, the son of Zeror, the son of Becorath, the son of Aphiah, a Benjamite, a mighty man of wealth and valor. Kish had a son named Saul, a choice young man and handsome; among all the Israelites there was not a man more handsome than he. He was a head taller than any of the people.*

Saul was from a wealthy powerful family. He was a chosen young man who stood out among his peers. Not just because he was tall, but because of his goodness - his character, charisma, and abilities. The fact that he was taller and more handsome than everyone, also increased his kingly nature. Saul's father was no doubt a role model for him, so he had everything he needed as a young man to succeed in life, and to even be a successful king.

Sidebar Wisdom: Many leaders have an upbringing like Saul. They do not have the testimonies of coming from broken homes, being saved from crack houses, being pulled from abandoned buildings. But even with a great beginning, you can end up being wounded. The challenge with Saul was he began to lead through his wounds. The wounds then cost him his kingdom.

Okay back to the story! It was evident that Saul would probably become king one day. And though the people wanted a king, unlike some of the leaders we choose today, Saul was initially God's choice as well. We see from the scripture passage we read concerning Saul, God gave the Israelites the best of the best. Saul was the best candidate in all of Israel. So even in their idolatry, God gave the Israelites a chance to succeed. God even gave Saul a new heart in hopes that he would live by his leading and will, and so that the people would discern that God's spirit was with Saul.

> *1Samuel 10:9 And it was so, that when he had turned his back to go from Samuel, God gave him another heart: and all those signs came to pass that day.*

With every opportunity fashioned upon Saul, successful kingship should have been inevitable. However, unhealed wounds would cause a turn in destiny where poor choices begin to override the identity and calling of the Lord. Let us also be mindful that man wanted a king to rule a Godly kingdom, but did not want God.

After finding out he was chosen as their king, Saul became wounded when a small group of people rejected him.

> *1Samuel 10:24-26 And they ran and fetched him thence: and when he stood among the people, he was higher than any of the people from his shoulders and upward. And Samuel said to all the people, See ye him whom the Lord hath chosen, that there is none like him among all the people? And all the people shouted, and said, God save the king. Then Samuel told the people the manner of the kingdom, and wrote it in a book, and laid it up before the Lord. And Samuel sent all the people away, every man to his house. And Saul also went home to Gibeah; and there went with him a band of men, whose hearts God had touched. But the children of Belial said, How shall this man save us? And they despised him, and brought him no presents. But he held his peace.*

The bible calls this group of people the "*children of Belial.*" *Belial* in the Hebrew means "*worthless, destructive, wicked, naughty, ungodly, without profit.*" They ridiculed Saul as king, while using their words to release who they were - their identity upon him. They despised and rejected him, and refused to honor him as king. Saul had already received an impartation of a new heart from God, and even walked in it with favor and signs following (*See 1Samuel 9-13*). Yet he let the *children of Belial* impart a false truth into him. He allowed their words to become bigger than the heart of God within him.

We would like to think that Saul holding his peace was a meek and temperate display of healthy emotion. But if you study the word "*peace*" and how it was used in the scripture, you will find that it has a unhealthy connotation.

Peace is haras and means:
1. to scratch, i.e. (by implication) to engrave, plough
2. hence (from the use of tools) to fabricate (of any material)
3. figuratively, to devise (in a bad sense)
4. hence (from the idea of secrecy) to be silent, to let alone; hence (by implication) to be deaf (as an accompaniment of dumbness)
5. to altogether, cease, conceal, be deaf, devise, ear, graven, imagine, leave off speaking

Verse 26 of the Amplified Bible reads: *But some worthless fellows said, How can this man save us? And they despised him and brought him no gift. But he held his peace and was as if deaf.*

Saul appeared as dead. Saul pretended to be okay and to have handled the situation appropriately, but really he was stunned and stupefied. Saul actually dissociated. He emotionally and psychologically separated himself from the situation. As a counselor in the mental health field, we find that many people dissociate when they are encountering an undesirable or painful experience, and are not sure how to cope with it. People initially dissociate when they have never had a painful or undesirable experience before, and they are striving to deal with or numb the pain of what is presently happening to them. Basically their soul leaves their body, or they emotionally hide inside a compartment of their mind when the encounter is happening, and then when it is over they come back. When people engage in this for long periods of time, they end up having split personalities, such that they incur mental disorders (e.g. multiple personality disorder, paranoid personality disorder, bipolar disorder, borderline personality disorder, major depression, schizophrenia, etc.).

Saul was not being meek or tempered. Seeming he grew up in a wealthy prominent family, popular, and chosen among his peers, he had never experienced being despised or rejected. He was most likely shocked and appalled, and when the people's word hit him, he was traumatized. Yet he tried to deal with the situation as best he could that moment.

The challenge with this is Saul buried his true feelings and went on a quest to prove he should be king. This began his initial wounding and it was murderous to his soul and destiny. Saul did not deal with his trauma, nor did anyone, not even Samuel, reveal to him that these people were operating as destiny killers. From that day forward, Saul's destiny path was altered as he set out to prove his abilities. Wounded King Saul SHIFTED into proving that he was worth being chosen by God and the people, and proving that he deserved to be king.

Sidebar Wisdom: The challenge with being chosen by the people is, "*they are fickle!*" The minute you are or become what they want, they change the rules and decide they want something else or they reject the truth of what they contended they wanted you to be. This is the reason knowing and being content in your identity is so essential. If you are insecure about who you are, you will yield to "proving sprees." You will go on the splurges of proving what is already the truth of you. And your identity and life will be dictated by the people's responses, rather than by God's imaged reality of who he created you to be.

Okay back to the story! God's spirit was upon Saul and in **1Samuel 11**, Saul delivered Israel out of the hands of the Ammonites. The Israelites were so pleased with their king until they wanted to kill the *children of Belial* for speaking ill of Saul. Saul, however, would not allow them to do this. And instead chose to celebrate the victory that had occurred that day.

> ***1Samuel 11:11-15*** *And it was so on the morrow, that Saul put the people in three companies; and they came into the midst of the host in the morning watch, and slew the Ammonites until the heat of the day: and it came to pass, that they which remained were scattered, so that two of them were not left together. And the people said unto Samuel, Who is he that said, Shall Saul reign over us? bring the men, that we may put them to death. And Saul said, There shall not a man be put to death this day: for to day the Lord hath wrought salvation in Israel. Then said Samuel to the people, Come, and let us go to Gilgal, and renew the kingdom there. And all the people went to Gilgal; and there they made Saul king before the Lord in Gilgal; and there they sacrificed sacrifices of peace offerings before the Lord; and there Saul and all the men of Israel rejoiced greatly.*

Though Saul spared the *children of Belial*, were pleased by his victory, and had gained the favor of the people, he still had buried unhealed hurt. As leaders, we have to be balanced in celebrating our victories, while dealing with our trials and tribulations. Saul appeared healthy, forgiving, and focused on being a sufficient reliable king. Yet later in the next chapter, as we dig more into Saul's life, we discern that what Saul was most proud of was winning the hearts of the people and proving he could be king.

Leaders must be chosen by God, not by the people. Once we are positioned, our focus and drive must be on pleasing God, being an example of his word, and establishing his will and plan in the earth. I decree that this is your foundation as a leader, and that you will never succumb to man pleasing and proving your identity. May you always know who you are, and whose you are, while remaining grounded in your identity, purpose, and destiny. SHIFT!

THE DYSFUNCTIONAL FUNCTIONING WOUNDED LEADER

Chapter 6

Some leaders are wounded and manage to still display a decent level fruit and success despite being dysfunctional. Many of them are anointed, gifted, charismatic, intelligent, hardworking, and well-educated. They have two lives, one that is public where their wounds are generally covered up by their gifts and efficiency, and a private life where their wounds are exposed, and bleeding all over the place. I equate them to a functioning alcoholic who has an obsessive addiction and affliction, yet is still able to hold down a job, make a decent living, and possibly even have a family and reasonable relationships. All of these avenues are infected and affected by the person's alcohol addiction, yet are overlooked or covered up because the person is able to maintain a sufficient level of success, despite his or her excessive drinking.

The dysfunctional functioning leader can operate in woundedness for years with minimal to no consequences. This is mainly because the dysfunctional functioning leader often has people around them that mask their wounds. Often such leaders have "fixers" around them that help them conceal sin issues and wounds. At times, the fixer is their spouse, children, close confidant, armor bearers, team members, and even overseers. We see this a lot with famous people. We wonder how can the wife remain in a marriage with a cheating, drug or alcohol addicted mate. They were either already fixers or learned to be fixers through years in a dysfunctional marriage.

When the wounded leader is exposed after years of dysfunction, everyone can look back and pinpoint signs that spiraled their downfall. Because many people are ashamed that they enabled and gain from the wounded leader's life, they SHIFT into an even greater effort to cover up the leader's mess, rather than get them help, or let the consequences of their actions be a catalyst for change. This is the reason many wounded leaders are able to remain in position despite being poison to the people, and a reproach to God and his word.

Moreover, the higher the platform, the less likely that wounded leader will adhere to truth about the dysfunction they operate in, and their need for help. When we read *1Samuel 15*, it appears as if Saul was convicted about being disobedient to God when sparing King Agag's life, even though God told him to kill him, and everything that concerns him. As we read with depth, we recognize that Saul is more convicted that the people will realize that God has left him. He therefore, sought to repent and worship God just so he could return to God's good graces, and show forth the favor of God upon his life. It was not so they he could truly be delivered and transformed from his rebellious ways. It was to trick the people into thinking he still had favor with God.

> *1Samuel 15:24-31 And Saul said unto Samuel, I have sinned: for I have transgressed the commandment of the Lord, and thy words: because I feared the people, and obeyed their*

voice. Now therefore, I pray thee, pardon my sin, and turn again with me, that I may worship the Lord. And Samuel said unto Saul, I will not return with thee: for thou hast rejected the word of the Lord, and the Lord hath rejected thee from being king over Israel. And as Samuel turned about to go away, he laid hold upon the skirt of his mantle, and it rent. And Samuel said unto him, The Lord hath rent the kingdom of Israel from thee this day, and hath given it to a neighbour of thine, that is better than thou. And also the Strength of Israel will not lie nor repent: for he is not a man, that he should repent. Then he said, I have sinned: yet honour me now, I pray thee, before the elders of my people, and before Israel, and turn again with me, that I may worship the Lord thy God. So Samuel turned again after Saul; and Saul worshipped the Lord.

This is often the heart posture of a dysfunctional functioning leader. They are only repented to the point of returning to the members' and vision carriers' good graces. Yet, pure repentance and a drive for true transformation is not in them. This is the reason God said he had chosen a replacement king that was after his own heart.

> ***1Samuel 13:14*** *But now your kingdom shall not endure. The LORD has sought out for Himself a man after His own heart, and the LORD has appointed him as ruler over His people, because you have not kept what the LORD commanded you.*

Many times the dysfunctional functioning leader has been rejected by God but:
- Refuses to acknowledge it or is not aware so they remain in position.
- Is the people's choice so they remain in position.
- The wounded leader and the people are reaping the consequences of their actions.
- The wounded leader is being used by God for talents and charisma, but God is not with him.
- The wounded leader operating in grace, as God has compassion for the souls of the people under their covering, but is not with the leader.

Even though David was anointed king, It was over 15 years before he actually took the throne. And even in knowing he was king, he had to serve a wounded dysfunctional leader who did not desire to be delivered and healed. God allowed Israel to reap the consequences of choosing man to judge and govern them rather than him being Lord over them.

Many times a dysfunctional functioning leader is over a mass of people who has chosen that leader above God. They are able to endure and tolerate the dysfunction because of their idolatry and enmeshment with that leader. And the "fixers" who work with that leader will attempt to find that leader the best medication to soothe his or her demons or refresh them where he or she can function for a time, while never really delivering, healing, and curing the leader's wounds.

> ***1Samuel 16:14-18*** *But the Spirit of the Lord departed from Saul, and an evil spirit from the Lord troubled him. And Saul's servants said unto him, Behold now, an evil spirit*

from God troubleth thee. Let our lord now command thy servants, which are before thee, to seek out a man, who is a cunning player on an harp: and it shall come to pass, when the evil spirit from God is upon thee, that he shall play with his hand, and thou shalt be well. And Saul said unto his servants, Provide me now a man that can play well, and bring him to me. Then answered one of the servants, and said, Behold, I have seen a son of Jesse the Bethlehemite, that is cunning in playing, and a mighty valiant man, and a man of war, and prudent in matters, and a comely person, and the Lord is with him.

Wherefore Saul sent messengers unto Jesse, and said, Send me David thy son, which is with the sheep. And Jesse took an ass laden with bread, and a bottle of wine, and a kid, and sent them by David his son unto Saul. And David came to Saul, and stood before him: and he loved him greatly; and he became his armourbearer. And Saul sent to Jesse, saying, Let David, I pray thee, stand before me; for he hath found favour in my sight. And it came to pass, when the evil spirit from God was upon Saul, that David took an harp, and played with his hand: so Saul was refreshed, and was well, and the evil spirit departed from him.

Everyone who is a part of the dysfunctional functioning leader's life becomes a key player in their woundedness. Everyone has a role in helping the person maintain and sustain despite the leader's dysfunction. Everyone is committed to their role and find their life's value in that role. They actually believe they were called to that role in life, and are protective of their position in that wounded leader's life. This is what made Johnathan's and David's love for one another so special. Jonathan willingly sacrificed his role as son and heir to Saul, for covenant with David.

1Samuel 18:1-4 *And it came to pass, when he had made an end of speaking unto Saul, that the soul of Jonathan was knit with the soul of David, and Jonathan loved him as his own soul. And Saul took him that day, and would let him go no more home to his father's house. Then Jonathan and David made a covenant, because he loved him as his own soul. And Jonathan stripped himself of the robe that was upon him, and gave it to David, and his garments, even to his sword, and to his bow, and to his girdle.*

David and Jonathan had pure relationship not a fixer relationship. Yet later in this chapter, we see others conspiring with Saul against David. They were key players in Saul's dysfunction, and in his woundedness wounding others.

1Samuel 18:20- 27 *And Michal Saul's daughter loved David: and they told Saul, and the thing pleased him. And Saul said, I will give him her, that she may be a snare to him, and that the hand of the Philistines may be against him. Wherefore Saul said to David, Thou shalt this day be my son in law in the one of the twain. And Saul commanded his servants, saying, Commune with David secretly, and say, Behold, the king hath delight in thee, and all his servants love thee: now therefore be the king's son in law. And Saul's servants spake those words in the ears of David. And David said, Seemeth it to you a light thing to be a king's son in law, seeing that I am a poor man, and lightly esteemed?*

> *And the servants of Saul told him, saying, On this manner spake David. And Saul said, Thus shall ye say to David, The king desireth not any dowry, but an hundred foreskins of the Philistines, to be avenged of the king's enemies. But Saul thought to make David fall by the hand of the Philistines. And when his servants told David these words, it pleased David well to be the king's son in law: and the days were not expired. Wherefore David arose and went, he and his men, and slew of the Philistines two hundred men; and David brought their foreskins, and they gave them in full tale to the king, that he might be the king's son in law. And Saul gave him Michal his daughter to wife.*

Though this plot of woundedness did not snare David, it was designed by Saul and his players to take David's life. Players aka fixers, are accessories to murder. Either they do not realize it or do not care. Many people who are under the covering of dysfunctional functioning leaders do not realize that their lives are at stake, as that leader is not able to adequately birth, cover, or spiritually govern and shepherd them. They operate in a form of God where their life and ministry looks like God, but is void of God's blessing, favor, power, purity, and Spirit. The challenge with this is many will see death and experience death, but will keep making excuses for what they discern. They hold on to optimism due to being enmeshed and bewitched by the charisma, words, and seduction of that leader and his fixers. And some are just like their leader, as dysfunction breeds and draws dysfunction.

Many ministries led by dysfunctional functioning leaders have a David in their midst. David is there by God's design to avenge God's name and word, and to be a covering for those who truly have a heart for God. Dysfunctional functioning leaders hate their David, but uses David for his gifts and talents. One minute they are trying to kill their David, and the next they love them, and want them close to them. This is because the wounded leader recognizes that God is with David, and is jealous and afraid of him.

> *1Samuel 16:21 And David came to Saul, and stood before him: and he loved him greatly; and he became his armourbearer.*

> *1Samuel 18:10-13 And it came to pass on the morrow, that the evil spirit from God came upon Saul, and he prophesied in the midst of the house: and David played with his hand, as at other times: and there was a javelin in Saul's hand. And Saul cast the javelin; for he said, I will smite David even to the wall with it. And David avoided out of his presence twice. And Saul was afraid of David, because the Lord was with him, and was departed from Saul. Therefore Saul removed him from him, and made him his captain over a thousand; and he went out and came in before the people.*

It is my belief that a dysfunctional functioning leader struggles with mental illness. They may admit it or they may not even recognize it. Though many of these leaders have times of functioning in wellness, generally, their nature is soultied to drama, chaos, instability, and mental torment. Because of the comfortability with disorder, they may not recognize that their dysfunction is unhealthy. Their personal and ministerial success, seasons of stability, along with the loyalty of their enablers, keeps them bound to the delusion that their life is alright. However, if they ventured into the counseling and psychiatric arena, many would probably be diagnosed with bipolar disorder, schizophrenia, major depression, multiple personality disorder, etc.

It is important that we begin to identify and address the issues and challenges of those operating as dysfunctional functioning leaders. Their actions may be going unnoticed and overlooked by man but not by God. Those under them and the body of Christ as a whole is infected and impacted by their actions and God is not pleased. It is quite amazing that non believers or inconsistent church goers can discern the heart and life of these leaders, yet the believers are hoodwinked and led astray. Many of these leaders are the examples people use for not coming to church, not believing in God, and not wanting to be saved. Many of these leaders are breeding other wounded dysfunctional leaders. The body of Christ is being viewed as a joke and a farce, and it is because we choose to live a lie. We let wounded leaders die in their lie, while sacrificing many sheep with their woundedness. I decree we shall rise up and begin to expose, deliver, and heal the leaders and ministries that operate in functioning dysfunction. SHIFT!

CHALLENGING OPPRESSIONS THAT INFLICT WOUNDS

Chapter 7

I would define the word drain as:
- to be bankrupt or exhausted of one's identity, abilities, resources and existence
- to deplete of strength, vigor, power, prosperity, and virtue
- to tire, empty, render useless and ineffective, or to slowly deplete until there is nothing left to give

There are many demonic spirits, attacks, character flaws, and challenging experiences that drain the leader and inflict wounds. This chapter will equip the leader with revelation to fortify against being wounded, drained, and depleted of a healthy identity, fulfilled life, successful ministry, and sustaining destiny.

Self-Pity - When engaging in self-pity, the leader is displaying pity for oneself, especially a self-indulgent attitude concerning one's own difficulties, hardships, ministry trials, and whatever else that life may unveil. Self-pity drains and steals the leader's joy, hope, fulfillment, faith in God and ability to trust and operate in Godly strength. Self-pity yields one's character to murmuring, complaining, groaning, turmoil, anxiety, restlessness, destitution, and false expectation regarding God and one's life. Self-pity opens the door to double mindedness, pride, depression and idolatry. Wounds are formed as the leader becomes angry and distrustful of God, and as the leader is hurt, appalled and even traumatized by the challenges of life. Trauma comes in as the leader is psychologically wounded, injured, and shocked due to being self focused rather than God focused.

> *James 1:2-4 My brethren, count it all joy when ye fall into divers temptations; Knowing this, that the trying of your faith worketh patience. But let patience have her perfect work, that ye may be perfect and entire, wanting nothing.*

Patience is the ability to be hopeful and cheerfully endure the trials of life and ministry, as God works in you and through you. When we "*count it all joy,*" we are continually reminding ourselves of what God has done and what he is going to do. Praise, thanksgiving, decreeing and declaring, is our weapon against self-pity. The more we engage in these weapons, we mature in steadfast faith and spiritual excellence, while reframing from being destitute in thinking that God is failing us.
As you receive deliverance from self-pity, be sure to cast out the spirit of destitution and heal wounds of trauma in this area. Build your spirit man up in the truth of God concerning your life, ministry, and destiny.

> *Romans 8:28 And we know that all things work together for good to them that love God, to them who are the called according to his purpose.*

Leech: Life Suckers - A leech is any bloodsucking or life sucking person or thing that clings to another with the intent to drain, for personal gain, and/or due to being enabled in things that they can really do for themselves. The leech usually attaches and latches on for personal gratification with no intent of giving anything in return. Whether intentionally or unintentionally, their actions operate like a parasite. They deplete and exhaust the other person's strength, power, life, and resources. Leeches steal your time, attention, energy and focus, while draining your anointing and ability to really invest in the things God desires you to fulfill and attend to. Wounds are formed as your blood is literally physically, emotionally, and spiritually drained, due to the leech feeding/feasting upon you. You are experiencing a tedious death from being sucked of all your energy, zeal, and anointing. Leeches love to come around when leaders are burned out, and have decided to take a sabbatical. They are usually in a self made crisis and draw on your compassion or "*need to fix people,*" such that you feel obligated to help them. Yet the leech is not interested in being transformed. They thrive off of drama, being unhealed, and being able to survive on the life they suck from others.

Using the redeeming blood of Jesus, cleanse out and break every soultie and mindset with the leech spirit and the fixer spirit. Close up every door and avenue with the leech spirit relationally and spiritually, and decree healing to the wounds that came to your soul, heart, mind, and body through the experience. Soak yourself in the refreshing power of the Holy Spirit to restore every way your life and anointing was drained from you.

Rejection - Rejection means *"to detest, refuse, cast out, vomit, disallow, disregard; to deem unfit or unsatisfactory."*

> *Mark 13:13 And ye shall be hated of all men for my name's sake: but he that shall endure unto the end, the same shall be saved.*
>
> *John 15:18-19 If the world hate you, ye know that it hated me before it hated you. If ye were of the world, the world would love his own: but because ye are not of the world, but I have chosen you out of the world, therefore the world hateth you.*
>
> ***The Message Bible*** *If you find the godless world is hating you, remember it got its start hating me. If you lived on the world's terms, the world would love you as one of its own. But since I picked you to live on God's terms and no longer on the world's terms, the world is going to hate you.*

We should expect rejection as it is a part of the daily life and warfare of the leader. Jesus has told us we will be hated. Not so much because of who we are, but because of who he is in us. This is inevitable and unavoidable, therefore, experiencing rejection will cause wounds for the leader. Rejection should be consistently released to Jesus, so that we can reign in a life of forgiveness and free from offense. Rejection drains the leader when it is taken personal, and when leaders allow wounds to go unhealed. The need to defend self and retaliate causes rejection to drain leaders of their desire to live for God, preach the gospel, and suffer for the sake of Jesus. Leaders will be drained of biblical truth, and will compromise the truth of the gospel, while trying to avoid rejection. When drained of truth, leaders become lukewarm, tainted, man pleasing, worldly, and idolatrous.

Ask the Holy Spirit for the ability to embrace rejection as a part of your kingdom walk. Repent for anyway you have yielded to rejection, cast out the spirit of rejection if necessary. Break any generational curses of rejection. Seek healing for experiences of rejection, and immediately seek deliverance and healing from all future experiences of rejection. Deal with it immediately before the Lord, so he can heal and restore you in his love, sonship, and spirit of adoption.

> **Romans 8:15** *For ye have not received the spirit of bondage again to fear; but ye have received the Spirit of adoption, whereby we cry, Abba, Father.*

Offense - Offense is a transgression. Offense means *"to step over the line, knowingly or unknowingly violate a law or moral standard, breech or break a covenant, vow, or boundary."* Offense causes anger, resentment, aggression, vexation, bitterness, contempt, hatred, mistrust, hurt and pain. Offenses can trap, ensnare, and be a stumbling block, where one yields to sin (fall into sin), and backsliding.

> **Luke 17:1-4** *Then He said to the disciples, "It is impossible that no offenses should come, but woe to him through whom they do come! It would be better for him if a millstone were hung around his neck, and he were thrown into the sea, than that he should offend one of these little ones. Take heed to yourselves. If your brother sins against you,[a] rebuke him; and if he repents, forgive him. And if he sins against you seven times in a day, and seven times in a day returns to you,[b] saying, 'I repent,' you shall forgive him."*

> **The Amplified Bible** *AND [Jesus] said to His disciples, Temptations (snares, traps set to entice to sin) are sure to come, but woe to him by or through whom they come! It would be more profitable for him if a millstone were hung around his neck and he were hurled into the sea than that he should cause to sin or be a snare to one of these little ones [lowly in rank or influence]. Pay attention and always be on your guard [looking out for one another]. If your brother sins (misses the mark), solemnly tell him so and reprove him, and if he repents (feels sorry for having sinned), forgive him. And even if he sins against you seven times in a day, and turns to you seven times and says, I repent [I am sorry], you must forgive him (give up resentment and consider the offense as recalled and annulled).*

The bible lets us know that it is impossible to avoid offenses. The bible uses the word "*woe*" which reveals that offense can be painful, grievous, afflicting and troubling. We should not cause others to be offended and we must release every experience of offense. Forgiveness is the cure for offense. This word *forgive* in this passage of scripture means "*to remit, depart, divorce.*" So you are literally divorcing the sin, and choosing to fall out of agreement with being offended. Any conscious, emotional, and justifiable contract you had with being offended is relinquished by your choice to breech the transgression with forgiveness. You transgress the boundary of offense with the principle of forgiveness. The offense is recalled and annulled as you withdraw the right to be offended and revoke its authority to lord over and between you and that person.

Offense drains the leader when they hold on to offense, are not able to forgive, or choose not to forgive. The bible likens offense to a millstone necklace. A millstone necklace is a heavy emotional or mental burden or hardship that physically feels like a humongous stone.

Metaphorically, it is a large stone around the neck, such that if you fall into the sea, you go straight to the bottom. The millstone is heavy and cannot float. You are not able to remove it, or to swim back up to the top with it around your neck, therefore you drown. In this case you drown in the offense. If you are drowning, you are suffocating. You are also rendered inaudible because you cannot talk underwater.

You are holding your breathe so you do not die, yet you are being drained of your life and ability to be an effective voice for God. His voice in you has been cut off as everything about you is immersed and filtered through offense. Resist any contracts with offense so that the milestone necklace does not become your portion.

Divorce the spirit of offense, break any spiritual, mental or emotional covenants made with offense, forgive your offender, use the hammer of God to break every millstone necklace, cast out any drowning or suffocation spirits that may have attached themselves to you, and spend time decreeing healing restoration to your heart, soul, mind, and spirit. Depending on the experience, offense can be threefold - against the person, against God, against the situation. Assess yourself before God concerning where your offense resides and deal accordingly with offense. Break the two or three fold cord if necessary, cast out any and all Spirits of offense, and allow God to heal every focused area of offense. Cancel every way your voice, ministry, and destiny has been cut off in the spirit and the natural, and assert your authority and right to be who God has ordained you to be.

Psychological Trauma - *Wikipedia* defines Psychological trauma *"as a type of damage to the psyche that occurs as a result of a severely distressing event. Trauma is often the result of an overwhelming amount of stress that exceeds one's ability to cope or integrate the emotions involved with that experience."* That event can be spiritual or personal, but can have such overwhelming effects that it causes trauma.

Dictionary.com defines trauma as:
1. Pathology: a body wound or shock produced by sudden physical injury, as from violence or accident
2. the condition produced by this; traumatism
3. Psychiatry: an experience that produces psychological injury or pain

In 2Samuel 13, Tamar is tricked and raped by her brother Amnon. Tamar was so distraught by the ordeal that she lived bound by trauma.

> *Verse 19-20 And Tamar put ashes on her head, and rent her garment of divers colours that was on her, and laid her hand on her head, and went on crying. And Absalom her brother said unto her, Hath Amnon thy brother been with thee? but hold now thy peace, my sister: he*

is thy brother; regard not this thing. So Tamar remained desolate in her brother Absalom's house.

<u>Desolate</u> in the Hebrew is *samem* and means:
1. to stun (or intransitively, grow numb), i.e.
2. devastate or (figuratively) stupefy (both usually in a passive sense)
3. make amazed, be astonied, (be an) astonish(-ment), (be, bring into, unto, lay, lie, make)
4. desolate(-ion, places), be destitute, destroy (self), (lay, lie, make) waste, wonder
5. to be desolate, be deflowered, be deserted, be appalled, to be awestruck
6. to be stunned, appalling, causing horror, show horror, to be astounded
7. to cause oneself desolation, cause oneself ruin

Tamar had experienced psychological trauma that put her emotions, heart, soul, and mind in shock, awe, horror, and devastation that was down right appalling. She was gripped by trauma as she was astounded that her brother would do such a horrible thing to her. Tamar definitely had a right to be dismayed, yet living in this place stole her life, identity, and destiny.

Tamar put ashes on her head, and rent her garment of divers colours. *Ashes* in this passage of scripture means "*worthless.*" Putting ashes on one's head was a sign of mourning for the dead, so Tamar viewed herself as dead. In her eyes, her life and value was gone. Tamar ripping her garments was a sign of her giving up her original purpose, favor, and identity in life, and taking on the shame, guilt, and shunning that resulted from her experience. Tamar could no longer accept who she was, and see it as her truth and ordained purpose in life.

When trauma is not dealt with, people live inside the shock of it. The bible says Tamar lived desolate inside her brothers house. She lived inside the shame, guilt and torment of her ordeal. It does not appear that she sought deliverance and healing so the trauma became the well to which she filtered and lived her life through.

Many people who experience psychological trauma build a house through their pain and devastation, and reside there.

- Most need help breaking free and releasing the shock and awe that they have experienced.
- Some do not know how to trust anyone again to be delivered and healed.
- And some are so gripped by trauma, that it has become their identity.

The gripping of trauma and pain lodged within, is what the person needs deliverance from. Trauma causes the person's life to stop, come to a halt, and they remain stuck in that experience. That experience has literally arrested - imprisoned - the person's life, and they need help breaking free from it.

Trauma can be lodged in a person's:
- Soul
- Heart
- Mind
- Body (Body Parts, Organs, Systems)
- Memories
- Personality
- Identity
- Senses

Trauma can be the result of:
- Accidents
- Sexual, Physical, Verbal Abuse
- Domestic Violence
- Control & Manipulation
- Rape
- Robbery
- Identity Theft
- Illnesses or Continual Health Problems
- Surgery or Intrusive Medical Procedures
- Separation & Abandonment
- Living in Unsafe Environments
- Divorce or Difficult/Sudden Break ups
- Bullying and/or Social Outcasting
- Unexpected Life Experiences or Sudden Difficult Life Changes
- Catastrophes: e.g. Tornados, Hurricanes, Fires, Floods, Terrorist Attacks
- Death of Loved Ones
- Warfare
- Hardships of Life and Ministry
- Offense/Betrayal
- Failure in Life and Ministry Endeavors
- Exposure of Sin Issues or Character Flaws that Cause Reproach on Self and the Ministry
- Rejection

Signs of Trauma
- The person constantly talks about the situation with no focus or ability to heal from it or move past it.
- The person constantly relives the pain over and over and lives inside of the pain.
- The person is appalled and in disbelief by what happened to them, and speaks of the situation with shock, awe, and horror even if it happened years ago.
- The person may waver between disbelief and denial of what happened to them.
- The person may be numb to their feelings, or in being able to express healthy emotion for themselves and for others.
- The person creates situations by sabotaging relationships and interactions in effort to prove or avenge what originally happened to them - to prove that this is their life's lot or that all people are bad.
- The person fears trusting, loving, or having faith in others.

- The person hates themselves because of their experience.
- The person has challenges trusting their judgement of others, and is skeptical of everyone. They exhibit continuous anxiety and paranoia. They think everyone is out to get them or do them harm.
- The person cannot forgive their offender or forgive themselves. They feel they did something to deserve what happened to them.
- The person is angry, enraged, resentful, bitter, negative, harsh, prideful, moody, irritable, discontent, and most of what they speak is filtered through these attributes.
- The person has a difficult time focusing, seems confused, edgy, easily agitated, and has problems being accountable and responsible for life decisions, and for progressing successfully in life.
- The person is focused and committed on retaliating against their offender. Much of this is psychological retaliation that consumes the heart and mind.
- The person is bound by sadness, depression and/or cycles of depression, and may experience other mental health problems.
- The person has identity problems, inferiority issues, inadequacy challenges, low self-esteem, low self-worth, and difficulty receiving compliments or encouragement.
- The person may use drugs and/or alcohol to numb pain. The person may use ministry works and assignments to numb the pain.
- The person may be promiscuous and sexually risk taking, but is not invested in committed relationships.
- They person lives from a place of hopelessness and destitution.
- The person lives in isolation, or latches on to people that they feel can protect them.
- The person is constantly and easily stressed, becomes tired easily and may experience constant fatigue. They may also use sleep as a coping mechanism to avoid pain and dealing with their trauma.
- The person is easily panicked and fearful. They often look for the worst to happen.
- The person has constant physical health issues. This could be an indication that trauma is lodged in the body.
- The person may have aches, pains, and health issues, but the doctor cannot find anything wrong with them.
- The person may have trouble sleeping and may experience nightmares related to their experiences.

Overcoming Shock and Trauma
1. Break the power and grip of shock and awe.
2. Cast out any demonic spirits of trauma, shock and awe, and any other spirits God reveals.
3. Be specific as Trauma can be lodged in a person's:
    - Soul
    - Heart
    - Mind

- Body (Body Parts, Organs, Systems)
- Memories
- Personality
- Identity
- Senses

4. Soak in the healing power of God to mend all wounds of trauma.

Hope Deferred - ***Proverbs 13:12** Hope deferred maketh the heart sick: but when the desire cometh, it is a tree of life.*

Hope deferred is when we are discouraged with waiting on the promises of God to manifest. This discouragement causes sickness in the heart, where we become depressed, and grieved, while experiencing literal heart aches and pains. This can also cause pain in the body, such as headaches, anxieties, restlessness, ulcers, tumors, cancer, irritation in the stomach, bowels, heart, physical body, imbalances in the hormones, blood levels, disease, affliction, weakness, grief, wounding, and on and on the sicknesses can manifest. The sickness occurs because the physical body is now manifesting the issues of the heart and soul.

> ***Proverbs 4:20-22** My son, attend to my words;incline thine ear unto my sayings. Let them not depart from thine eyes; keep them in the midst of thine heart. For they are life unto those that find them, and health to all their flesh. Keep thy heart with all diligence; for out of it are the issues of life.*

When there is discontentment in our heart and soul, we will feed on things that can cause cycles, habits and addictions in us. Our taste buds and desires begin to crave the unpleasant things we feed them, in hopes of fulfilling a void that really only God can fulfill. These cravings lodge in our flesh, appetite, taste buds, thought life, soul, heart and emotions. As we feed the growing web inside of us, other parts of us become weak, sick, and even die, because of the malnourishment it is receiving from false satisfaction, unfruitful satisfaction, void filling, and feeding the lust of the flesh, the lust of the eyes and prides of life. These areas of our identity can only be fulfilled when our spirit is fulfilled, and rooted and grounded in God. Otherwise we become a bottomless pit that gluttons for what it cannot contain and maintain by human means and standards.

> ***Psalms 6:2-4** Have mercy upon me, O Lord; for I am weak: O Lord, heal me; for my bones are vexed. My soul is also sore vexed: but thou, O Lord, how long? Return, O Lord, deliver my soul: oh save me for thy mercies' sake.*

> ***The Amplified Bible** Have mercy on me and be gracious to me, O Lord, for I am weak (faint and withered away); O Lord, heal me, for my bones are troubled. My [inner] self [as well as my body] is also exceedingly disturbed and troubled. But You, O Lord, how long [until You return and speak peace to me]? Return [to my relief], O Lord, deliver my life; save me for the sake of Your steadfast love and mercy.*

Delays in God are not necessarily denials. Also if God is not releasing a promise, then position yourself to expect something better. God could be desiring to go above and beyond what is intended.

>*Ephesians 3:20* Now unto him that is able to do exceeding abundantly above all that we ask or think, according to the power that worketh in us.

It is okay to ask God the reason a promise or desire is delayed, and to expect an answer. Be cautious however, in becoming sick and wounded over not receiving something from God. This is where balance is necessary. We must remain in truth about who God is. He will never leave you lacking or unfulfilled. Examine if what you are seeking is beneficial or necessary, and efficiently aligns with your destiny plan. Be okay with relinquishing that matter, if it does not prove beneficial, or if you are not receiving a clear answer regarding your promise or desire. As you relinquish it, you remove any blockages to hearing God, while opening the door to receiving, expecting, and further standing in faith for what is promised or desired.

Refuse to be fed from soulish, demonic, emotional, and immediately gratifying tables, that only cause temporary fulfillment, rather than eternal fullness in Jesus. Practice valuing the journey process, that which is generationally sustaining and fruitful, and what breeds eternal fulfillment. This will fortify you against hope deferred.

>*Psalms 16:11 The NET Bible* You lead me in the path of life; I experience absolute joy in your presence; you always give me sheer delight.

>*The Message Bible* Now you've got my feet on the life path, all radiant from the shining of your face. Ever since you took my hand, I'm on the right way.

Anger - Ephesians 4:26 *Be ye angry, and sin not: let not the sun go down upon your wrath.*

Interestingly, the word *angry* in this passage means "*to be enraged, be exasperated, irritated, aggravated, disturbed, wroth.*" When a person is "*wroth*" they are FEELING violent, turbulent in anger, where they are ready to blow a gasket. Becoming this angry is not a sin. How you DISPLAY the anger determines whether you have yielded to sin.

<u>Sin</u> in this scriptures means:
1. do not transgress, offended, to be without a share in, to miss the mark, to err
2. be mistaken, to miss or wander from the path of uprightness and honor
3. to do or go wrong, to wander from the law of God, violate God's law, sin

A lot of times we want time to calm ourselves before discussing a matter. We believe this is beneficial to avoid sining in our anger. Yet, the bible tells us to not let the sun go down on our wrath.

> ***The Message Bible reads:*** *Go ahead and be angry. You do well to be angry – but don't use your anger as fuel for revenge. And don't stay angry. Don't go to bed angry. Don't give the Devil that kind of foothold in your life.*

The bible is letting us know that it is important to resolve conflict quickly and efficiently, as it is not safe to go to bed angry. When we go to bed angry, we risk the anger settling into our soul and heart. What was a feeling has become a part of us. Also when we are sleep we are defenseless, and because there is transgressed anger in us, the enemy has a legal right to prey on us, and sow more seeds of wrath and indignation. The more anger brews in us, the more we yield to negative and venomous thoughts. This yields the potential to sin in our heart. Our emotions feed thoughts of retaliation, rage, and aggression. We lend to releasing curses through our thoughts and words, which is passive aggressive sin. Since anger is a transgression, it tears our soul and heart. Thus causing wounds that need to be healed.

If you cannot resolve a matter before bedtime, spend time in prayer, releasing your anger to the Lord, forgiving where necessary, repenting and using the blood of Jesus to cleanse any negative emotions that have settled in your soul and heart. Journaling your feelings and writing a plan for how you plan to resolve the matter the next day is also beneficial. But be sure to spend time with God acknowledging and dealing with your feelings. This will help you remain biblical in how you deal with your anger.

Meekness, temperance and love are key character traits to being able to resolve conflict when angry.

> ***Galatians* 5:22-25** *But the fruit of the Spirit is love, joy, peace, longsuffering, gentleness, goodness, faith, Meekness, temperance: against such there is no law. And they that are Christ's have crucified the flesh with the affections and lusts. If we live in the Spirit, let us also walk in the Spirit. Let us not be desirous of vain glory, provoking one another, envying one another.*

Meekness enables us to be teachable, humble, where we are focused on how we can learn and grow from an experience. When we are meek, we are postured in the gentleness and submission of God. We are focused on resolving the matter in a healthy manner that pleases and edifies God. When we are tempered, we are self-controlled. Our passions, feelings, and desires are governed by our spirit, and not in our sensual appetites and emotions. ***1Corinthians 13*** gives us great revelation on the benefits of having God's unconditional love.

> ***Verse 4-7 The Amplified Bible*** *Love endures long and is patient and kind; love never is envious nor boils over with jealousy, is not boastful or vainglorious, does not display itself haughtily. It is not conceited (arrogant and inflated with pride); it is not rude (unmannerly) and does not act unbecomingly. Love (God's love in us) does not insist on its own rights or its own way, for it is not self-seeking; it is not touchy or fretful or resentful; it takes no account of the evil done to it [it pays no attention to a suffered*

wrong]. It does not rejoice at injustice and unrighteousness, but rejoices when right and truth prevail. Love bears up under anything and everything that comes, is ever ready to believe the best of every person, its hopes are fadeless under all circumstances, and it endures everything [without weakening].

Spend consistent time through your walk asking the Holy Spirit to fill you with his fruit and character so that you can possess and operate in the nature and principles of God.

Envy and Discontentment - Proverbs 14:30 sound heart is the life of the flesh: but envy the rottenness of the bones.

> *The Amplified Bible A calm and undisturbed mind and heart are the life and health of the body, but envy, jealousy, and wrath are like rottenness of the bones.*
>
> *The Message Bible A sound mind makes for a robust body, but runaway emotions corrode the bones.*

Envy is a jealous, intense burning passion or a demonic, unhealthy zeal and desire, that usually derives from personal discontentment and insecurity. I believe that envy not only creates wounds in the soul and heart, but also causes wounds in one's identity, personality, and character. I say this because envy provokes a person to alter how they would normally respond to a person or situation. Their identity and self-perception becomes distorted as the person is challenged with not being, or having what someone else has or is experiencing.

Rottenness is *raqab* in this scripture and means "*decay.*"

Dictionary.com defines *rottenness* as:
1. decomposing or decaying; putrid; tainted, foul, or bad-smelling
2. corrupt or morally offensive
3. wretchedly bad, unpleasant, or unsatisfactory; miserable
4. contemptible; despicable
5. (of soil, rocks, etc.) soft, yielding, or friable as the result of decomposition

Envy causes the bones - the skeletal structure of your life - to be miserable, to be weak, to rot, to smell, to die.

Sound is *marpe* in the Hebrew and means:
1. curative, i.e. literally (concretely) a medicine, or (abstractly) a cure
2. figuratively (concretely) deliverance, or (abstractly) placidity
3. (in-) cure(-able), healing(-lth), remedy, sound, wholesome, yielding
4. health, healing, cure healing, cure health, profit, sound (of mind) healing

In order to have a sound heart, you must abide in the contentment of who you are, who God is, and what he has called you to do in the earth.

> ***Philippians 4:11-13 states:*** *Not that I speak in respect of want: for I have learned, in whatsoever state I am, therewith to be content. -- I know both how to be abased, and I know how to abound: every where and in all things I am instructed both to be full and to be hungry, both to abound and to suffer need. I can do all things through Christ which strengtheneth me.*

<u>Contentment is *autarkēs* in the Greek and means:</u>
1. self-complacent, i.e. contented
2. sufficient for one's self
3. strong enough or processing enough to need no aid or support
4. independent of external circumstances
5. contented with one's lot, with one's means, though the slenderest

Paul said that no matter what season of life he is in, he is instructed in how to be content. Instructed means that he is learned, trained, accustomed, and has an intimate understanding and knowledge in this area. It is so essential as leaders that we become skilled in being content. Not just when life and ministry is good, but in seasons of lack and suffering. This is an intimate equipping that comes overtime as we walk with the Lord, grow in the identity of who we are and who's he has called us to be, and learn to trust and lean on God for everything.

> ***2Corinthians 9:8*** *And God is able to make all grace abound toward you; that ye, always having all sufficiency in all things, may abound to every good work:*

> ***Hebrews 13:5*** *Let your conversation be without covetousness; and be content with such things as ye have: for he hath said, I will never leave thee, nor forsake thee.*

It is important not to yield conversation, thoughts and your heart to coveting who others are and what they have. And when you sense yourself yielding to this, get before God, be honest about your thoughts and feelings and reasons for discontentment; let him reveal and deliver you from hidden discontentment that you may not have been aware of, pursue healing and Holy Spirit empowerment in the areas of your identity, and ask him to train and equip you with abounding in every season of life with him. As he instructs you, practice journeying in a lifestyle of contentment with him.

Bitterness - Hebrew 12:15 *Looking diligently lest any man fail of the grace of God; lest any root of bitterness springing up trouble you, and thereby many be defiled.*

<u>*Bitterness*</u> in the Greek *pikria* and means:
1. acridity (especially poison), literally or figuratively, bitterness
2. bitter gall, extreme wickednessa bitter root, and so producing a bitter fruit
3. metaph. bitterness, bitter hatred

<u>Dictionary.com defines *acridity*</u>:
1. sharp or biting to the taste or smell; bitterly pungent; irritating to the eyes, nose, etc.
2. extremely or sharply stinging or bitter; exceedingly caustic

The bible also speaks of bitter waters that causes a person to be cursed. We know that if not contained, waters have the ability to spread, and cover any and everything.

> ***Numbers 5:24*** *And he shall cause the woman to drink the bitter water that causeth the curse: and the water that causeth the curse shall enter into her, and become bitter.*

Bitterness has embedded roots which poisons our spirits, souls, hearts, thoughts and emotions. Whatever we say or do has an irritating or harsh affect to it. We become pessimistic, negative, condescending, slanderous, unforgiving, and hopeless. Our outlook and disposition wreaks defeat, and we spew that onto whatever people or situations we are a part of. It is obvious that something in our soul is troubled just by what is being defiled through our words and actions, but often we are unable to receive revelation of our bitterness, because bitterness has us believing everyone is against us.

Bitterness has to be cleansed, purified and sacrificed for the exchange of a broken and contrite heart and spirit.

> ***Psalms 51:10-17 The Amplified Bible*** *Create in me a clean heart, O God, and renew a right, persevering, and steadfast spirit within me. Cast me not away from Your presence and take not Your Holy Spirit from me. Restore to me the joy of Your salvation and uphold me with a willing spirit. Deliver me from bloodguiltiness and death, O God, the God of my salvation, and my tongue shall sing aloud of Your righteousness (Your rightness and Your justice).*
>
> *O Lord, open my lips, and my mouth shall show forth Your praise. For You delight not in sacrifice, or else would I give it; You find no pleasure in burnt offering. My sacrifice [the sacrifice acceptable] to God is a broken spirit; a broken and a contrite heart [broken down with sorrow for sin and humbly and thoroughly penitent], such, O God, You will not despise.*

A broken and contrite spirit and heart yields relentless repentance and humility, where the person can be restored in his or her perception and feelings regarding life, people, God, ministry, and his or her destiny. You are literally casting yourself before God, and throwing bitterness upon the altar as a sacrifice before him. As bitterness is sacrificed and released, you are purged and restored in your heart, spirit, and soul.

Depression and Spirits of Heaviness - Depression comes to drain, distract, steal our focus, make us self-absorbed, helpless, and hopeless where we do not want to live or partake of life, or fulfill destiny. Often when we become depressed and heavy, we assume it is our issue. This is understandable if we battle cycles and the stronghold of depression, and if it is a generational stronghold that has not been cleansed out the family line. But as leaders, we can incur heaviness from:
- The people we are leading (we feel their issues and challenges)
- The region we minister in (we may live in a region that battles territorial spirits and principalities of depression; e.g. where I live depression is strong in the region during the winter months)
- Witches, warlocks, and demons (witches, warlocks, and demons send heaviness to distract and oppress us)

We therefore, must be discerning of where the heaviness is coming from so we can deal with the roots accordingly. We must use our weapons to totally dismantle its attack against us. The bible talks about the Spirit of the Lord being upon us to break the powers of depression and heaviness.

> ***Isa 61:2-3*** *To proclaim the acceptable year of the Lord, and the day of vengeance of our God; to comfort all that mourn; To appoint unto them that mourn in Zion, to give unto them beauty for ashes, the oil of joy for mourning, the garment of praise for the spirit of heaviness; that they might be called trees of righteousness, the planting of the Lord, that he might be glorified.*

<u>Garment is *ma'ateh* in the Hebrew and means:</u>
1. a vestment: — garment, wrap, mantle
2. to clothe, dress, or cover
3. blanket, wrap, veil, envelope, conceal, cover

A *garment of praise i*s armor that protects and conceals us. As we praise, we are clothed in the praise and glory that we release unto God. As he is glorified, the garments liquidate and consume heaviness and any other burdens that attempt to yoke us. The mantle of praise becomes a weapon of destruction where it literally causes an exchange by smothering heaviness, making it obsolete upon us. We then become righteous trees which means we become pillars, door posts, jambs, pilasters, strong men and women, leaders, chiefs, that assert God's governmental authority and justice. We establish God's glory in the earth.

Spirit of Fear - ***2Timothy 1:7*** *For God hath not given us the spirit of fear; but of power, and of love, and of a sound mind.*

Fear drains us of confidence, love, soundness of heart and mind, focus, and power. Fear wounds our self-esteem, self-worth, and our security in God. Fear is a bewitching sent from the enemy to:
- Render us powerless (God gives power)
- Make us feel devalued, unworthy, unlovable (God gives love)
- Cause double mindedness, turmoil, agony, confusion, instability and imbalance (God gives soundness of mind)

Fear is a real or imaginary threat sent to coward, distract, immobilize, and spiritually or naturally kill us and the destiny work we are doing.

Fear is the very opposite of the characteristics and nature of God. It is in opposition of his will for us, and our ability to represent him.

God would not cause us to fear. Fear renders us incapable of the very desires and intention that God wants us to achieve.

Though you may run into fear at some point, these fears should not stop your destiny journey. Fear only has power over us when we relinquish our power to it. When we succumb to fear, we have SHIFTED from God being our source, our strength, and the ruler of our lives, to leaning in our own ability and strength. We are also yielding to the headship, lies, intimidations, and misperceptions of the enemy. Enemy as in a person or enemy as in demonic forces.

> ***Philippians 4:19*** *But my God shall supply all your need according to his riches in glory by Christ Jesus.*
>
> ***Philippians 4:13*** *I can do all things through Christ which strengtheneth me.*
>
> ***Psalms 55:22*** *Cast thy burden upon the LORD, and he shall sustain thee: he shall never suffer the righteous to be moved.*
>
> ***1Peter 5:7*** *Casting all your care (anxiety) upon him; for he careth for you.*
>
> ***Psalms 37:24*** *Though he fall, he shall not be utterly cast down: for the LORD upholdeth him with his hand.*
>
> ***Proverbs 6:3*** *Commit thy works unto the LORD, and thy thoughts shall be established.*
>
> ***Gods Word Bible*** *Entrust your efforts to the LORD, and your plans will succeed.*

God is all about empowerment, while instilling and revealing value, and stability. His thoughts towards you are good - for your success - so that his destiny plan can prevail in your life.

Jeremiah 29:11 For I know the thoughts that I think toward you, saith the Lord, thoughts of peace, and not of evil, to give you an expected end.

Unforgiveness - As I studied forgiveness in the scriptures, I noticed that forgiveness is always mentioned in relations to sin. So whether the sin was done by us or against us, unforgiveness is linked to a sin or transgression.

When we need to forgive, it is often because someone has hurt us. But the challenge with the need to forgive is it is a sin not to forgive. Even though someone hurts us, we cause further hurt and transgression, by holding onto that hurt and hurtful experience.

Sometimes we need to forgive ourselves and ask God for forgiveness, because we put ourselves in a position to be hurt. Even as we want people to acknowledge their hurt towards us, we must take responsibility in transgressing against our own self and even against God.

True forgiveness is:
- When you are no longer trying to punish the person for what they have done to you.
- When you can talk to them and about them without wanting to subtly or blatantly put them in their place.
- When you are not constantly putting up barriers with them or others to protect yourself from being hurt again. You are peacefully resting in the wisdom you gained from that situation, and you know you have the skills not to let it happen again. You are confident in your power not to let it happen again. You are not insecure where you have walls erected for fear of being hurt again.
- When you can talk or testify of that situation without reliving the pain, hatred, animosity, agony of it. Numbness is not the same as forgiveness. So if you feel numb about a situation, then you have stuffed your pain due to deep hurt and bitterness, or in effort not to feel it. If you are numb you have not forgiven.
- When you are not trying or needing that person to change to feel and be healed, or feel like you can finally forgive.
- When you do not have to see or no longer need and desire for that person to experience hurt, or to experience demise to feel justice has been serviced on your behalf. Your justice is in knowing you have overcome not in what they do and do not do, or experience in their life.

Being cordial with someone does not mean you forgive them. It definitely does not mean you respect them, or that you are granting them grace. You cannot grant someone grace unless you truly forgive them. Being cordial just means you are tolerating them, or you could be operating in unconscious pride to prove you are the better person, but that is not forgiveness. Even though your actions are not lashing out, your heart and soul is still bound which causes you to relive the pain, frustrations, and memories in your mind every time you interact with that person, or a similar situation. Or it causes you to erect and display walls out of fear of *"that will never happen to me again."*

Forgiveness is not a verbal declaration of *"I forgive you."* It is also not an act you can will to occur. Forgiveness is a internal heart transformation. You can actually feel when you have forgiven someone. There will be a liberation in your heart and soul of knowing you are no longer bound by that person or situation. If you do not feel such a freedom from them you have not forgiven.

I say this because there is an exchange of God's freedom for our pains and bondages that takes place when we forgive.

> ***Mark 11:25-26*** *And when ye stand praying, forgive, if ye have ought against any: that your Father also which is in heaven may forgive you your trespasses. But if ye do not forgive, neither will your Father which is in heaven forgive your trespasses.*

<u>Forgive</u> is *aphiēmi* in the Greek and means:
1. cry, forgive, forsake, lay aside, leave, let (alone, be, go, have)
2. omit, put (send) away, remit, suffer, yield
3. let alone, to send away, to bid going away or depart
4. to expire to let go, let alone, let be, to disregard, to leave, not to discuss now

<u>Trespass</u> is *paraptōma* and means:
1. a side-slip (lapse or deviation), i.e. (unintentional) error or (willful) transgression
2. fall, fault, offence, sin, trespass
3. to fall beside or near something, a lapse or deviation from truth and uprightness, a sin, misdeed

When we harbor unforgiveness:
- We side-slip from handling matters from a righteous manner.
- We also may be yielding to willful sin, because we are offended and choose to remain bound to offense.
- The situation is so hurtful we know we should forgive, but we are so focused and bound by the hurt, that we have believed a lie that we cannot forgive. It is not that we cannot forgive, we have allowed hurt to consume us such that it has blocked truth. To God this is a sin, because we are not supposed to allow anything to consume us. Unhealthy consumptions become a stronghold and even an idol in our lives. The unforgiveness starts to dictate and rule us rather than God ruling us. Even though we have a right to be upset, it is a transgression to serve any other God. Even if that God is in the form of a hurtful situation.

As we consider these thoughts and the scriptures on forgiveness, we have to let go of our hurts and pains. God then forgives us for harboring those hurts and pains. When all of this is released, a freedom comes of not being bound by the situation, nor by our own agony of the situation. Let's explore how to let go and forgive.

In order to really forgive you have to sacrifice your right to be hurt and avenged. You have to give up your need to be vindicated to God, and trust him to handle the matter however he chooses. ***Psalm 51:17*** *The sacrifices of God are a broken spirit; a broken and contrite heart, O God, you will not despise.* You are already broken and contrite. You feel crushed, destroyed, ripped apart, mentally and physically distraught. However, those feelings must be sacrificed. A sacrifice is the killing or offering of something.

This word *sacrifice* means:
1. sacrifices of righteousness
2. sacrifices of strife
3. sacrifices to dead things
4. the covenant sacrifice (for the sake of covenant with God or sacrifice an ungodly covenant for God's covenant
5. the passover
6. annual sacrifice
7. thank offering

You have to release your justifications for remaining angry, resentful, and bitter. You have a right to be angry, but you do not have a right to stay angry. You have a right to be angry, but you do not have a right to be vengeful.

> ***Matthew 11:28-30*** *Come to me, all who labor and are heavy laden, and I will give you rest. Take my yoke upon you, and learn from me, for I am gentle and lowly in heart, and you will find rest for your souls. For my yoke is easy, and my burden is light.*

Labor is *kopiao* in the Greek and means:
1. to feel fatigue; by implication, to work hard
2. (bestow) labour, toil, be wearied, bestow labour
3. to grow weary, tired, exhausted (with toil or burdens or grief)
4. to labour with wearisome effort, to toil

Heavy laden is *phortizo* in the Greek and means:
1. to load up (properly, as a vessel or animal), i.e. (figuratively) to overburden with ceremony (or spiritual anxiety)
2. lade, by heavy laden, to place a burden upon, to load
3. metaph. to load one with a burden (of rites and unwarranted precepts)

You have to acknowledge and be honest about your feelings and pains. God does not want you to lie about how you feel, or deny how you feel. His desire is that you are able to be honest while exchanging your hurts for his healing.

> *Psalms 56:8* *Thou tellest my wanderings: put thou my tears into thy bottle: are they not in thy book?*
>
> ***The Good News Bible*** *You know how troubled I am; you have kept a record of my tears.*
>
> ***Hebrews 4:15 New International Bible*** *For we do not have a high priest who is unable to empathize with our weaknesses, but we have one who has been tempted in every way, just as we are--yet he did not sin.*

You have to keep sharing your thoughts and feelings with God until pure forgiveness sets in. Some experiences are so painful it takes a while to get over them. God understands that, but we have to understand that. Sometimes there are generational roots and propensities of anger, bitterness, unforgiveness, resentment, retaliation, etc., lodged within us. There can also be a generational propensity to experience what happened to us. When a negative situation intertwines with these roots and propensities, it can make it hard to forgive. The roots and propensities have to be dealt with, along with the situation we are experiencing. Otherwise it can prolong healing. More time in prayer is needed to intercede for yourself and the family, to gut out those roots and propensities so true healing can occur.

> ***Psalms 34:18-19*** *The Lord is nigh unto them that are of a broken heart; and saveth such as be of a contrite spirit. Many are the afflictions of the righteous: but the Lord delivereth him out of them all.*

Destiny Killing Spirit - *John 10:10 The thief cometh not, but for to steal, and to kill, and to destroy: I am come that they might have life, and that they might have it more abundantly.*

The destiny killing spirit attacks personally and generationally. It wants to kill your destiny, and any way God's plan for your life impacts your lineage, and present and future generations. This spirit usually begins its attack at a young age, even at birth, and then attempts to kill the person's identity, purpose, and hope, at a young age. This is the reason so many Christians, especially leaders, experience challenging childhoods. The enemy is striving to kill the person before they realize there is a plan for their lives.

Most parents tend to cultivate a child's talents and giftings, rather than really seek God about the child's purpose and destiny. This allows the destiny killing spirit to have free reign. This spirit comes in and wreak havoc by interjecting negative experiences that alters the child's destiny, or tie the child to desires and behaviors, where he or she wants to use his or gifts and talents for the devil rather than God. Please understand that talents and gifts are a part of our identity, but do not necessarily determine our purpose and destiny. Many of us do things very well because of the supernatural ability in us. That does not necessarily mean that it is God's will and plan for our lives.

- Jesus was a carpenter, but his destiny was to save the entire world.

- David was a shepherd and talented musician who tended to sheep, but his destiny was to be king.
- Joseph was a dreamer and dream interpreter, but his destiny was to be appointed second-in-command to King Pharaoh, while leading the nation in a strategy to prosper during a time of famine.
- Many of the disciples were fisherman by trade, but their destiny was to be fishers of men.

Most times we operate in our gifts and talents and never move from that dimension of destiny success. Gifts and talents make room for your destiny, but do not necessarily determine what you will fully accomplish or be in destiny. After we begin moving in our gifts and talents, we should be asking, what are we to be doing to really give God glory, as that is what the enemy is after.

Proverbs 18:16 A man's gift maketh room for him, and bringeth him before great men.

New International Bible *A gift opens the way and ushers the giver into the presence of the great.*

The devil will let you move in your gifts and talents as long as you do not SHIFT into operating in your destiny. This is the reason the secular world is full of great singers, dancers, and actors that we idolize for their talents, but their lives have not SHIFTED into destiny. We assume their talent is their purpose. However, it just opens a greater realm for destiny to unfold. Many do not pursue destiny after being successful in their talent, because destiny is tied to our creator - the Lord himself. You cannot really know true destiny without God.
- Without him you are just winging it.
- Without him you are just trying to keep the spotlight that your gift acquired for you.
- Without him you have success, but no true fulfillment.
- Without him you are just doing good things that may glorify him, but not the ordained purpose that is sure to give him glory.

Psalms 16:2 O my soul, thou hast said unto the LORD, Thou art my Lord: my goodness extendeth not to thee.

New International Bible I say to the LORD, "You are my Lord; apart from you I have no good thing."

Jeremiah 10:23 I know, O LORD, that the way of man is not in himself, that it is not in man who walks to direct his steps.

Matthew 4:4 But he answered, "It is written, 'Man shall not live by bread alone, but by every word that comes from the mouth of God.'

> *John 15:5* *I am the vine, ye are the branches: He that abideth in me, and I in him, the same bringeth forth much fruit: for without me ye can do nothing.*
>
> *John 15:16* *Ye have not chosen me, but I have chosen you, and ordained you, that ye should go and bring forth fruit, and that your fruit should remain: that whatsoever ye shall ask of the Father in my name, he may give it you.*

The fruit of most people die with them, because it is rooted in gifts and talents, and not destiny. Their name may last through generations, but their works die with them. We honor the name legacy when it's nothing more than idolatry through the exaltation of a person's abilities. We have no regard to how or even if they impacted generations, or whether God received glory. If God is not glorified, then it is talents and works, but not destiny.

> *John 4:34* *Jesus saith unto them, My meat is to do the will of him that sent me, and to finish his work.*
>
> *The Amplified Bible* *Jesus said to them, My food (nourishment) is to do the will (pleasure) of Him Who sent Me and to accomplish and completely finish His work.*
>
> *John 5:30* *I can of mine own self do nothing: as I hear, I judge: and my judgment is just; because I seek not mine own will, but the will of the Father which hath sent me.*
>
> *Luke 2:48-49* *And when they [Joseph and Mary] saw Him, they were amazed; and His mother said to Him, Child, why have You treated us like this? Here Your father and I have been anxiously looking for You [distressed and tormented]. And He said to them, How is it that you had to look for Me? Did you not see and know that it is necessary [as a duty] for Me to be in My Father's house and [occupied] about My Father's business?*
>
> *John 5:19* *So Jesus explained, "I tell you the truth, the Son can do nothing by himself. He does only what he sees the Father doing. Whatever the Father does, the Son also does."*

This is vital for leaders because we assume that destiny occurs when we obtain the position and the platform. This is just your gifts and talents making room for you. Now that you have it, how will you use it such that God gets the glory.

The challenge with this is, by the time many of us become leaders,
- We do not know what our destiny and purpose is.
- We are more validated by our status and position than God getting glory.
- Our character is not mature enough to handle the position and platform.
- We SHIFT to being platform and fame driven than God driven.
- That we do not consider what God's ordained purpose for our life is.

We have been conditioned since birth that our talents is who we are and so we keep being talented as we equate that with a successful destiny. Since the destiny killing spirit is on the prowl and clear about his assignment, he creates platforms and opportunities to keep leaders bound to talents, so we will not focus on destiny, or he attacks us so we do not believe destiny is attainable.

The destiny killing spirit is always prowling for an open door, but will surely strike when the leader is:
- In a wilderness, isolation, or loneliness season.
- Weak in maturity in his spirit man, where flesh and soul is ruling and governing his or her life.
- In a season of isolation with God, or needs a time of consecration with God.
- Hungry for more of God.
- Hungry for more success and life advancement.
- Desires a greater platform and position.
- Driven by fame and fortune.
- In a season of transition.
- At a crossroads with God concerning his or her life and destiny.
- In a season of SHIFTING from gifting to calling.
- In a season of SHIFTING to another dimension of destiny.

When the devil tested Jesus in the wilderness, he was striving to get Jesus to exchange destiny for his talents and abilities (***Study Matthew 4:1-11, Luke 4:1-13***). But Jesus knew his purpose.
- He had nothing to prove to Satan.
- Did not need validation regarding his identity and purpose.
- Understood that his life was not about self glory, but God getting glory

Leaders must be clear and grounded in these areas, so that when the destiny killing spirit attacks, he will not find any claim to overtake them.

> ***John 14:30-31*** *I will not talk with you much more, for the prince (evil genius, ruler) of the world is coming. And he has no claim on Me. [He has nothing in common with Me; there is nothing in Me that belongs to him, and he has no power over Me.]. But [Satan is coming and] I do as the Father has commanded Me, so that the world may know (be convinced) that I love the Father and that I do only what the Father has instructed Me to do. [I act in full agreement with His orders.] Rise, let us go away from here.*

Sexual Immorality - Due to the pleasure and need for love and belonging, sexual sin can be difficult to overcome. We have been given the perception in Christendom that sex is a bad thing, and that even to desire it is a sin. Sex is not a sin if done in the context of marriage between a husband and wife. God has created us where it is natural to desire fulfillment in this area, which is one of his purposes for marriage.

Sexuality immortality works through the well of a destiny killing spirit. It is tied to perversion, burning lust, and inordinate affections that are rooted in our flesh. The flesh cannot be fed. It must be mortified, or it will seek to lead you into spiritual and eternal death. As a counselor, it has been my experience that many leaders live on the edge, where they are receiving just enough pleasure to feed their desires for love and belonging, but not enough to mortify the flesh. Many then contend they are living a pure life. In their minds they are doing just enough to feel like they are not sinning, but not enough to say they are at risk to sin. The challenge with sexual immortality is that any small window leaves opportunity for full blown sin to operate.

> **Romans 7:21-23** *I find then a law, that, when I would do good, evil is present with me. For I delight in the law of God after the inward man: But I see another law in my members, warring against the law of my mind, and bringing me into captivity to the law of sin which is in my members.*

There is always a law in our flesh that is trying to work to override our spirit. This law cannot be reasoned with, negotiated with, or offered a compromise. It must be killed. This is where we have to desire and love purity, and practice the fullness of purity in our lives. In this day and age where perversion and lust has infiltrated every major platform of life, we have to up our game with guarding our gates and righteous standards. The more we become desensitized and lukewarm, the more sexual immorality will become common place in our lives and ministries. Leaders have to want to be the standard for righteous indignation and purity. We need male leaders to rise up in the standard of purity. Female leaders are open about their desire and stance for purity, yet most male leaders do not assert God's word and truth in this area. I am not sure if this is because it is not macho to boast of purity or what, but it seems that men are bound in secret sexual sin because there are no public role models in this area. Moreover, many women are starting to feel helpless in sustaining in their purity, because there does not appear to be any men who are upholding or living the standards of righteousness. One of the most devastating challenges that kept Tamar bound to desolation after her brother raped her was that he had defiled her purity (*2Samuel 13*). She understood that purity was essential to her identity and she was appalled that it was ripped away from her.

The infiltration of sexual immorality in this day and age is comparable to rape, because we are being stripped of our right to choose what is appropriate for us or not. Yet, we are not appalled by it.
- It is called Facebook, and we deem it as our platform and page, but we are not given a choice as to what comes on our page or not. We are infiltrated, and then after infiltration, we have a right to choose if it remains or not.
- It is our TV, but we are not given a choice of what commercials come on in between programs, and whether what we are watching will suddenly implement an immoral act. We only have the option to change it after we are exposed to it.
- We are not given an option of whether our children are taught about same sexual relationships and contraceptives in school. We are only given the choice to teach

them from a biblical standpoint, and hope they choose God's values over the world's standards.

I could go on and on with examples, but the point is we are being violated, and do not even realize it. These infiltrations come to weaken and steal our standard of purity and righteousness. We have to view this as an attack against God and his word, hate anything that steals the purity and context of his word, standards for our lives, and refuse to allow them to become common place in our lives and ministries.

It begins with the leader being the standard of God's word, and wanting to be the standard. Wanting to please God and be an example of his word, while being appalled, defying, and fleeing anything that would contradict your purity in God.

> ***1Corinthians 6:9-10*** *Know ye not that the unrighteous shall not inherit the kingdom of God? Be not deceived: neither fornicators, nor idolaters, nor adulterers, nor effeminate, nor abusers of themselves with mankind, Nor thieves, nor covetous, nor drunkards, nor revilers, nor extortioners, shall inherit the kingdom of God. And such were some of you: but ye are washed, but ye are sanctified, but ye are justified in the name of the Lord Jesus, and by the Spirit of our God.*
>
> ***1Corinthians 6:18*** *Flee fornication. Every sin that a man doeth is without the body; but he that committeth fornication sinneth against his own body.*
>
> ***1Corinthians 10:13*** *There hath no temptation taken you but such as is common to man: but God [is] faithful, who will not suffer you to be tempted above that ye are able; but will with the temptation also makes a way to escape, that ye may be able to bear [it].*
>
> ***Matthew 5:28*** *But I say unto you, That whosoever looketh on a woman to lust after her hath committed adultery with her already in his heart.*
>
> ***Colossians 3:5*** *Mortify therefore your members which are upon the earth; fornication, uncleanness, inordinate affection, evil concupiscence, and covetousness, which is idolatry.*

Since **Romans 7** tells us that there is a war between the flesh and the spirit, even as we are delivered, we must view and approach sexual immorality as a war. The societal infiltration alone lets us know that it is always seeking to steal, kill, and destroy us.

Rebellious Spirit and Acts - 1Samuel 15:23 For rebellion is as the sin of witchcraft, and stubbornness is as iniquity and idolatry. Because thou hast rejected the word of the LORD, he hath also rejected thee from being king.

Dictionary.com defines *rebellion* as:
1. open, organized, and armed resistance to one's government or ruler
2. resistance to or defiance of any authority, control, or tradition

Dictionary.com defines a rebel as:
1. a person who refuses allegiance to, resists, or rises in arms against the government or ruler of his or her country
2. a person who resists any authority, control, or tradition
3. rebellious; defiant

Rebellion engineers as a destiny killing spirit. When we operate in rebellion it bewitches us into thinking our actions are okay and even justifiable. This spirit gives the assumption that we are entitled to behave rebelliously and even makes us stubborn and idolatrous where we only think of ourselves. Nothing or no one else is considered in the choices we make as the aim is to please self and fulfill some justifiable need within ourselves.

Dictionary.com *defines* defiant as:
1. Generally insubordinate
2. Contumacious-stubbornly perverse or rebellious; willfully and obstinately disobedient
3. Refractory-hard or impossible to manage, hard to fuse, resistant to ordinary methods of treatment
4. Recalcitrant-noncompliant
5. Rebellious, insolent; daring, resistant, challenging

Rebellious people will have:
- Challenges unifying with the plan and direction of the Lord, ministry and team members.
- Resist direction and redirection from God, overseers, and those who help carry the vision of their lives and ministry.
- Have challenges following or complying to the rules and regulations, and vision God has provided for their lives and ministry.
- Resist following requirements for preparing themselves for ministry engagements.
- Unifies just enough to say they are obeying God or to say they are compromising with ministry endeavors, but not enough to be a true team player, or to avoid being disobedient and defiant to God, the team, and ministry.
- Can easily fall into backsliding, as they do just enough at times to comply, but not enough to be truly transformed.
- Will attempt to coast off his or her gifting and will get away with sins because of his or her gift, charisma, and status, but will be a disruption and open door to bringing warfare, reproach and impurity to ministry, to those they oversee or minister to, and to his or her own destiny.

Saul's destiny was thwarted because of rebellion. God raises up apostles and prophets. He does not raise up witches and warlocks. God will use your gifts and talents to advance his kingdom, while rejecting you as his leader, and stripping you of your destiny.

1Samuel 1:15:23 For rebellion is as the sin of witchcraft, and stubbornness is as iniquity and idolatry. Because thou hast rejected the word of the Lord, he hath also rejected thee from being king.

Verse 28 And Samuel said unto him, The Lord hath rent the kingdom of Israel from thee this day, and hath given it to a neighbour of thine, that is better than thou.

1Corinthians 9:27 But I keep under my body, and bring it into subjection: lest that by any means, when I have preached to others, I myself should be a castaway.

2Corinthians 13:5 Examine and test and evaluate your own selves to see whether you are holding to your faith and showing the proper fruits of it. Test and prove yourselves [not Christ]. Do you not yourselves realize and know [thoroughly by an ever-increasing experience] that Jesus Christ is in you – unless you are [counterfeits] disapproved on trial and rejected?

It is important to do consistent self checks of your spirit and fruit, as rebellion comes to drain you of your obedience and humility unto God. You cannot implement half of God's vision for your life and ministry, and think God is pleased. Especially if you changed it because of your own pride and self glory. You will mistake fruit as God's will, without considering that God will never compromise his word for our kingdom advancement. Consistent self-exploration will posture you in Godly truth regarding your motives and intent, and whether God is guiding, pleased and being glorified by your decisions and actions.

Spirits and Trials of the Past - Philippians 3:12-14 Not as though I had already attained, either were already perfect: but I follow after, if that I may apprehend that for which also I am apprehended of Christ Jesus. Brethren, I count not myself to have apprehended: but this one thing I do, forgetting those things which are behind, and reaching forth unto those things which are before, I press toward the mark for the prize of the high calling of God in Christ Jesus.

Such spirits keep people bound to past painful experiences, and to generational strongholds. They keep people remembering and reliving the past, even though God has brought deliverance and healing through the works of Jesus Christ. Spirits of the past keep leaders bound in hardship. Even if the leader is advancing, they experience constant trials, or keep leaders from going beyond a certain point of success. Spirits of the past also keep leaders bound in torment, shame, guilt, and condemnation. They constantly remind them of who they were, and what they have experienced. The leader battles inadequacy and insecurity regarding being a sufficient leader, and being able to progress in the plan God has ordained for their lives.

Cast the spirit of the past out and any trauma attached to them, break soulties from your heart, mind, emotions and memories that may be tied to the past. Repent, forgive, and release all hurtful and inadequate thoughts and emotions related to the experiences. Ask God to heal painful memories and experiences of the past, and any guilt, shame, and condemnation attached to them. Receive God's healing and move forward to focusing on future endeavors.

Warfare and Sufferings as Vision Carriers - 2Corinthians 10:3-4 *For though we walk in the flesh, we do not war after the flesh: (For the weapons of our warfare are not carnal , but mighty through God to the pulling down of strong holds).*

<u>Warfare is *strateia* in the Greek and means:</u>
1. military service, i.e. (figuratively) the apostolic career (as one of hardship and danger): — warfare
2. an expedition, campaign, military service, warfare
3. metaph. Paul likens his contest with the difficulties that oppose him in the discharge of his apostolic duties, as warfare

As leaders, apostles, fivefold ministers, and saints of Jesus Christ, warfare is a part of our calling. Depending on the type of leader you are and the position you hold, the warfare is a career of warfare and danger. Paul likens warfare to being in a military service. He used his calling as an apostle to express that for some leaders, it is part of ones' calling to be opposed and to contend for the gospel of Jesus Christ. Therefore, the warfare should not be a shock or a challenge to you. It should be expected and embraced as a part of your calling.

This is so important because often we equate warfare as:
- Being out of the will of God or in sin.
- Not having enough faith or maturity concerning the things of God.
- Being in demonic oppression or bondage.
- An indicator that we are not successful, or we are failing in our destiny or ministry.

Or we may not adequately discern when warfare is not about our destiny and calling, such that we are not aware of the open doors in our lives and ministries.

Some leaders contend that grace, or not acknowledging or focusing on the devil guards them from warfare. I have not found this to be biblical or reality. Our entire walk is rooted in asserting our authority over the enemy. Acting like the devil does not exist is not going to make him go away. He is coming for you whether you like it or not or whether you want to fight or not.

> **Matthew 11:12** *And from the days of John the Baptist until now the kingdom of heaven suffereth violence, and the violent take it by force.*

There has to be a balance in understanding that warfare is a part of a leader's position, and the importance of closing doors to unnecessary warfare. Since we know warfare is inevitable, leaders must engage from an offensive position. Often as leaders we are trying to defend ourselves from the warfare we are encountering, rather than being offensive in training ourselves as skilled warriors so we can attack the enemy before he attacks us, or close off doors and gateways to attacks. In becoming offensive, we are asserting our authority and power over the enemy, and our kingly right as saints, and leading governmental officials in the earth. When we are offensive, we achieve and receive the victory that Jesus gave us through the works of the cross, because we are asserting our authority over blessings and successes that rightfully belong to us. When we are defensive, it is like trying to do Jesus works all over again. We are trying to win something that is already ours. Instead of exercising our authority over what has already been won for us.

> *1John 5:4 For whatever is born of God overcomes the world; and this is the victory that has overcome the world-- our faith.*

We do not have to be afraid of warfare because:
- God is a God of war (*Exodus 15:3*)
- God teaches us how to war (*Psalms 18:44, Psalms 144*)
- God gives us insight into the enemy's camp, and how to defeat the enemy (*2Timothy 2:7, Daniel 9:22, 1Corinthians 2:12, Matthew 16:18-19*)
- We are already victorious (*Romans 8:37*)
- God provides insight concerning our calling and the warfare it entails (*Ephesians 1:18-19*)
- We have power over all the power of the enemy (*Luke 9:1, Luke 10:19*)
- The battles is not really ours, we are just vessels God uses; the battle is the Lords (*2Chronicles 20:25, Isaiah 54:17*)

As leaders we should be seeking God for insight on the movements and activities of the enemy, and pursuing strategy on how to stop him and defeat him. The devil should dread coming to our address, because he knows we will be waiting on him, and even attacking him before he gets there.

> *Psalms 44:5 Through You we will push down our enemies; through Your name we will trample those who rise up against us. For I will not trust in my bow, nor shall my sword save me. But You have saved us from our enemies, and have put to shame those who hated us. In God we boast all day long, and praise Your name forever.*

WHEN GOD REQUIRES YOU TO MINISTER WOUNDED!

Chapter 8

When I experienced betrayal, I was very wounded deeply. God had released me to leave the church I was attending, and focus on further launching my own ministry. I had already been walking in my ministry while at my present church, as it had been established for about four years. Now it was time for me to take my ministry to the next dimension in God, and it required my total attention. I was simply doing as God led me, but sometimes within the body of Christ, we have a difficult time letting go. We mistake someone's leaving and advancing to a new dimension in God as abandonment, impure motives, and intent to harm or desecrate, divide, etc. Misperceived fears and hurts from these perceptions, created an open door for betrayal to occur.

Since I was leaving a church, I thought I was going to get to sit down, hide, or at least take some time to heal. I thought those who were my accountability partners were going to tell me to sit down too. They were very mature, balanced, and stable in God, and in my thoughts, would never recommend I minister unhealed. And I surely thought my new overseer was going to say *"girl sat down some where and heal."* Unlike many others, I was openly honest in saying *"I am in pain, my heart hurts; it hurts like a stabbing knife, it feels like someone is ripping my heart out."* But God told me I would heal as I go, and those in authority over me confirmed that.

I wish I could say, I got over my woundedness quickly, as I usually get over stuff pretty fast. As a counselor and spiritual warrior, I have a lot of tools for dealing with challenging situations. By the time you try to help me, me and the Lord have already dealt with it, and I have moved on to being about my father's business again. I also pride myself on being a representation of healing, so l do not let stuff linger. I however, had to walk this healing out. And I had to do it in front of my team, those I ministered too, and those who wounded me, while towering over the principalities that wanted to use my woundedness to annihilate me.

I wish I could say it only took a few days, a week or month, or even a year. It took me two years to completely heal. That was two years ago, and I still have to check myself from time to time, to make sure I am living and operating from a healthy place. This is where you have to value process, and where you have to want to live in the character and nature of God.

Some leaders will contend God told them not take time away from ministry to heal, even though they have transgressed in a sin or they are wounded. The challenge with this is there is:
- No conviction for where they are in their spiritual walk.
- No true demonstration to want to be delivered and healed, or to pursue deliverance and healing.

- Minimal to no fruit that the character and nature of God is birthed and operating through their lives.

Even though I had not sinned, I had conviction because I was not healed. I had concern for how my woundedness would impact those I led, those I ministered to, and the vision I was planting and plowing.

Often times people mistake conviction for condemnation and they rebuke it, or ignore it, because they think it is demonic.

> ***John 14:26*** *But the Comforter, which is the Holy Ghost, whom the Father will send in my name, he shall teach you all things, and bring all things to your remembrance, whatsoever I have said unto you.*

> ***John 15:26*** *But when the Comforter is come, whom I will send unto you from the Father, even the Spirit of truth, which proceedeth from the Father, he shall testify of me:*

<u>Comforter</u> in the Greek is *paraklētos* and means:
1. intercessor, consoler: — advocate, comforter
2. summoned, called to one's side, esp. called to one's aid, one who pleads another's cause before a judge
3. a pleader, counsel for defense, legal assistant, an advocate
4. one who pleads another's cause with one, an intercessor of Christ in his exaltation at God's right hand, pleading with God the Father for the pardon of our sins
5. in the widest sense, a helper, succourer, aider, assistant of the Holy Spirit destined to take the place of Christ with the apostles (after his ascension to the Father)
6. to lead them to a deeper knowledge of the gospel truth, and give them divine strength needed to enable them to undergo trials and persecutions on behalf of the divine kingdom

How can the Holy Spirit teach us all things, right and wrong, right from wrong, the truth of Jesus Christ, be an advocate, intercessor, teacher, trainer, imparter of doctrine, be the spirit of truth, if he does not convict us when we operate contrary to God's principles?

> ***Romans 8:1*** *There is therefore now no condemnation to them which are in Christ Jesus, who walk not after the flesh, but after the Spirit.*

> ***The Amplified Bible*** *THEREFORE, [there is] now no condemnation (no adjudging guilty of wrong) for those who are in Christ Jesus, who live [and] walk not after the dictates of the flesh, but after the dictates of the Spirit.*

If you are in Christ and are walking after the Spirit, you should not feel condemned. But if you are walking in the flesh - sining and transgressing, you should feel condemnation. There is no way to walk after the spirit and sin. At that point you are operating in flesh and therefore, condemnation of your sin comes upon you. Moreover, you should want to experience condemnation at that moment, as it is an indicator that you are no longer "*in Christ.*"

Condemnation actually means to be judged as guilt or to incur damnation. It means you are unfit or have failed. Somewhere we have misinterpreted that condemnation means shame and guilt, and that we should not have any shame and guilt as a believer in Christ. If we have sinned or we are living beneath or contrary to the principles of God, we should have some remorse, shame, and guilt about that. Now I am not saying we should be shamed by people or be damned to hell, but we should feel shame and guilt, such that we have conviction and want to change.

Many leaders have no conviction and even with condemnation upon them, have no shame and guilt about their sin or wounded state. Paul was given a thorn in his side that buffered him, to keep him humbled, due to the revelations he received from Jesus.

> ***2Corinthians 12:7-10*** *And lest I should be exalted above measure through the abundance of the revelations, there was given to me a thorn in the flesh, the messenger of Satan to buffet me, lest I should be exalted above measure. For this thing I besought the Lord thrice, that it might depart from me. And he said unto me, My grace is sufficient for thee: for my strength is made perfect in weakness. Most gladly therefore will I rather glory in my infirmities, that the power of Christ may rest upon me. Therefore I take pleasure in infirmities, in reproaches, in necessities, in persecutions, in distresses for Christ's sake: for when I am weak, then am I strong.*

Paul was so challenged by this buffeting that he sought God three times to remove the thorns. He had a concern about having a wound that yielded the impression that he was unhealed or in sin. This is so key for leaders. If we are going to be true representations of Jesus Christ, we should display concern when anything in our lives does not represent him sufficiently. We should never loose our conviction in this area, and when we do, we should check to make sure we are "*in Christ.*" Only *in Christ* do we experience the dictates of the Holy Spirit.

My heart felt like a never ending bleeding painful wound that I thought everyone could see. I thought it was so evident that I just looked like brokenness. This was really the enemy tormenting me. Even still, I knew that if I was going to minister in healthiness despite being wounded, I had to abide "*in Christ.*" I had to live inside of his presence, so that everything I did or said was filtered through him, and not through my woundedness. Though I already thought I lived "*in Christ,*" as a lifestyle. I learned very quickly that there is a difference in experiencing Christ and literally living inside of him.

> ***John 15:3-4*** *Now ye are clean through the word which I have spoken unto you. Abide in me, and I in you. As the branch cannot bear fruit of itself, except it abide in the vine; no*

more can ye, except ye abide in me. I am the vine, ye are the branches: He that abideth in me, and I in him, the same bringeth forth much fruit: for without me ye can do nothing.

<u>Abide</u> in the Greek is *memo* and means:
1. abide
2. in reference to place: to sojourn, tarry
3. not to depart
4. to continue to be present
5. to be held, kept, continually
6. in reference to time: to continue to be, not to perish, to last, endure
7. in reference to people: to survive, live
8. to remain as one, not to become another or different

Dictionary.com contends that *abide* means, "*to continue or last in a particular condition, attitude, relationship, etc. last.*"

If we abide with God then it is not a place we go to when in need or want, it is where we live. We are housed inside of him. It is the place where we dwell - we are housed inside of him. We never depart from his presence.

So abiding in God is about continually:
- Living inside of him
- Building a relationship with him
- Resting in whoever we are in him and whatever we do for him

Abiding is never ending. Therefore, abiding in God denotes a continuous planting and plowing in our relationship with him. It is about initiation and operating in a continual cultivating of growing in relationship, and in the maturity of the character, nature, will and plan of God.

Additionally, abiding in God is about ability and capability. It is about that which is not of God dying, and the ability and capability to continually produce and reproduce that which is of him.

> **The Amplified Bible of John 15:1-2 reads like this:** *I AM the True Vine, and My Father is the Vinedresser. Any branch in Me that does not bear fruit [that stops bearing] He cuts away (trims off, takes away); and He cleanses and repeatedly prunes every branch that continues to bear fruit, to make it bear more and richer and more excellent fruit.*

If we as leaders, are really abiding in God, there should be continual development and transformation of who we are, and who he has created us to be. As we are continually developed and transformed, his character and nature, will and plan should be produced in us so that we can reproduce his character, nature, will, and plan in others.

As we abide, what is being done in and through us, should be getting better and better – richer and richer - as God's work and fruit is being produced and reproduced in us. So my question as we consider whether a leader can really govern ministry when wounded, is are we abiding in his glory when leading while wounded?

- Is the leader getting better?
- Are those or that which we are producing and reproducing getting better and richer?

In my experience, as I learned to lived in God's presence, I did get better, and those I led got better. Even though my process took two years, I was literally being shaped into the character and nature of God. Because of the pain I endured and the ministry that was being granted to my hands, I spent much of my free time with the Lord. If I was not working or doing ministry, I was with the Lord. For those who know me that read this book, they will contend that I already did this. But my abiding place was so different. I was not just seeking to have revelation and knowledge of the character, nature, plan, and will of Christ. I was seeking to literally become the character, nature, plan, and will of Christ. I was seeking to be the walking embodiment, a living carrier of God. I SHIFTED from pursuing to being. I believe God took me through a slow process of healing from woundedness, so it could become my lifestyle, and so I could role model and teach others that this is what true salvation is all about. Where we live in Jesus, and he lives in us. Anything else is a facade of glory. And we are fooling ourselves to think he is a part of it.

One of the fads we see in this day and age, is many quote and apply the principles of God's character and nature, will and plan, and thus display the ability and capability to produce and reproduce what appears to be God's fruit. But what we must understand is that quoting and applying principles is nothing more than activating a formula.

Formulas get results but if we are not truly abiding in God where development and transformation of his character, nature, will and plan is taking place in us and in what he has granted to our hands, then the formula is producing and reproducing what is in us. We are producing and reproducing after our own kind, rather than the authenticity of the true and living God.

We can call it God all we want, but if we do not look like God, act like God, produce and reproduce God, it is not being cultivated in God's abiding presence. We have mistaken production and reproduction as an derivative to it being God. We also have mistaken our ability to produce and reproduce after our own kind, as it being God.

But that is a formula. It is not authentic fruit of abiding in God. It is not supposed to look like us, act like us, and produce/reproduce us, it is supposed to look like, act like, produce, and reproduce God. Let's explore what authenticity is.

Dictionary.com defines *authenticity* as:
1. not false or copied; genuine; real
2. having the origin supported by unquestionable evidence; authenticated; verified
3. entitled to acceptance or belief because of agreement with known facts or experience; reliable; trustworthy
4. Law: executed with all due formalities (strict adherence to established rules and procedures; rigidity)
5. Credible, dependable, actual, legitimate, factual, bona fide, the real deal

What does the legitimate, bona fide, fruit of the Lord look like, act like?

Since Jesus is the vine, we are the branch, God is the vine dresser, we have to understand that God is not going to dress us with fruit that is not of him. As we abide in him, we go through a continual, never ending purging process. The word purge in this scripture means *"to expiate, to prune, to cleanse from filth and impurities."*

Expiate means *"to atone for; make amends or reparation,"* which means as God purges us, we are continually being reconciled unto God for our wrong doings through the works that Jesus Christ did for us through the cross.

Dictionary.com defines *prune* as:
1. to cut or lop off (twigs, branches, or roots).
2. to cut or lop superfluous (sur-per-flu-ous) (being more than is sufficient or required; excessive, unnecessary or needless) or undesired twigs, branches, or roots from; trim.
3. to rid or clear of (anything superfluous or undesirable).
4. to remove (anything considered superfluous or undesirable).

So as we are abiding in God, living in his presence, he is constantly pruning anything that is ungodly, impure, sinful, filthy, unhealthy, undesirable, not needed, excessive, so that the works of Jesus can be evident in our lives. These branches are constantly being cut off and lopped off - constantly being pruned - so we can bear the fruit of God, and produce and reproduce his fruit in the earth.

> *Matthew 7:16-20 Ye shall know them by their fruits. Do men gather grapes of thorns, or figs of thistles? Even so every good tree bringeth forth good fruit; but a corrupt tree bringeth forth evil fruit. A good tree cannot bring forth evil fruit, neither can a corrupt tree bring forth good fruit. Every tree that bringeth not forth good fruit is hewn down, and cast into the fire. Wherefore by their fruits ye shall know them.*

> *2Corinthians 3:18 But we all, with open face beholding as in a glass the glory of the Lord, are changed into the same image from glory to glory, even as by the Spirit of the Lord.*

If we are living in the glory, then the glory is serving as a mirror where we see our authentic selves, what needs to be changed in us, and seeing who God wants us to become. We are then being transformed into the authentic image of the Lord the more we abide in his glory – the more we shift into deeper realms of his glory.

As we continue to learn how to live in and from the presence of the Lord, we have to continuously check ourselves and check our fruit. Our fruit will let us know if we are really living in the presence of God - engaging the authentic presence of God or working a formula. If we are not changing, getting better, if we have the same ungodly attitude and habits, if we are drawing people who look and act like us, rather than look and act like the God in us, then we are not truly abiding in the glory of the Lord.

- We are doing works and principles but not relationship.
- We are applying principles but the principles are not activated in our lives and interactions with the Lord.
- We maybe having encounters with God but not truly living inside the continual authentic presence of God.
    - Encounters are temporary and fleeting; abiding is eternal.
    - Encounters are a quick fixes like a drug – a high - that eventually leaves you empty and wanting; abiding is fulfilling and takes you from level to level in feasting in God.
    - Encounters leave open doors to your fruit being stolen by the enemy, the world and by people; abiding keeps you hedged in your deliverance, healing and breakthrough where the fruit of God is sustained and advancing in your life.
    - Encounters disconnect you from God such that you are vulnerable to connecting to other vines and letting other sources dress you in their fruit. Abiding keeps you hooked to the vine of Jesus where only God dresses you with his fruit.
    - Encounters produce/reproduce what and for what is occurring in that moment. Abiding produces/reproduces what is needed and plentiful for the future, while constantly sustaining you inside present glory.
    - Encounters have you striving to create experiences with God and even build high places on encounters you deem powerful or most divine. Abiding builds revelation, confidence, and faith that everything about your life is an experience with and in God.

Humility is essential to abiding in "*in Christ.*" When God had me minister through a season of woundedness, I had to humble myself under the hand of God and inside the presence of God. I had to be open and accepting of truth about where I was in my walk, what I needed to be whole, and receiving truth from those who had to walk with me in that season. I had to understand that even as I needed God, it was not about me, while at the same time, knowing that I needed God and was nothing without him. I had to also understand that I needed him like never before, and part of my transparency before the people, was demonstrating that so they too could draw into him.

A lot of leaders who are in sin or woundedness lend to pride to overcompensate for their transgression and/or deficiency. Then as they are trying to explain their situation to the people, they present themselves as prideful, inconsiderate, immature, unaccountable, and unreliable. They make God and his word look cheap, mundane, and impossible to achieve. The people take on the mindset that if the leader cannot be whole, then how can they be whole.

> ***1Peter 5:6*** *Humble yourselves therefore under the mighty hand of God, that he may exalt you in due time.*

<u>Humble</u> is *tapeinoō* in the Greek and means:
1. to depress; figuratively, to humiliate (in condition or heart): — abase, bring low, humble (self)
2. to make low, bring low, to level, reduce to a plain
3. metaph. to bring into a humble condition, reduce to meaner circumstances
4. to assign a lower rank or place to, to abase, to be ranked below others who are honoured or rewarded, to humble or abase myself by humble living
5. to lower, depress of one's soul bring down one's pride, to have a modest opinion of one's self, to behave in an unassuming manner devoid of all haughtiness

You cannot truly abide in God and view that as a necessary lifestyle, until you have humbled yourself. Without humility you go in and out of his presence. It is more of an experience or dwelling when you need God, more so than knowing you have to live every moment from his glory. Many leaders are more challenged that their sin is exposed or that their woundedness is put on display, than debasing themselves so people will know that our walk is not about us, but about God. In that, people will know there is more to God than what they are presenting him to be. Even Jesus humbled himself, even unto death. He was willing to become death so that God could be honored, exalted and glorified.

> ***Philippians 2:7-8*** *But made himself of no reputation, and took upon him the form of a servant, and was made in the likeness of men: And being found in fashion as a man, he humbled himself, and became obedient unto death, even the death of the cross.*

When God requires you to minister wounded, it is because he can trust you with the vision he has given you. He can also trust you with the people, while he uses the process of your woundedness for his glory.

If God allows you to minister wounded, it is because he believes he can trust you with:
- the souls of people
- the vision he has given you
- his word
- his glory

When God allows you to minister wounded:
- If you hurt his people you are quick to repent to God and the people you hurt, and correct your actions.

- If you hurt the vision, you are quick to repent to God, your team and those that are helping you to carry the vision. You rectify your actions, and correct and cleanse out anything you have imparted and done to the vision that is not of God.

- You do not make excuses for your sins, and you do not use your wounds as an excuse not to accept responsibility for your actions. You are also quick to demonstrate true repentance through your actions.

- You do not water down, twist, confuse, or contaminate God's word to cover up or negate your sin or wounds. You will not misrepresent God's word where others begin to stumble and become complacent with living in sins and wounds.

- You do not steal God's glory by making the people feel guilty about wanting you to be accountable to being healed of your sins and wounds. You release glory to God by being a walking demonstration of his deliverance, healing, and covenant restoration.

- You will not infect the people where they are producing and reproducing after your sins and woundedness. Those you lead and impart into will begin to look more and more like God as you are cultivated and demonstrating his image.

- People will clearly see God's sufficiency of grace upon you, as it would be a testament of his supernatural power. In this fashion, the wound would not get the glory, the person would not get the glory, the devil would not get the glory; God would get the glory.

Is God getting glory from your broken place or you just too haughty to take time to learn to abide in Christ?

We have a lot of ministers claiming God told them to minister while in sin and woundedness and God is not getting glory out of their lives. Because they will not hear truth or we withhold truth, these leaders are not healing, and the people in the pews are not healing. They are producing after their own kind and calling it God. And we are what they are producing and we are calling it God. It is a delusion that has gripped many in the body of Christ, such that the world does not even believe in our bible or our God anymore. I decree a SHIFT in truth and Holy Ghost conviction is returning to God's leaders and people. I decree scales are falling from our eyes, and we are falling before God; seeking to know him and to live inside of his essence and glory. SHIFT!

Wisdom Keys For Abiding In Christ
- Renew your mind in the revelation of living "in Christ" and abiding in him.
- Renew your mind in the spirit of humility and begin to practice debasing yourself for God as a lifestyle.
- Spend time soaking and resting in the glory of God rather than pursuing encounters.
- Ask God to make you his character, nature, image, plan, and to reveal his identity that is already within you so that you can become one with it and embrace it as your truth.
- Give up anything that is not the truth of who God is.
- Receive deliverance and healing from anything that is not the truth of God.
- Practice giving up spiritual and religious gimmicks, fads, and movements that appear as God encounters, but are just formulas producing and reproducing after their own kind.
- Do self checks to make sure you have his DNA, such that you produce and reproduce him.
- If God requires you to minister wounded, be conscious in making sure you abide in him, so that everything you say and do is filtered through him.
- Seek him for healing of your sin and woundedness, and remain accountable to abiding in the process until you are healed.
- Do whatever God tells you to do as he is processing you to wholeness. Stick with the process no matter how long it takes for you to be delivered, healed, and walking in sustaining wholeness. Make sure you have fruit that you are whole, and can demonstrate that consistently in your everyday life.
- Do not make excuses for your sin and woundedness. Repent quickly when you hurt others, the vision of the ministry, or grieve the Holy Spirit.
- Be honest with yourself when God has not told you to continue ministering in sin and woundedness, but it is you that do not want to take time away from ministry. Recognize that this is unhealthy; take time away from ministry to receive deliverance and healing, so that you will not be producing and reproducing sin and woundedness, but God's fruit and glory.

ABIDING IN CHRIST DECREE

Chapter 9

We know from the previous chapter that when we abide in Jesus we become the essence of him - who he is, what he is, how he is, and what he has. We become his character, his nature, his existence, his prototype, his image.

We are able to remove and kick anything out simply by abiding in him and declaring over ourselves, the essence of who, what, and how he is in us, to us, and through us.

> *Galatians 2:20 I have been crucified with Christ; and it is no longer I who live, but Christ lives in me; and the life which I now live in the flesh I live by faith in the Son of God, who loved me and gave Himself up for me.*
>
> *Colossians 2:6 Therefore as you have received Christ Jesus the Lord, so walk in Him.*
>
> *1John 2:6 the one who says he abides in Him ought himself to walk in the same manner as He walked.*
>
> *1John 3:24 The one who keeps His commandments abides in Him, and He in him We know by this that He abides in us, by the Spirit (essence) whom He has given us.*
>
> *John 6:56 He who eats My flesh (my essence) and drinks My blood (my essence) abides in Me, and I in him.*
>
> *John 15:4-9 Abide in Me, and I in you. As the branch cannot bear fruit of itself unless it abides in the vine, so neither can you unless you abide in Me. I am the vine, you are the branches; he who abides in Me and I in him, he bears much fruit, for apart from Me you can do nothing. If anyone does not abide in Me, he is thrown away as a branch and dries up; and they gather them, and cast them into the fire and they are burned.*

Spend five to ten minutes a day soaking yourself in this truth: *I am the literal deliverance, healing, wellness, prosperity, wholeness, essence, truth, and miracle working power of Jesus Christ.* As things try to challenge this truth, kick it out of your body, soul, heart, mind, spirit, life, and situations.

Abide In Christ Decree!
I am delivered because I am Deliverance.
I am healed because I am Healing.
I am boundary-less and limitless because I am Breakthrough.
I am saved because I am Salvation.
I am a living miracle because my daddy JESUS is The Miracle Worker.
I am miraculous because I am a Miracle Worker.
I perform miracles because I am Dunamis Power.

I am demon and stronghold free because I am Supreme Power Over Every Enemy.
I am victorious because I am Victory.
I am free because I am Holy Ghost Liberation.
I am sin free because I am the Habitation of God.
I am Holy fire because I am Baptized By Fire.
I am a glory carrier because I am Rivers Of Living Water.
I am healthy because I am Wellness.
I am complete because I am Wholeness.
I am blessed because I embody Blessings.
I am wealthy because I am Prosperity.
I am generous by I am Generosity.
I am a lender to nations because I am a Commandment Keeper.
I have the Spirit of excellence because I am Excellency.
I am unwavering faith because I am Radical Faith.
I am a mountain mover because I am Belief.
I am rooted and grounded because I am divine Foundation.
I am gifted because I have God's Substance.
I am the epitome of God because I am his Essence.
I lack nothing because I have God's Fullness.
I am integral because I am Godly Character.
I am the existence of God because I have his Nature.
I know truth because I am Truth.
I am uniquely me because I have God's Identity.
I am valiant because I am Strength.
I am fulfilled because I am Joy.
I love unconditionally because I am Love.
I work miracles because I am Compassion.
I am embracing because I am Gentleness.
I am loved because I am Kindness.
I am docile because I am Meekness.
I am humble because I am Humility.
I am balanced because I am Temperance.
I conquer tribulation because I am Peace.
I am patient because I am Patience.
I endure all because I am Long Suffering.
I have instruction because I am Counsel.
I have clarity because I am Understanding.
I am empowerment because I am Revelation.
I have information because I am Knowledge.
I have direction because I am Wisdom.
I have supernatural capability because I have Divine Might.
I worship Jesus only because I am worship.
I honor Jesus because I am Reverence.
I serve Jesus because I am The Fear of The Lord.
I have destiny because I am Destiny.

I am marvelous because I am Magnificence.
I am successful because I am Greatness.
I create because I am Creation.
I recreate because I am like my Creator.
I transform because I am Transformation.
I establish the kingdom because I am Kingdom.
I advance the earth because I am a Trailblazer.
I am fruitful because I am Production.
I generate and regenerate because I am Reproduction.
I bring increase because I am Multiplication.
I have dominion in the earth because I am Subduer.
I govern the earth because I am a Dominion Heir and King.
I judge because I am Justice.
I birth and give life because I am Life.
I raise the dead because I am Resurrection.
I live forever because I am Eternal life.

DISMANTLING THE WOUNDS OF BETRAYAL

Chapter 10

Betrayal seems to be inevitable in ministry. Though there may be some who have dodged the knife, I do not know any leader who has not experienced betrayal. I guess if Jesus experienced betrayal, then we should expect for it to come to our doorstep at some point in our Christian walk. I would have to admit that I have not experienced pain so treacherous than when being betrayed. It was like an exposed, bleeding, painful wound that I thought would never stop hurting, throbbing, and revealing itself, while spilling all over me. The pain consumed my heart, my soul, my thoughts, my body. And even though I clearly knew who I was, whose I was, my calling and destiny, the betrayal sought to consume my perception of myself, my perception of others, my perception of God, and what he has called me to do. The betrayal tried to define and redefine me. It was after my identity.

See betrayal comes for your existence, worth, position, and purpose. Betrayal tries to get you to prove who you are, even though it clearly knows who you are, and wants you dead. This is the reason Jesus would not save himself from being crucified - he had nothing to prove.

> ***John 10:17-18*** *Therefore doth my Father love me, because I lay down my life, that I might take it again. No man taketh it from me, but I lay it down of myself. I have power to lay it down, and I have power to take it again. This commandment have I received of my Father.*

Betrayal usually occurs with someone who has partaken of who you are. They are aware of your identity, your value, your ability, and your purpose, but they are willing to sacrifice who you are for their personal gain.

Though not always the case, often times betrayers do not realize that are betrayers or that they are going to betray you. Most betrayers think they are doing a good deed by sacrificing you for what they perceive to be the greater good. If they gain from their good deed then "all is well in love and war." Their payment - their advancement - is simply a reward for a job well done.

Though betrayal is meant to ignite death, the betrayer may not consider this when they are sacrificing you. Many of them do not realize they have opened a portal to your demise. Many do not realize this until it is too late, as whether done ignorantly or unintentionally, there is no undoing of betrayal.

Though not always the case, often times relationships of betrayal cannot be mended because the betrayer either cannot forgive themselves, or cannot SHIFT pass what they did to you. Your very presence is a constant reminder of their actions, and so in order to have relationship with you, they have to see you from a new place. Not from what they can gain from you being sacrificed, but what they gain from you being a valuable part of their life and the world at large. They must be delivered and healed to acquire a new enlightenment about you. And often times they are so bound by shame and guilt, that even if they obtain a measure of healing, it rarely lends itself to restoration of the relationship, because the spirit of condemnation kills it. This is the reason Judas killed himself. He could not bear the affliction of his folly.

> ***Matthew 27:3-5 The Amplified Bible*** *When Judas, His betrayer, saw that [Jesus] was condemned, [Judas was afflicted in mind and troubled for his former folly; and] with remorse [with little more than a selfish dread of the consequences] he brought back the thirty pieces of silver to the chief priests and the elders, Saying, I have sinned in betraying innocent blood. They replied, What is that to us? See to that yourself. And casting the pieces of silver [forward] into the [Holy Place of the sanctuary of the] temple, he departed; and he went off and hanged himself.*

Many betrayers will not physically take their life, but they will kill the relationship with you, because they cannot stomach the responsibility of their actions toward you.

When betrayal spirals, it causes others to betray you. Even if they do not agree or have no clue why you are being betrayed, they just jump on the band wagon, "*crucify him,*" simply because the others around them are doing it.

> *Luke 23:20-24 Once more Pilate called to them, wishing to release Jesus; But they kept shouting out, Crucify, crucify Him! A third time he said to them, Why? What wrong has He done? I have found [no offense or crime or guilt] in Him nothing deserving of death; I will therefore chastise Him [in order to teach Him better] and release Him. But they were insistent and urgent, demanding with loud cries that He should be crucified. And their voices prevailed (accomplished their purpose). And Pilate gave sentence, that what they asked should be done.*

This is the reason Jesus said: "*Forgive them for they know not what they do*" (**Luke 23:34**).

Though not always the case, often when leaders are betrayed, the only thing you have done wrong is be you. Most times the only transgression that occurred was that you were about your father's business. You were walking in destiny and the enemy wanted to thwart it. He rattled a few haters and had them whisper in an insecure person's ear that had access to you; or maybe he had haters show their indignation towards you, and that insecure person became the catalyst for the spirit of betrayal to

operate. This happened to Jesus. Jesus was just "*doing him*" and in came the vile of betrayal. Fact is, you are who you are and there is nothing betrayers or devils can do about it.

> *Matthew 26:60-65 But they found none, though many witnesses came forward [to testify]. At last two men came forward And testified, ThisFellow said, I am able to tear down the sanctuary of the temple of God and to build it up again in three days. And the high priest stood up and said, Have You no answer to make? What about this that these men testify against You? But Jesus kept silent. And the high priest said to Him, I call upon you to swear by the living God, and tell us whether you are the Christ, the Son of God. Jesus said to him, You have stated [the fact]. More than that, I tell you: You will in the future see the Son of Man seated at the right hand of the Almighty and coming on the clouds of the sky. Then the high priest tore his clothes and exclaimed, He has uttered blasphemy! What need have we of further evidence? You have now heard His blasphemy.*

Many of the people who you did not expect to get on the ban wagon, those you ministered to and poured into, well - they are insecure too. Many of them do not know their identity and are broken in their identity. While jumping on the band wagon, they now feel betrayed by you for doing God's will, and being an example of how they need to grow up, mature in the Lord, and stop using you to identify and bring worth to them. They are not ready to grow up even though you have been equipping them. Since betrayal is nobody's friend and has exposed them, they will be forced to mature or reap the consequences of their actions. But let me leave that alone. You get the point right????

Below are some wisdom keys to help leaders dismantle and heal from betrayal.

Wisdom Keys for Dismantling Betrayal:
Know your Identity - Know who you are and whose you are, so when you experience betrayal, no matter how confusing or baffling, you will not be shaken in your identity.

Do Not Defend Yourself - Do not defend who you are to jealous, covetous, and hating people. Even those in authority will come for you and try to shake you in your identity, make you feel like what has occurred is your fault and you should rectify it. They will try to use their platform and position to get you to agree with lies that have been spoken about you and untruths regarding your identity. Speak the facts - the truth in love and meekness. Do not argue and do not defend. Respect whatever they believe is their truth, while peacefully not wavering in yours. Just be who you are, and let the God in you speak for itself.

Choose Your Battles - Even as God will redeem you, you will have to pick and choose when to stay silent as the process of betrayal unfolds, and when to speak truth. Jesus said that all would know the truth after the betrayal was over, and he was sitting at the right hand of God, and floating in the clouds. The power, miracles, signs and wonders after the betrayal is where your life really speaks and defends you. This may not come for days, months, or years later. But be okay with allowing it to be your voice rather than you defending yourself from an experience that has already unfolded and cannot be stopped. Yes! Once betrayal begins, it fulfills its agenda whether we like it or not. The pain, reproach, and death is inevitable. I would have to say you die a spiritual death then you are raised to life in resurrected power. The challenge is that once the betrayal unfolds, many people try to stop it. This just makes matters worse and makes you look guilty. You are fighting against a transaction that has taken on a spiritual assault within the minds and ideologies of the people, and within the spirit realm. The best way to combat this is to walk it out, and let God and your destiny avenge you.

Forgive - Forgive and release those who persecute you no matter how hard it is to let the pain go. When considering my experience with betrayal, since I had done everything as God had required, I was not expecting to be betrayed. I mean I should have expected it as all the signs were there. But I was still hoping to be celebrated and supported by those who knew me, knew my character, who was close to me, and who I had spent years pouring my life into. I had to diligently pray until real forgiveness was birthed in my heart. I spent countless days and hours in prayer releasing those who betrayed me, begging God to stop the bleeding, and take away the pain. Sometimes my mind would be tormented with thoughts of those who betrayed me. I also have a gift of being able to hear what is going on in the enemy's camp, and the thoughts of others. I was plagued by the continual betraying that was occurring. I could confront people with literal words they had spoken about me, and they would stand awed, unable to deny what I shared. Sometimes I spent days rebuking thoughts and releasing forgiveness, all while working a full time job and doing ministry.

I share this because forgiveness is not a choice. It is a commandment. It poses a contingency where you are only forgiven if you forgive.

> *Matthew 6:14-15* *For if ye forgive men their trespasses, your heavenly Father will also forgive you: But if you do not forgive others their sins, your Father will not forgive your sins.*

> *Matthew 18: 21-22* *Then Peter came to Jesus and asked, "Lord, how many times shall I forgive my brother when he sins against me? Up to seven times? "Jesus answered, "I tell you, not seven times, but seventy-seven times."*

> *Colossians 3:13* *Forbearing one another, and forgiving one another, if any man have a quarrel against any: even as Christ forgave you.*

I wanted to forgive because I wanted to heal and be healthy. I also wanted God to be pleased with me and how I handled the situation. Others were watching me, so I knew it was important for me to handle my experience in a healthy manner. In addition, I never want to put myself in a position to wound others. Wounded people wound others. For that reason alone, it was worth doing whatever necessary to forgive. You have to figure out what is more important to you, retaliating, begrudging, or forgiving and healing? It may be difficult to process through it, but it is so worth it. You are worth it! Your destiny is worth it!

Release the Pain - You are going to be bitter, angry, enraged, appalled, baffled, confused, tormented, feel rejected, and etc. You are going to want to fight, retaliate, defend yourself, prove yourself, slander those who slandered you, tell your side of the story to whoever will listen. You are going to feel shame, guilt, reproach; wonder why you did not discern it, condemned that it is happening to you, and reproached by being in the negative spotlight. You are going to cry and cry and be grieved by what happened. Even grieve the relationships you lost due to the betrayal. You are going to grieve the loss of the betrayer, especially if they were close to you. You are going to want to quit ministry and never help people again. You are going to want to distrust everyone, even those who support you. Every part of you may hurt, and you will just want it to stop. I felt like I was being stabbed over and over and over, in my heart and soul. Sometimes I would be bowed over in agony, while asking God to heal me. Though I wanted to get a knife and get to cutting some folks up, I did not lash out at anyone. I took my pains and tortured feelings to God, and I kept taking them and kept taking them and kept taking them, until he healed me.

> *Ephesians 4:31-32 Get rid of all bitterness, rage and anger, brawling and slander, along with every form of malice. Be kind and compassionate to one another, forgiving each other, just as in Christ God forgave you.*

> *The Amplified Bible Let all bitterness and indignation and wrath (passion, rage, bad temper) and resentment (anger, animosity) and quarreling (brawling, clamor, contention) and slander (evil-speaking, abusive or blasphemous language) be banished from you, with all malice (spite, ill will, or baseness of any kind). And become useful and helpful and kind to one another, tenderhearted (compassionate, understanding, loving-hearted), forgiving one another [readily and freely], as God in Christ forgave you.*

This may not be what you want to hear, but I am revealing a process to you that will save you a lot of extended heartache. You already in pain, why add to it?

Conquer the Shock & Trauma - Do not get stuck inside the shock, trauma, and pain of betrayal. Do not bury the trauma and woundedness of betrayal. Jesus could have died and refused to raise up as savior. But Jesus had work to do. He had purpose beyond the betrayal. You will want to quit, you will want to hide, you will be trying to figure out how to get the pain to stop, so you can deal with what you are experiencing. You will have to be wise in not quitting, hiding, stuffing, and blowing a gasket, as you walk through the betrayal and deal with the aftermath.

Your body, heart, and soul, will start to go numb in effort to deal with the shock and trauma of the ordeal. Do not see this as a good thing, as it will feel like the pain has lessened. But please do not mistake this as healing, because it is not healing. You are actually absorbing the feelings and pain, and it is becoming a part of you. It is becoming a part of your soul, heart, spirit, body, personality, and identity. If you do not get true healing, it will overtake your ministry and destiny. Remember these are bleeding wounds that are spilling on everything. You have to purpose to "*get rid*" of them. That means you are not agreeing with them. You are opposing them, rejecting them, and refusing to allow them to become your truth.

Just as you did with forgiveness, you will have to spend time before God being honest about your feelings, releasing your pain to him, receiving his healing, while rebuking and casting out any demonic spirits, thoughts, and feelings that are trying to become a part of you. Deal with trauma and shock as demonic spirits as they are like weapons that lodge inside of you that create knife like wounds. You may literally feel these spirits lodged in your heart, back, spine, etc. Deal with the spirit of betrayal as a death spirit as it did come to kill your identity and destiny.

Break Powers of Fiery Darts - Break the powers of shame, guilt, public reproach and accuser of the brethren. Declare favor and blessings over yourself with man and God. Cleanse yourself of all fiery darts, daggers, and word curses that will be sent by those who jumped on the band wagon.

Stand in Your Godly Truth - Confusion and bewitchment will come for your truth. They will come for your truth concerning the situation, your identity, who God is, your purpose, authority, and destiny. God is not the author of confusion (***1Corinthians 14:33***). This is the work of the enemy trying to further entangle you in the bondage of betrayal. Spend consistent time, declaring out your truth in every area, and be quick in rebuking thoughts of confusion and bewitchment that come for your truth.

Annihilate Depression & Loneliness - Depression and loneliness will also come for you. Study the story of Jesus in the garden of Gethsemane (***Matthew 26:36-56***). He had disciples not too far from him, and they meant well, but there was only so much support they could give him in this time of betrayal and preparing for the cross. Jesus felt depressed, grieved, and lonely. He rebuked the disciples for not staying awake and praying with him. He even asked God to take the cup of destiny away from him. Jesus could have just sat in the garden and drowned in his sorrow. Instead he chose to commune with God. In these instances, you have to know that you are not down trodden or alone. God is with you and journeying with you. Resist yielding to depression and loneliness, while drawing nigh to God for strength and rejuvenation to press forward in the battle.

Give up the Need to Avenge - Please know that you have to give up your drive and burning lust for revenge and to be avenged, in order to really forgive and heal. With the experiencing of betrayal, God does the judging and avenging. God is going to bring justice to you, redeem you, and bless you right in the midst of your enemies. But it is by his design and timing. And you have to trust him with this part of the experience. As I pondered on revenge in my prayer times, it became scary to think about the fact that people had to be judged and chastened by God, rather than to be avenged by me. I actually began to have pity and mercy for them. Truth is we should want people to be delivered and saved over being destroyed. When I gained this revelation, I was excited;

it revealed maturity in my healing process, and that I had fully released this situation to God.

> ***2Chronicles 20:15*** *And he said, Hearken ye, all Judah, and ye inhabitants of Jerusalem, and thou king Jehoshaphat, Thus saith the LORD unto you, Be not afraid nor dismayed by reason of this great multitude; for the battle [is] not yours, but God's.*

> ***Romans 12:19*** *Dearly beloved, avenge not yourselves, but rather give place unto wrath: for it is written, Vengeance is mine; I will repay, saith the Lord.*

Possess God's Eyes - Ask God to give you a love and compassion for those who betrayed you, and to help you discern and engage them as he sees them. This will help you as you continue to deal with the betrayal, the aftermath, and process forward in complete healing. This will also help you in times where you may have to interact with those who betrayed you. Operating through the love and compassion of God will give you a desire to want to see them delivered rather than destroyed. In my ordeal, God had placed such a love in me, that I was praying for him to take the judgment he had released against my betrayers away. I was standing in the gap asking God to forgive them for what they did to me, repenting on their behalf, and to spare them of hardship. Even to this day, I have and I will be given the opportunity to minister deliverance and healing to them. The very persons that betrayed me, will one day need me to save their life. You may be chosen to save those that betrayed you. Leave the justice to God, and ask him for the ability to love the unworthy and the unlovable.

Be Watchful, Meek & Temperate - Ask God for a meek and temperate spirit to deal with conflicts and challenges that will arise during the aftermath of the betrayal. Also be slow to speak. And slow to become offended. Rest in the truth of God and search God for what to say and how to speak it.

> ***James 1:19*** *Understand this, my dear brothers and sisters: You must all be quick to listen, slow to speak, and slow to get angry.*

Be okay when you do not have an answer right away for what is being asked of you. Let the person/people know that you need time to pray and consider what is being spoken, and you will yield and answer when God has released you to speak. This is important because you will be enthralled with debates and gossip regarding the betrayal. People may testify wrongly against you to further strengthen what has been spoken. People you do not know or barely know may make you feel obligated to defend gossip. They will come to you as middle men claiming that God sent them as mediators to bring restoration with those that betrayed you. Be careful not to end up in a lion's den situation that God has delivered you from. A lion's den situation is when someone is trying to get you to reenter a situation that God has already delivered you from. They claim that they want to reunify and bring healing between you and your betrayers, and this may very well be their heart. But if it is not God's will, then it is a set up to devour you through a false unification that God has not designed. If Judas wants to apologize and restore relationship, he will come on his own accord. He will not send a mediator to do his work for him.

People are going to come to you in private appearing to have your best interest at heart, but they will just be seeking to obtain more information to further slander you. Be watchful and diligent so you will not be tricked into speaking and doing something that will incite drama or grieve God.

Avoid Re-Wounding - Those who support you will want to discuss the situation over and over, as they are trying to process their pain and challenges too. But you have to guard your heart in making sure you do not continuously relive the betrayal over and over, through those who are players in the experience. You are before God and he is healing you, but your healing is stolen by those who still mean bad for you, or those who are trying to understand the situation. Jesus never relived the situation with the disciples. Not even those who denied him, or those who did not believe that he was savior. And he never relived it with those who witnessed him being betrayed or raised from the dead. Nor did Jesus return to those who betrayed him, and try to get them to acknowledge what they had did to him. I had to learn that these actions, even if well intended, reopened my wounds, and restarted my healing process. So to stop the reopening of wounds, the re-bleeding, I began to guard my heart.

> **Proverbs 4:20-23** *My son, attend to my words; incline thine ear unto my sayings. Let them not depart from thine eyes; keep them in the midst of thine heart. For they are life unto those that find them, and health to all their flesh. Keep thy heart with all diligence; for out of it are the issues of life.*

Have Accountability Partners - I only had a few people that I would discuss the betrayal with. They were mature leaders committed to making sure I had healthy dialog that kept me focused on God healing me. They did not feed into my pain. They acknowledged my pain, provided wisdom as God led, and prayed for me in that moment so that I could be strengthened in my process to complete healing.

Resist Gossip - If people came to me discussing the betrayal, even if they had my best interest at heart, I would tell them I do not care to discuss the matter. I respected their hurt and shared how I was taking my pain and challenges to the Lord. I encouraged them to do the same. I also would share keys I was receiving to deal with the betrayal in a healthy way.

If gossipers came to me, I would immediately stop them from being messy. I would bless my betrayer and speak well of them. That often silenced the slanders, or they would try to change what they were speaking of. If they were trying to get me to share my story, I would tell them I do not care to discuss the matter. Gossipers cannot defend you, as they are not able to carry truth. By the time they repeat whatever is stated, a lie has already intertwined with it. Save yourself some heartache by not entertaining their slanderous character.

When I did share my story, it was at God's leading. Sometimes I knew the purpose and sometimes I did not know the reason God led me to share. This was few and far between, and was for God's glory. In those moments, I did not see God redeeming me. I saw the supernatural strength and character he had given me to endure the situation.

Be A Godly Example - Be cognizant of the people watching you. Even if they are waiting for you to fall, they are learning from your experience. You are teaching them how to overcome betrayal. The more we have people dealing with betrayal in a healthy manner, the less hurt and drama we will have in the body of Christ.

Consistently Check Yourself - Conduct healing checks with the Lord. Ask him if you are healed yet and allow him to show you areas where you are still wounded. This is important because the more you process towards healing, the better you will feel, and the more confident you will be. But you want to make sure nothing is hiding, nothing has been stuffed, and that there is no residue of betrayal on you. You want to be fully resurrected in the new place and identity that you are to journey into.

Wisdom Keys for Reconciling - Some of those that betrayed you, particularly the band wagon betrayers, will want to restore relationship with you. Though not always the case, the most you may achieve is the initial part of reconciliation, yet full reconciliation where the relationship can be restored takes work.

> *2Corinthians 5:18-21 And all things are of God, who hath reconciled us to himself by Jesus Christ, and hath given to us the ministry of reconciliation; To wit, that God was in Christ, reconciling the world unto himself, not imputing their trespasses unto them; and hath committed unto us the word of reconciliation. Now then we are ambassadors for Christ, as though God did beseech you by us: we pray you in Christ's stead, be ye reconciled to God. For he hath made him to be sin for us, who knew no sin; that we might be made the righteousness of God in him.*

If we consider this scripture, reconciliation is a two step process. Initial reconciliation says we have acknowledged our faults and forgiven one another. Now we have SHIFTED to a place where we favor one another enough to consider relationship again. But the latter end of reconciliation means that I am accepting all that comes with being forgiven, and want to be restored with the intent to rebuild, revive, and reestablish our covenant relationship. This means we are committed to learning one another from this new restored place; learning our potential in this new restored place, and practicing engaging one another from this place until a new unimpaired relationship forms between us.

The challenge with this is that the original relationship was killed by betrayal. Paul told the people to be reconciled as ambassadors of Christ. Christ as they knew him had changed, and their position as resurrected believers had changed. You are now a different resurrected person because of betrayal, so you cannot go back to that person even if you wanted to. You are not sure if the other person is just sorry or has really changed. You cannot know that just from the initial exchange of reconciliation. You can only know that by relationship.

Let me say it another way: Initial reconciliation is the resolving of an alt, a breech, or transgression. The relationship part of reconciliation is the mending of that alt, breech, or transgression, where division no longer exists. That is the reason many believe in God and acknowledge him as their savior, but they are not fully reconciled back to him. They are sorry, and want a savior, but not truly converted into salvation. They believe he is the savior and want the fruit of that. Though God has forgiven them of their sins, they are not fully converted into salvation, such that they receive all it entails, as that only comes with journeying in relationship with him.

It takes a strong person, to really accept forgiveness of their sin, especially betrayal, and then commit to walking in a renewed covenant relationship from a new place. They have to trust that you have forgiven them, forgiven themselves, have received deliverance and healing, and are willing to live out that deliverance and healing in a relationship with you. Many say that is what they want, but do not do the work to see that come to pass. Therefore, do not be surprised if you reconcile with Judas, but do not restore covenant with them.

Those that betrayed you may assume that because you all have initially reconciled that there is restoration of relationship. Let me say it another way: Relationship means we are actively working on building healthy interactions with one another beyond toleration. If we are just tolerating one another, then we are being cordial and respectful, while sharing a common space. God does this all the time with people. They contend they are walking in relationship with him, but he does not have covenant with them.

Rest in your Healing Process - It is important to receive peace concerning those who you have cordial reconciliation with, and even those who have betrayed you, and never tried to reconcile. It may feel awkward to be around them, but do not succumb to being fearful. No, you are not going to give them a chance to betray you again, but you are not going to engage them from an unhealthy place either. Remain loving, compassionate and discerning, while guarding your heart through the truth of who you are in God. If something is not right then God will let you know, and he will direct you in how to deal with it. I know you are probably saying "*God didn't guard me the first time.*" Well he did not leave you either. He was right there with you, helping you to overcome. And if you are really towering in your resurrected place, then you will know the real reason the enemy wanted to kill you. He did not want you to walk in that power that would save masses and set captives free. He could not thwart your destiny then, and he cannot thwart it now. Stand strong in your identity and conquer in destiny, as betrayal SHIFTS you to operating in resurrection power. You are re-birthed in Jesus' resurrection power! SHIFT

MOSES! THE DELIVERER NEEDING DELIVERANCE
Chapter 11

Spiritual Enlightenment
Moses was a deliverer, but had areas where he needed deliverance. His issues stemmed all the way back to childhood.

He was abandoned as a baby, and raised in the palace under a king who had enslaved his people. As a young adult, he rebelled against his privileged life by killing a guard who was attacking his people. Fearing persecution he ran and took refuge in Midian, where he married and raised a family.

Moses encountered God in a burning bush and was cohered to return to Egypt to deliver his people. He had all types of excuses for the reason he was not equipped, but God had chosen him, so he reluctantly accepted his calling. Moses the deliverer had a lot of unhealed wounds that only confounded as he began to journey in his deliverance ministry.

We see this a lot in the body of Christ where leaders have particular callings yet, need deliverance and healing in that same area.

- The leader will have a healing ministry, but is bound by all types of sicknesses.
- The leader will have a men's ministry, but is challenged in his identity and manhood.
- The leader will be called to youth ministry, but is immature and struggles with arrested development.

Moses actually had a God designed team, Aaron and Miriam, that helped offset his inadequacies. Yet, because Moses the deliverer needed deliverance, he made mistakes that hindered him from entering the promised land.

Moreover, Moses delivered the people from Egypt, but an entire generation would die in the wilderness before reaching the promised land.

Though we may save many, and perform some mighty acts, woundedness costs. It does not matter how many you have saved and wowed, if you killed just as many in the process. Our woundedness impacts us, those we oversee, and the generations. For Moses an entire generation entered the promise land without parents. They were left to cover themselves, and to complete a vision that had wandered in limbo for 40 years.

Even as they entered the promised land uncovered, Joshua rose up and led them. When he died, no leader was positioned to carry the torch. The Israelites therefore, had judges in leadership for years, many who did not uphold the standards of the Lord.

We cannot be so caught up in building ministries, in doing miracles, signs, and wonders, and content with those we did save, that we are not cognizant of those we are sacrificing due to our woundedness.

I employ you to get delivered and healed, so you can be an adequate representation of the ministry you have been called to lead and establish in the earth. SHIFT!

Study Exploration:
1. Study the story of Moses.
2. What gifts and calling did Moses have?
3. What ministry successes did Moses have?
4. What ministry failures did Moses have?
5. What was Moses' strengths?
6. What was his weaknesses and character flaws?
7. How did his weaknesses and impact the people and his ministry?
8. How would being delivered and healed generate a different outcome for Moses' destiny?
9. What are your gifts and callings?
10. In what ways can you identify with Moses?
11. How have your unhealed wounds impacted your life and ministry?
12. Who has been negatively impacted by your unhealed wounds and character flaws?
13. What needs to be healed in you, such that you operate as a healthy leader?

SAMPSON! THE IMMATURE CARELESS LEADER

Chapter 12

Wisdom Keys From Sampson's Story

Sampson was chosen before birth to be a deliverer of Israel. God had given him a clear vision for his life and destiny, endowed him with his Spirit and supernatural might, but Sampson felt being chosen exempt him from exercising restraint, and living through the destiny plan of the Lord as a lifestyle.

Sampson was driven and governed by his desires, his prideful personality, and his strong will, rather than the Spirit of the Lord.

Sampson would not take the time to mature and grow in the Lord. He was powerfully gifted and made sure everyone knew it. He just wanted to walk in his power (gifting), but was not interested in how to properly govern the strength (anointing) on his life.

Sampson would not listen to the guidance of his mother and father who had rule over him and his gift, and understood the destiny plan and calling on his life. He used familiarity to manipulate them into yielding to his carnal demands.

Sampson felt he could use his enemies for his personal pleasure and entertainment. He assumed power trumped strategy, intellect, and cleverness.

Sampson loved the spotlight, loved taking risks, and loved the chase of people trying to figure him out. He took pleasure in being complex, and used his peculiarity to ridicule and belittle others.

Sampson joyed in slaying principalities and powers (the deep assignments of the Lord), with an immature character and nature. Though he was naturally equipped for the assignments, he was not spiritually mature enough for them.

Sampson webbed the truth of his identity and anointing into lies, games, and riddles. While he was playing and taunting his enemy, his enemy was persistent in rendering his demise.

Sampson thought he could judge those who persecuted him and make a public spectacle of them.

Sampson did not realize he was not indispensable. He thought his strength - his gifts and calling made him untouchable. He thought that because he was anointed, he could do and say as he pleased.

Sampson was careless. He assumed because he was called and had power, no one could touch or judge him.

Sampson had a sexual addiction and lust for women. He did not discern that it weakened his anointing, and bound him to the bed of the enemy.

Sampson believed shaking himself - shaking off his sins and mishaps - delivered him of the bondage and consequences of his actions. Yet the cords were spiritual representations of him being weeded into the webbing of the enemy.

Sampson's weakness - women - constantly betrayed him. His manhood caused him to overlook the deceptions of his lustful addiction.

Sampson trusted his life's destiny plan - the secret to his strength - to his lustful addiction, while becoming comfortable in the lap of the enemy.

Sampson was vengeful. He did not care if he perished, or who he hurt along the way, as long as he killed his enemies.

Sampson was his own destiny killer. He spent his life endangering the giftings and calling on his life.

Sampson did not discern that God already knew that he would self-sabotage and destroy himself, while fulfilling his destiny calling.

Since Sampson was not teachable, God had to use his mistakes to bring forth his destiny.

Sampson had not regard for the fact that he was the only child, so when he died, his lineage died with him.

Exposing the Immature Careless Leader
We have a lot of careless leaders who take their anointing for granted. They are driven by the anointing and calling upon their lives, and believe they are indispensable. They assume being used of God makes them exempt of the consequences of their immature and careless actions.

Many of them tend to be renegades. They are not interested in submitting their gifts under sufficient leadership that can teach them how to properly govern the anointing on their lives. And if they do have covering, it is under someone who is too timid and laid back. They are not equipped to deal with their personality. Such overseers allow them to be loose cannons and destroyers of their own destiny.

Many immature leaders have some type of propensity for sin. They will sacrifice their gifts and calling to fulfill desires of the flesh and soul. These sins are usually done in secret though others know of them, because of the immaturity and carelessness of the leader. They often leave clues behind, then dare someone to confront them. They use their bold personality to intimidate people into not speaking truth to them.

The enemy however, is not afraid of such leaders. The enemy is not intimidated by their giftings, calling, and is only concerned with gaining the secret to the leader's anointing, so he can cut it off and destroy the leader's destiny.

The spirit of self-sabotage aka destiny killing spirit, and the enemy works hand in hand to create the demise of the leader. It is often the sin weakness of the leader that is key in his or her destruction. The leader usually becomes comfortable with sin, and with playing games with the enemy. The leader loves the thrill of winning and seeing what he or she can get away with, but the devil does not mind losing. He is persistent in getting that one win to trap and destroy his prey.

Usually this leader has to sacrifice his destiny to restore honor to God's kingdom. Many leaders are pridefully at peace with this as long as they win in the end. The leader is not cognizant of how his or her death also destroys their lineage by cutting off future generations.

Study Exploration:
1. Listen to Judges 13-16 several times on audio.
2. As you listen, consider the wisdom keys that were given regarding Sampson in this chapter.
3. Journal other wisdom keys God may reveal to you.
4. As you consider your upbringing, what is the vision plan that has always followed your life.
5. Spend time examining your own life.
6. What ways have you been careless with the gifts and calling on your life?
7. What areas of your character and personality are immature?
8. How has your carelessness and immaturity impacted your decision making and the calling on your life?
9. Have there been times you have endangered your gifts and calling due to carelessness and immaturity?
10. Are you a risk taker? If this is not subjected unto the Lord, what consequences can it pose to your walk?
11. Share at least three instances whether saved or unsaved that you were a risk taker, and it negatively impacted or endangered your life?
12. Ask God to show you areas in your character where you are prideful, disobedient, self-absorbed, and focused on getting your way? Focused on winning despite the cost? Ask God to kill this in you.
13. Are you submissive to leadership that can adequately cover you and speak truth to you? If not, then get under leadership that can. If you are, further submit your whole heart under their training and guidance.

14. Seek God and leadership for ways you can mature in your character and personality, and be more responsible to the gifts and calling on your life. Practice this as a lifestyle.
15. SHIFT!

DELIVERANCE FROM THE FIXER SPIRIT!
Chapter 13

This chapter is to help the leader identify the fixer spirit, so they can be aware of those in ministry that may operate in this spirit, and to be delivered from it if they are the fixer. This is a broad revelation of the fixer spirit. Some may not possess all these qualities, but still be bound by the fixer spirit.

Dictionary.com defines *fixer* as:
1. a person or thing that fixes
2. Informal. a person who arranges matters in advance through bribery or influence

Dictionary.com defines *fix* as:
1. to repair; mend
2. to put in order or in good condition; adjust or arrange
3. to make fast, firm, or stable
4. to place definitely and more or less permanently
5. to settle definitely; determine
6. to direct (the eyes, the attention, etc.) steadily
7. to attract and hold (the eye, the attention, etc.).
8. to make set or rigid
9. to put into permanent form
10. to put or place (responsibility, blame, etc.) on a person

A fixer has a driven need to repair, rescue, or help someone, while fitting them into a perception of how they believe someone should be, or what they feel would perfect the person or their lives. The fixer tends to bombard the person with ideas or perceptions of what they think will make them perfect, and tend to only accept the person if they conform to these perceptions, and yield to what the fixer thinks will perfect their lives.

A fixer can also be someone who has the best interest of others at heart, sees their potential, but cares more about the person changing than the person has for themselves. Such a person ends up playing roles in the person's life that they should not. The fixer resorts to being more to the person than they should be.

The fixer is striving to be the rescuer and though some of their perceptions can be useful and beneficial, the well to which these ideas are filtered, is usually through critical mess, negativity, a need to control, a need to be needed, and to fix others. Most fixers have unresolved hurts and past painful or challenging experiences, so they use their fixer mindset in effort to rescue others from hardship.

Some fixers fear being hurt due to past unresolved issues, so they strive to perfect those who desire relationship with them. The challenge is they will make the person constantly fix things about themselves in order to please them, and be in their lives. By the time the person fixes one thing about themselves, the fixer has already presented another thing to fix. The person finds themselves constantly jumping through hoops to try and please the fixer. However, the fixer cannot be pleased because their issue is really not that person, but is their own need to be healed. They engage in their relationships through their past unhealed pains and fears of being hurt again.

Some fixers have the heart and compassion of God, gift of discernment and helps, administration and are called to lead, shepherd, train and equip people. Yet, they use their gifts in a unhealthy or unbalanced manner. They end up being God and/or enablers in peoples' lives. Their need or drive to be the savior causes them to be more to people than God has said or to take on more than God is requiring. This type of fixer possesses great positive qualities and giftings, but requires balance in making sure they are allowing God to be God. And that they do not start hating their lives and callings, while resenting those they are called to help by being and bearing more than God has intended.

Fixers tend to build a lifestyle of false peace and false perfection. They do this by keeping people in superficial and surface relationships. If you penetrate their walls, you will find some mental instabilities, and an inability for them to truly trust, relax, and rest in the love and security of the relationship.

Anytime you are imperfect, the fixer takes this as a personal attack against them. They view your downfalls as you hurting them, betraying them, and dishonoring them. Especially if they gave you advice on a matter, and you did not implement it, or were not consistent with utilizing it. *"How dare you not take their advice and run with it."* The fixer tends to punish the person by ending the relationship or threatening to end it, if you do not correct this betrayal immediately.

The fixer will also use silence and abusive threats to control and manipulate a person into feeling guilty and shamed about not following through with their advice. The person will often feel beat down, condemned, confused and double-minded by the negative words, and negative perceptions the fixers speaks towards them. They will feel confused and double-minded, because what the fixer says, or is suggesting may have a point of truth, but the method is all wrong. Therefore, the person wavers between wanting to submit, and rebelling against what the fixer is suggesting. Also unless the person does everything the fixer says, the fixer negates any progress the person makes. It is usually all or nothing for a fixer, so the person tends to be abusively corrected and chastened, despite any progress they have made.

There are instances where the fixer will obtain information about the person's past failures, and then when the fixer is correcting and chastising the person, the fixer will belittle them with these failures. They use these failures to make the person feel they will never change, and will never have success unless they adhere to what is being demanded of them.

Sometimes the fixer's perceptions of the person are rooted in their own past hurtful experiences with other people. The fixer however, cast these perceptions on the person, and assume they are that way too, even if the person is nothing like the person that hurt them.

A fixer checks up on the person to make sure they are doing what is demanded of them. The fixer will also ask certain questions in effort to get the person to admit they have not changed, or followed through with what was requested. The fixer tends to attack the person's character, and place them in a situation where they are defending themselves, lying so they will not get rebuked, or having to shut down all together for fear of being rebuked if they have not done what was required of them. Anyone of these positions causes the fixer to become angry and betrayed, and usually verbally abusive or controlling manipulative acts follow, to bring the person into subjection to the fixers demands.

Though the fixer appears to celebrate you when you achieve success from doing what they say, their motive of celebration is not due to you being transformed, but that you implemented their ideas. You will recognize this when they take credit for your achievement even though you did the work. They will contend you only acquired victory because of them, and without them you are a failure waiting to happen.

Because the fixer views themselves as the helper, it is very difficult to get them to pursue deliverance and healing from their fixer mindset. If they do acknowledge their issues, it is generally with the mindset that the only reason why they are broken is because of the person they are fixing, and if they fix you then that fixes them.

The fixer relationship tends to resemble Jezebel and Ahab from the bible. To Jezebel, Ahab was inadequate, and she was always using control, fear, manipulation, threats, murder, and negative methods to fix situations that King Ahab had reign over (**1Kings 18-19**).

Because of the emotional soulties and bewitchment that occurs between the fixer and the fixee, it can take years before the fixee realizes they are being abused and need to end the relationship. They have close calls of ending it, but tend to talk themselves out of it when they are rewarded with the fixer's attention and seductive accolades, due to their good behavior of submitting to what is required of them. But soon the fixers behaviors return and they are entertained again with striving to comprehend whether the confusion and chastising they are receiving is really abuse and unhealthy to their overall wellbeing.

Also the fixer can possess a lot of good qualities that makes the fixee want to work on the relationship, to please the fixer, and even prove themselves to the fixer. The fixer tends to have the person so bewitched that the person feels like they are losing out by ending the relationship, or that they are hopeless, and cannot life without the fixer. It is these very misconceptions that keeps the cycle of the relationship going. The fixer tends to eventually leave the relationship with regret, due to years of their life waisted on something that never could be healthy, or losing themselves in a relationship that only breeds unhealthiness and identity theft.

Some of us have become fixers or have been groomed as fixers through our family roles and traditions. We have been the smart one, successful one, the responsible one or reliable one in the family. We have been the oldest kid, the family curse breaker, or have had to step up due to insufficient parental roles in the family. Some have had to rely on themselves and take care of others, particularly siblings. We thus have been molded and shaped into the fixers.

Some of us have become successful and feel obligated to go back and fix or take care of capable family members. Or we feel obligated because they are our family and so we feel unrealistic pressure to take care of them or enable them. This is a fixer mentality that has been groomed in us due to wounds of a difficult childhood, false obligations and unhealthy cultural obligations, guilt and shame of being successful, while other family members remain in poverty, role reversals where the child has had to be the parent or has had to fulfill parental duties as a child or teenager. This is not your burden to bear. Let God lead you on when to assist and help your family. Do not engage in savior roles that only God can fulfill. God is the only fixer and he has promised that if we walk with him, he will perfect (make sound) the things which concern us.

> ***Psalms 138:8*** *The Lord will perfect (make sound) that which concerneth me: thy mercy, O LORD, endureth for ever: forsake not the works of thine own hands.*

Deliverance from a Relationship with a Fixer:
1. Break the soul ties between you and the fixer.
2. Break word curses and bewitchment used through words.
3. Cleanse yourself of confusion, double mindedness, helplessness, hopelessness and a need to please and prove yourself to the fixer.
4. Break and cleanse the powers of shame, guilt and condemnation.
5. Reclaim your identity.
6. Forgive yourself for yielding to the fixer relationship.
7. Forgive the fixer for abusing you.
8. Reestablish God as the head and fixer of your life and let him work with you on what needs to be changed in you.
9. Work on building your self esteem and self worth so you won't succumb to this type of relation ever again.

Deliverance from the Fixer Mentality:

1. Acknowledge you are a fixer and need deliverance and healing.
2. Explore underlying issues to fixer behaviors and receive deliverance and healing in those areas.
3. Explore and receive healing of areas related to fear of being hurt and a need to control your life and the lives of others.
4. Repent for fixer behaviors and how they have impacted others.
5. Explore your gifts of discernment, healing, and helps, and how to use them in a healthy manner.
6. Reestablish God as the head of your life and submit to his leading.
7. Work on building your trust and faith in God, so you can trust him to lead you in your relationships.

DISCERNING UNHEALED AREAS IN TESTIMONIES

Chapter 14

A lot of times people will come before the service and testify or share their testimony while ministering. So many are caught up in what is being shared, the commonality with what was shared, the charisma and/or the emotionalism to which it was shared in, and even being excited that God moved, that we do not discern the deliverance, and processing to wholeness that is needed in many of these testimonies. We are also not discerning of how the testimonies draw people to the person and not to God. We become fascinated with the person sharing the testimony and not of God who is the deliverer, the savior.

> **John 4:28-29** *The woman then left her waterpot, and went her way into the city, and saith to the men. Come, see a man, which told me all things that ever I did: is not this the Christ? Then they went out of the city, and came unto him.*

When Jesus brought deliverance to the Samaritan woman, the woman went into the city, declaring all God had revealed and did in her, while encouraging them to come experience Jesus for themselves. She did not draw the people to her or even to the deliverance that was done in her. She drew the people to Jesus. Because of her deliverance and focus on her deliverer, a people who did not normally worship Jesus, left their town and came into him.

> **Verse 39-42** *And many of the Samaritans of that city believed on him for the saying of the woman, which testified, He told me all that ever I did. So when the Samaritans were come unto him, they besought him that he would tarry with them: and he abode there two days. And many more believed because of his own word; And said unto the woman, Now we believe, not because of thy saying: for we have heard him ourselves, and know that this is indeed the Christ, the Saviour of the world.*

The Samaritan's woman made them want to inquire of Jesus for themselves and when they did, they believed on him as savior of the world. This is so essential because our ministries are filling up with fans and groupies, but not believers who are rooted and grounded in Christ. We have a lot of *"follow me as I am just like you."* But people are not being delivered, healed, and transformed. They are not being converted into salvation because testimonies in and of themselves, do not save, only the power of Jesus Christ saves lives.

> **John 12:32** *And I, if I be lifted up from the earth, will draw all men unto me.*

> **The Amplified Bible** *And I, if and when I am lifted up from the earth [on the cross], will draw and attract all men [Gentiles as well as Jews] to Myself.*

Draw is *helkyō* in the Greek and means:
1. to drag (literally or figuratively)
2. draw, to draw, drag off
3. metaph., to draw by inward power, lead, impel (incite to action)

Dictionary.com defines *drag* as, "*to draw with force, effort, or difficulty; pull heavily or slowly along; haul; trail.*"

When we testify, people should enter a process of salvation with Jesus, where the literal force of our testimony is dragging them out of sin, discouragement, helplessness, and into alignment with him. As he is exalted, they are pulled out of darkness into the light and truth concerning Jesus' power to save, deliver and heal them.

Our testimonies serve as reports and witnesses of how Jesus' blood and works on the cross have impacted our lives. People want what we have, so they seek Jesus for the workings that they discern through us.

> **Revelations 12:11 The Amplified Bible** *And they have overcome (conquered) him by means of the blood of the Lamb and by the utterance of their testimony, for they did not love and cling to life even when faced with death [holding their lives cheap till they had to die for their witnessing].*

Our testimonies should be example worthy, such that people see God working, and living in our lives. It should also be a sign that the devil has lost in your life, and there is nothing he can do about it.

> ***Philippians 1:27-30*** *Only be sure as citizens so to conduct yourselves [that] your manner of life [will be] worthy of the good news (the Gospel) of Christ, so that whether I [do] come and see you or am absent, I may hear this of you: that you are standing firm in united spirit and purpose, striving side by side and contending with a single mind for the faith of the glad tidings (the Gospel). And do not [for a moment] be frightened or intimidated in anything by your opponents and adversaries, for such [constancy and fearlessness] will be a clear sign (proof and seal) to them of [their impending] destruction, but [a sure token and evidence] of your deliverance and salvation, and that from God. For you have been granted [the privilege] for Christ's sake not only to believe in (adhere to, rely on, and trust in) Him, but also to suffer in His behalf. So you are engaged in the same conflict which you saw me [wage] and which you now hear to be mine [still].*

Testimonies are not platform opportunities. Testimonies are life long testaments of God's wonders that are passed down through the generations. A testimony is not just one event. Your entire life should continually boast of the wonders of God.

> ***Psalms 71:15-18 The Amplified Bible*** *My mouth shall tell of Your righteous acts and of Your deeds of salvation all the day, for their number is more than I know. I will come in the strength and with the mighty acts of the Lord God; I will mention and praise Your*

righteousness, even Yours alone. O God, You have taught me from my youth, and hitherto have I declared Your wondrous works. Yes, even when I am old and gray-headed, O God, forsake me not, [but keep me alive] until I have declared Your mighty strength to [this] generation, and Your might and power to all that are to come.

We should not be ashamed to testify, and we should not be ashamed of the transformation we have received. We also should not bring shame upon our testimony as through Christ, we should be living in the transformation power of his workings in us. That means we should be demonstrating a lifestyle of a converted life that yields truth and validation of our testimony.

> ***2Timothy 1:8-9 The Amplified Bible*** *Do not blush or be ashamed then, to testify to and for our Lord, nor of me, a prisoner for His sake, but [with me] take your share of the suffering [to which the preaching] of the Gospel [may expose you, and do it] in the power of God. [For it is He] Who delivered and saved us and called us with a calling in itself holy and leading to holiness [to a life of consecration, a vocation of holiness]; [He did it] not because of anything of merit that we have done, but because of and to further His own purpose and grace (unmerited favor) which was given us in Christ Jesus before the world began [eternal ages ago].*

Testimonies are a proclamation of Jesus, and they reveal Jesus to the world. It is not a proclamation of self and receiving fame and platform from the world or from Christendom.

> ***Matthew 10:32 The Amplified Bible*** *Therefore, everyone who acknowledges Me before men and confesses Me [out of a state of oneness with Me], I will also acknowledge him before My Father Who is in heaven and confess [that I am abiding in] him.*

Testimonies advance the kingdom of God. You may also be persecuted for sharing how God has delivered you, and for the other ways in which you advance the kingdom of God. The persecutions will also open up doors for you to further spread the gospel of Jesus Christ.

> ***Philippians 1:12-14*** *I want to report to you, friends, that my imprisonment here has had the opposite of its intended effect. Instead of being squelched, the Message has actually prospered. All the soldiers here, and everyone else too, found out that I'm in jail because of this Messiah. That piqued their curiosity, and now they've learned all about him. Not only that, but most of the Christians here have become far more sure of themselves in the faith than ever, speaking out fearlessly about God, about the Messiah.*

We see here that Jesus received glory out of Paul's testimony, and from him being further persecuted for his testimony. Doors were open not for him to advance his career and ministry, but to proclaim the gospel of Jesus Christ, whereby others may be saved. We do reap the benefits of status, fame, favor, and blessings, when we are about his business, but this must not be our motive for doing ministry. We must remain humble and pure in spreading the gospel and drawing souls to Jesus Christ.

There is a difference between boasting your testimony in pride, and boasting your testimony where God can be glorified. When we boast in pride we are stealing glory from God. We are inviting people to do religious acts that we really are not living ourselves. We are not really caught up in a drawing with God, but we are inviting others to do it. Not for Jesus glory, but as an abuse of our own power, platform and ability to manipulate and coerce others. We are also subjecting ourselves to having to people please in order to keep the accolades, rewards, and statuses derived from boasting in our testimony.

> ***Galatians 6:12-14 The Amplified Bible*** *Those who want to make a good impression and a fine show in the flesh would try to compel you to receive circumcision, simply so that they may escape being persecuted for allegiance to the cross of Christ (the Messiah, the Anointed One). For even the circumcised [Jews] themselves do not [really] keep the Law, but they want to have you circumcised in order that they may glory in your flesh (your subjection to external rites). But far be it from me to glory [in anything or anyone] except in the cross of our Lord Jesus Christ (the Messiah) through Whom the world has been crucified to me, and I to the world!*
>
> ***The Message Bible*** *These people who are attempting to force the ways of circumcision on you have only one motive: They want an easy way to look good before others, lacking the courage to live by a faith that shares Christ's suffering and death. All their talk about the law is gas. They themselves don't keep the law! And they are highly selective in the laws they do observe. They only want you to be circumcised so they can boast of their success in recruiting you to their side. That is contemptible! For my part, I am going to boast about nothing but the Cross of our Master, Jesus Christ. Because of that Cross, I have been crucified in relation to the world, set free from the stifling atmosphere of pleasing others and fitting into the little patterns that they dictate.*

When you leave out the works of Jesus Christ in your testimony, you void it of his saving power - of the drawing power.

As leaders, we cannot get caught up in gimmicking the people to get them to follow us. And we especially cannot taint, corrupt, or use our testimony as manipulation to draw numbers and platforms.

We have to be so very cautious of this in this day and age, where we have so many social media outlets and opportunities to draw crowds and build platforms. And where we have so many opportunities within the world and Christendom to advance, without the direction and approval of God.

> ***Psalms 75:7*** *But God is the judge: he putteth down one, and setteth up another.*
>
> ***Ecclesiastes 3:14*** *I know that, whatsoever God doeth, it shall be for ever: nothing can be put to it, nor any thing taken from it: and God doeth it, that men should fear before him.*
>
> ***Philippians 2:3*** *Let nothing be done through strife or vainglory; but in lowliness of mind let each esteem other better than themselves.*

A lot of proclamations that we are calling testimonies are really just words of encouragement, which is not a bad thing necessarily, or encounters with God and his presence, but not true transformation in God's presence. We are feeling God, feeling better, even feeling convicted about changing, and even provoked enough to take some steps to change, but we have not been truly transformed where our salvation, deliverance, and/or healing, is truly bonafide testimony where God can be sufficiently glorified.

> ***Acts 1:8*** *But ye shall receive power, after that the Holy Ghost is come upon you: and ye shall be witnesses unto me both in Jerusalem, and in all Judaea, and in Samaria, and unto the uttermost part of the earth.*

<u>Witness in the Greek is *martys* and means:</u>
1. of uncertain affinity; a witness (literally (judicially) or figuratively (genitive case))
2. by analogy, a "martyr": martyr, record, witness
3. a witness in a legal sense, an historical sense one who is a spectator of anything, e.g. of a contest
4. in an ethical sense those who after his example have proved the strength and genuineness of their faith in Christ by undergoing a violent death

The scriptures says "*you shall be a witness.*" When you are a witness that means a court proceeding has taken place, and something or somebody is being judged. When we testify, our word and lifestyle is being judged. We are essentially standing before people and God, declaring that we have died a horrible death through the works of Jesus Christ, and through allowing him to process us as we walk in the relationship with him. And now we are resurrected examples of his workings through the life that we live. The works that JESUS has done in us are definable, recordable, and recorded as documented deaths of being delivered from sin and death. We no longer have a desire or propensity for that thing as it was martyred, and when you look at us and our lifestyle, you do not see it. You just see Christ. So basically you are a dead person that has been killed for the sake of the gospel, and now you travel all over the world, revealing and drawing souls to Christ. Whether the people discern that you are a fraud, manipulator, or embellisher, God knows. The people may judge and approve you, but what really matters is whether God has judged and approved you as a valid martyr for his glory.

As leaders we must recognize that we cannot fool God even if we fool people. Our testimonies must be rooted in him, about him, and for his glory. Our testimonies must demonstrate transformation of the revealed resurrection power of Jesus Christ.

> ***Galatians 2:20-21 The Amplified Bible*** *I have been crucified with Christ [in Him I have shared His crucifixion]; it is no longer I who live, but Christ (the Messiah) lives in me; and the life I now live in the body I live by faith in (by adherence to and reliance on and complete trust in) the Son of God, Who loved me and gave Himself up for me. [Therefore, I do not treat God's gracious gift as something of minor importance and defeat its very purpose]; I do not set aside and invalidate and frustrate and nullify the grace (unmerited favor) of God. For if justification (righteousness, acquittal from guilt) comes through [observing the ritual of] the Law, then Christ (the Messiah) died groundlessly and to no purpose and in vain. [His death was then wholly superfluous.]*

> ***The Message Bible*** *Christ's life showed me how, and enabled me to do it. I identified myself completely with him. Indeed, I have been crucified with Christ. My ego is no longer central. It is no longer important that I appear righteous before you or have your good opinion, and I am no longer driven to impress God. Christ lives in me. The life you see me living is not "mine," but it is lived by faith in the Son of God, who loved me and gave himself for me. I am not going to go back on that. Is it not clear to you that to go back to that old rule-keeping, peer-pleasing religion would be an abandonment of everything personal and free in my relationship with God? I refuse to do that, to repudiate God's grace. If a living relationship with God could come by rule-keeping, then Christ died unnecessarily.*

As leaders we must not engage in this behavior, and we must be discerning of those who testify in our midst, that may really be sharing a word of encouragement, but not truly walking in the demonstration of a true testimony. Many times these people are revealing that they need further processing of deliverance and wholeness. Especially if they are struggling with the same thing every few months, or every other season of their lives. And then when they have an encounter with God and feel free again, they are testifying of deliverance. When we do not address such testimonies, people go unhealed, while struggling in secret bondages. We as well have to address how these testimonies will have everyone shouting and praising the Lord, and even will draw souls to the altar, as in that moment they appear to glorify God. And sometimes they are, if they are a word of encouragement. The person is receiving their few minutes of fame, and is feeling great about themselves, but because they are not truly healed, the enemy catches them in their private struggle and binds them even more in their woundedness. They end up more challenged, shamed, and condemned than they were. They fear seeking help, due to publicly contending they are already delivered and healed. Such cycles and actions must be discerned and exposed for what they are, so the person can be connected with a counselor and/or mentor that can journey with them to complete wholeness.

Sometimes people call themselves "*testifying*," yet they are really acquiring attention. Often these people just want to be seen, valued, and validated. They present themselves as glorifying God, but really they are getting their ego stroked, and their self esteem and self worth boosted. This is so they can feel good about themselves. There is an air of pride connected to their testimony as once they share, they feel a sense of connection to the people, to God, and even to the moment of success that they are standing in. Many tend to want to tell their testimony at the most random time. It is usually when God is getting glory, or when someone else has given God glory through a bonafide testimony. And most of the time what they are sharing is off subject, fruitless, not necessary at the time, and takes the attention away from what the Holy Spirit is doing in the service. As leaders we must not engage in this behavior, neither should we promote or allow it. We are responsible for the move of God and for not quenching the Holy Spirit. We must be cognizant of how the enemy will use these people to kill a move of God. We must also recommend counseling and/or mentoring to these people, so they can be healed in their identity and self-worth. This is essential because, most often these attention seeking behaviors are manifesting and affecting other areas of their lives. Being healed will stop these attention seeking behaviors and enable the person to live a confident life in who they are in God and to the world.

Ingredients of a Jesus Focused Testimony:
1. Should draw people to God that is in the person. Once impacted by the testimony, people should seek Jesus, rather than be driven with being a groupie of the person giving the testimony, for this is idolatry.
2. Should be given with pure motives to edifying God - giving him glory and drawing souls unto him.
3. Should make God famous all over the earth.
4. Should be factual with clear evidence of God's workings in the person's life. These facts should be able to be proven by the person's lifestyle.
5. Should have factual demonstrated evidence that the person has totally subdued, overcome, prevailed, and obtained victory over whatever it is he or she is testifying about. The person is not overcoming. The person has overcome and is an evident demonstration of victory. Otherwise it is encouragement and not a testimony.
   Romans 12:11 *And they overcame him by the blood of the Lamb, and by the word of their testimony; and they loved not their lives unto the death.*
6. Should be factual as if the person were in a court of law; what the person is declaring and proposing is the truth and nothing but the truth.
7. Should demonstrate that the person's life is a witness to he or she being martyred with Christ, and now living a life resurrected with him.
8. Should be void of embellishment, exaggeration, manipulation, seduction, attention seeking behaviors, and gimmicks. **1Corinthians 2:4** *And my speech and my preaching was not with enticing words of man's wisdom, but in demonstration of the Spirit and of power.*
9. Though doors will open and blessings will follow, testimonies should be void of this being the motive for sharing them.

10. Should be recordable where the testimony can be passed down and shared from generation to generation. ***Psalms 145:4*** *One generation shall praise thy works to another, and shall declare thy mighty acts.*
11. Should be judged accordingly. If it does not have the fruit of a testimony then do not call or record it as a testimony. To lie in a natural or spiritual court is a punishable sin by law. ***1Corinthians 3:13*** *Every man's work shall be made manifest: for the day shall declare it, because it shall be revealed by fire; and the fire shall try every man's work of what sort it is.*

***John 5:29-32 The Amplified Bible** And they shall come out – those who have practiced doing good [will come out] to the resurrection of [new] life, and those who have done evil will be raised for judgment [raised to meet their sentence]. I am able to do nothing from Myself [independently, of My own accord – but only as I am taught by God and as I get His orders]. Even as I hear, I judge [I decide as I am bidden to decide. As the voice comes to Me, so I give a decision], and My judgment is right (just, righteous), because I do not seek or consult My own will [I have no desire to do what is pleasing to Myself, My own aim, My own purpose] but only the will and pleasure of the Father Who sent Me. If I alone testify in My behalf, My testimony is not valid and cannot be worth anything. There is Another Who testifies concerning Me, and I know and am certain that His evidence on My behalf is true and valid.*

EMBRACING PROCESS AS A LIFESTYLE
Chapter 15

Dictionary.com defines *process* as:
1. a systematic series of actions directed to some end
2. a continuous action, operation, or series of changes taking place in a definite manner
3. a series of actions that produce something or that lead to a particular result

A process takes us from level to level, glory to glory, dimension to dimension, in God. In our walk with God, there will always be something we will be attaining. This is because our relationship with God is a lifetime and a lifestyle. Our destiny is acquired over the course of a lifetime, and therefore is a lifetime.

If there are deep rooted issues, the process of attainment can become compacted, but the art of processing is always necessary for deliverance, healing, elevation, growth, success, and constantly maturing in the likeness of the Lord.

> **2Corinthians 3:17-18** *Now the Lord is that Spirit: and where the Spirit of the Lord is, there is liberty. But we all, with open face beholding as in a glass the glory of the Lord, are changed into the same image from glory to glory, even as by the Spirit of the Lord.*

Glory is *doxa* in this scripture and means:
1. honor, renown; glory, splendor, an especially divine quality
2. the unspoken manifestation of God, dignity, opinion, judgement

When we go from glory to glory, we go from honor to honor, splendor to splendor, revealing quality after quality, of God's divine nature. We also display manifestations of who God is that have not been revealed in us or in the earth. This lets us know that there is a unique manifestation of God in us that the world needs, and that only we can reveal to the world.

As we go from glory to glory, *doxa* also reveals our opinions and judgments, which basically speaks for our character and nature. As we mature in *doxa*, our opinions and judgments should align and resemble God's precepts, such that it is like looking in a mirror (glass) at the likeness of Jesus.

The word changed in this scripture means "*metamorphose.*" Per dictionary.com, *metamorphosis* denotes "*a profound change in form from one stage to the next in the life history of an organism.*" Basically you are being transfigured as you enter each stage of life development. According to the scripture, our process in any given season should be as followed. The more we partake of God, experience his presence, and are led by his spirit, the more we should be transformed to look like him. Once we are processed to look like God, continual life processing is needed to maintain our transformation.

A lot of times we want to control the process, but the process is by the Spirit of God. This word *Spirit* in this scripture refers to the Holy Spirit. *Spirit* is *pneuma* in the Greek and means "*breath.*" Just like we cannot live without breathing, we cannot live without being processed from glory to glory in God. It is vital to our life process.

> ***John 16:13*** *Howbeit when he, the Spirit of truth, is come, he will guide you into all truth: for he shall not speak of himself; but whatsoever he shall hear, that shall he speak: and he will shew you things to come.*

Though the disciples saw Jesus perform miracles, and Jesus used them to do miracles, aside from being rescued from danger or hardship, rarely were they the recipients of personal miracles. Much of their deliverance and healing came through being mentored by Jesus and being processed to wholeness. As we consider the disciples we can conclude the following:

- Processing is an indication that God desires more than interaction with you or that which he is seeking you to attain. He desires relationship and for you to become or to come into covenant with the very thing he desires you to achieve.

- Processes create a solid foundation that helps to sustain progress and success.

- The main goal in every season of processing is for us to become more and more like God, and to further unveil the uniqueness of who we are in him.

- Because the steps in a process are chain linked, avoiding or bypassing steps can hinder the success of the process. This can also thwart the work you have already put into and sacrificed in the process.

- It takes vulnerability and a relinquishing of control to be processed to breakthrough.

- The process is not designed for you to know everything, do everything or to figure everything out. The process is intended for you to be in a posture of humility and attentiveness to the voice and direction of God and those he has ordained to walk in the process with you.

  > ***Proverbs 3:5-6*** *Trust in the Lord with all thine heart; and lean not unto thine own understanding. In all thy ways acknowledge him, and he shall direct thy paths.*

  > ***Hebrews 13:17*** *Obey them that have the rule over you, and submit yourselves: for they watch for your souls, as they that must give account, that they may do it with joy, and not with grief: for that is unprofitable for you.*

- If you cannot give up control then you are trying be God or the leader in the process, and since you are in the wrong position, the process will be unnecessarily challenging and even aborted.

- The more you seek to be God by trying to control the process or remain prideful in being unwilling to be vulnerable in the process, the longer it will take you to actually begin, or establish within that season of processing.

- You can abort or stagnate your progress when you rush the process.

- Quick fixes can equal temporary results. Process equals skills and knowledge that produce lasting results.

- The process is not intended to keep healing and knowledge from you. The fact that you battle this wrong thinking, while experiencing hope deferred, is proof that processing is needed so that you can mature in your relationship, and with understanding God; and even in appreciating the processes of life.

    - ***Proverbs 13:12*** *Hope deferred maketh the heart sick: but when the desire cometh, it is a tree of life.*

- The inability to submit to the process exposes deeply rooted issues within your soul and heart. Dealing with root issues is a process all on its own, as it takes energy and time to dig up roots. At times when dealing with underlying roots, it can feel and is like being processed within a process. The twofold processing can be intense and increasingly painful. That is because digging up roots is like gutting out parts of your identity that does not reflect God's image. You are literally being separated from parts of yourself that are not beneficial to who you are and where you are going in God. Anytime we lose parts of ourself whether good or bad, it hurts. But, the twofold processing of gutting out roots is worth it. It is best to sustain in the original process while dealing with roots so you do not prolong this season of processing. Setting yourself aside in consecration can be beneficial in maintaining during seasons of twofold processing.

- When there is a lack of submission and obedience to the process, God and/or those who are helping us end up processing us as if we were babies drinking bottled milk, and being spoon fed rather than as mature adults. Where we should be able to receive, retain, attain, and maintain sufficient knowledge and revelation that keeps the process unfolding effectively, we end up receiving just enough to keep us in the process. Yet, the focus is more about breaking our will so we become submitted to God's will more so than about the process itself.

    Isaiah 28:10 *For precept must be upon precept, precept upon precept; line upon line, line upon line; here a little, and there a little.*

> ***Psalms 51:17*** *The sacrifices of God are a broken spirit: a broken and a contrite heart, O God, thou wilt not despise.*

- Focusing on being perfect or focusing on your lack of perfection will hinder and even abort the process, as the process is designed to expose what is of God and what is not of God. If you cannot handle truths about your imperfections, it will be difficult to relinquish control of the process to God where he can deliver and heal you.

  > ***Psalms 138:8*** *The Lord will perfect that which concerneth me: thy mercy, O Lord, endureth for ever: forsake not the works of thine own hands.*

  > ***2Corinthians 3:18 The Amplified Bible*** *So all of us who have had that veil removed can see and reflect the glory of the Lord. And the Lord – who is the Spirit – makes us more and more like him as we are changed into his glorious image.*

Decreeing that you embrace process as a lifestyle and be content in seasons where additional processing is required to bring greater maturity to your deliverance, healing, and wholeness. SHIFT!

RESTORING THE SPIRIT OF COUNSEL IN THE BODY OF CHRIST

Chapter 16

One of the biggest mistakes we make in Christendom, is when people come to God, we cast the devil out of them, heal areas that they may not be ready to be healed in, while stripping them of their walls of protection, identity, and supports, without adequately filling these areas of their lives with tools to help them maintain in deliverance and healing. We throw bible scriptures, principles, and cliches at them, and expect them to know how to implement them in their lives with no proper equipping, skills development, or tools to help them further improve and sustain in life. Then we rebuke people for being carnal, worldly, lost, confused, lukewarm, backslidden, and unable to mature in the Lord. This mentality has created so much damage until people are resistant to attending church, lack faith that church can help them, and do not believe in God or his saving power. Because of such folly, restoration of the Spirit of Counsel is needed in the body of Christ like never before.

Not only should leaders equip themselves as sufficient counselors, physical counseling centers and educated degree certified counselors should be established in ministries for the purposes of processing people and communities to wholeness.

Jesus had the Spirit of Counsel & Might
> *Isaiah 11:1-2 A shoot will come up from the stump of Jesse; from his root a branch will bear fruit. The spirit of the Lord will rest on him-the Spirit of wisdom and of understanding, the Spirit of counsel and of power, the Spirit of knowledge and of the fear of the Lord.*

The word *"counsel"* in the Hebrew is *etsah*, which means *"to counsel, advice, purpose."* The root word *ya`ats* means, *"to advise, consult, give counsel, counsel, purpose, devise, plan."*

The word *"spirit"* in the Hebrew is *ruwach*, which *"means wind, breath, mind, spirit."*

The "*ruwach*" aka *spirit* of God is the vigor, breath, life, power of counseling. The counsel is the wisdom, consultation, and deliberation of God's spirit. Therefore, the intent of the spirit of counseling is to breathe life into a person and help progress them into their destined purpose in God.

Jesus the Wonderful Counselor
> *Isaiah 9:6 For to us a child is born, to us a son is given, and the government will be on his shoulders. And he will be called Wonderful Counselor, Mighty God, Everlasting Father, Prince of Peace.*

Counseling is a mantle that serves as a governmental rule and voice in the lives of people and nations.

The Counsel of a Learned Tongue Anointing
> **Isaiah 50:4-5** *The Lord God hath given me the tongue of the learned, that I should know how to speak a word in season to him that is weary: he wakeneth morning by morning, he wakeneth mine ear to hear as the learned. The Lord God hath opened mine ear, and I was not rebellious, neither turned away back.*

A person that is learned has been instructed, taught, and discipled. A counselor is one who has been under the training and discipleship of the Lord, so he or she can acquire revelation for those in need of refreshing, empowerment, and transformation. A counselor receives daily word from the Lord, and is obedient to what he or she hears. This scripture also lets us know that it is beneficial for a counselor to have some educational experience as a counselor. A person that has a Bachelors, Masters, or Ph.D in counseling or social work, can be more effective in leading clients through a process of deliverance, healing, and wholeness. Further educational training in the areas of licensure, certification, and attending workshops is beneficial in equipping and maturing the spirit of counsel upon your life.

Lack of Counsel Breeds Death
> **Proverbs 11:14** *Where no counsel is, the people fall: but in the multitude of counsellors there is safety.*

"*Safety*" in the Hebrew is *tshuah* and means:
1. rescue, deliverance, help, victory
2. deliverance (usually by God through human agency)
3. salvation (spiritual in sense)

We see from this definition that counseling brings
- recovery
- freedom
- enlightenment
- protection
- breakthrough
- spiritual enlightenment
- deliverance
- healing
- redemption

> *New International Bible* *For lack of guidance a nation falls, but many advisers make victory sure.*

There will be people who will perish if they fail to receive counsel. Where there is no existence of counsel, there is sure to be death. People, regions, nations, generations will die.

Nations Voided from a Lack of Counsel
> **Deuteronomy 32:28** *For they are a nation void of counsel, neither is there any understanding in them.*

This scripture reveals that the plans and purposes of God can derive from counseling, People and nations error without sufficient counsel.

Counseling Ministry
In *Exodus 18:15-26*, we see the people coming to Moses for counseling. Because so many required counseling, Moses father in law, Jethro, administrated a counseling ministry that comprised of mature believers who were trained to assist with counseling, judging, and leading the people.

> *And Moses said unto his father in law, Because the people come unto me to enquire of God: When they have a matter, they come unto me; and I judge between one and another, and I do make them know the statutes of God, and his laws. And Moses' father in law said unto him, The thing that thou doest is not good. Thou wilt surely wear away, both thou, and this people that is with thee: for this thing is too heavy for thee; thou art not able to perform it thyself alone. Hearken now unto my voice, I will give thee counsel, and God shall be with thee: Be thou for the people to God-ward, And it came to pass on the morrow, that Moses sat to judge the people: and the people stood by Moses from the morning unto the evening.*

> *And when Moses' father in law saw all that he did to the people, he said, What is this thing that thou doest to the people? why sittest thou thyself alone, and all the people stand by thee from morning unto even? And Moses said unto his father in law, Because the people come unto me to enquire of God: When they have a matter, they come unto me; and I judge between one and another, and I do make them know the statutes of God, and his laws. And Moses' father in law said unto him, The thing that thou doest is not good. Thou wilt surely wear away, both thou, and this people that is with thee: for this thing is too heavy for thee; thou art not able to perform it thyself alone. Hearken now unto my voice, I will give thee counsel, and God shall be with thee: Be thou for the people to God-ward, that thou mayest bring the causes unto God: And thou shalt teach them ordinances and laws, and shalt shew them the way wherein they must walk, and the work that they must do. Moreover thou shalt provide out of all the people able men, such as fear God, men of truth, hating covetousness; and place such over them, to be rulers of thousands, and rulers of hundreds, rulers of fifties, and rulers of tens: And let*

them judge the people at all seasons: and it shall be, that every great matter they shall bring unto thee, but every small matter they shall judge: so shall it be easier for thyself, and they shall bear the burden with thee. If thou shalt do this thing, and God command thee so, then thou shalt be able to endure, and all this people shall also go to their place in peace. So Moses hearkened to the voice of his father in law, and did all that he had said. And Moses chose able men out of all Israel, and made them heads over the people, rulers of thousands, rulers of hundreds, rulers of fifties, and rulers of tens. And they judged the people at all seasons: the hard causes they brought unto Moses, but every small matter they judged themselves.

Counseling Center

In *Judges 4:4-5*, we have Prophetess Deborah who set up a counseling center under a tree such that the people of Israel came to her for direction, justice, judgements, counsel, and advice.

> *And Deborah, a prophetess, the wife of Lapidoth, she judged Israel at that time. And she dwelt under the palm tree of Deborah between Ramah and Bethel in mount Ephraim: and the children of Israel came up to her for judgment.*

New Testament Equipping & Training

In the New Testament, Jesus implemented fivefold ministry offices to govern ministries. He expected them to implement services and trainings to equip and advance the lives of the people.

> ***Ephesians 4:11-12 The Amplified Bible*** *And His gifts were [varied; He Himself appointed and gave men to us] some to be apostles (special messengers), some prophets (inspired preachers and expounders), some evangelists (preachers of the Gospel, traveling missionaries), some pastors (shepherds of His flock) and teachers. His intention was the perfecting and the full equipping of the saints (His consecrated people), [that they should do] the work of ministering toward building up Christ's body (the church).*

It seems that most ministries have been focused on people working their vision, or equipping people in gifts and callings, that counseling and counseling centers have been removed from the body of Christ. We also have the challenge of leaders attempting to counsel saints without having the time, and sufficient skill set to be balanced in helping people process to wholeness. Moreover, a false mindset has developed in the body of Christ and in cultures, that it is unhealthy and weak to attend counseling. When we reject counseling, we reject Jesus as he is the Spirit of Counsel. He is the Wonderful Counselor.

It is obvious with so many confused, wounded, hurt, backsliding, falling Christians that church, bible study, Sunday school, conferences and training workshops are not bringing complete healing to many people in the body of Christ. People and ministries are perishing and need effective processing, guidance, mentoring, support and empowerment, so that they can be revived and equipped to walk in destiny. Leaders have to view counseling as a necessity and begin to establish accredited centers within their ministries, so that people can receive help after the altar, after they have gone home and considered their encounter with God, after they have been tempted with the very thing they just got delivered and healed from.

We often ask who pours into leaders, superstars, public figures, or those who live their lives giving to others. Leaders must see the need for counseling for themselves. Leaders need a confidential place to:
- Vent and be themselves without feeling judged for their position, stature or need for breakthrough.
- Be replenished, encouraged, and poured into.
- Be held accountable to maintaining balance in their schedule, interactions, relationships, and in taking time for themselves.
- Receive deliverance and healing in areas where restoration is needed due life challenges, moral discrepancies, unresolved trials and wounds, and/or character issues.
- Receive wise counsel, while exploring direction and accountability to maintaining and achieving personal goals that are essential to their wellness and overall wellbeing.

Leaders are relying on other leaders who are too busy, too burned out, or too desensitized to the things of God to provide sufficient accountability and guidance to help heal and restore wounded leaders.

The main purpose for the churches in the bible was to be an edifice where people in the community could come to seek assistance. In this day and age, churches have become a place to gather on Sundays, and most people go else where to be assisted, supported, healed, and directed regarding life issues. Most people do not see the church as a counseling center, healing ground or a place where they can get help of all kinds. Furthermore, the church raves about wanting to help people from the pulpit, but when people do come forward for assistance, the church does not have the funds or organizations in place to sufficiently impact people's lives. Most churches are referring people to organizations outside the church. At some point we have to see this as negligence to *Ephesians 4*, where we are to be perfecting peoples lives, such that they see God as their source and savior.

LEADERS!!!! Today I prick your spirit to discern your needs, your communities needs, and the needs of those that cycle in your ministry, who are mentally ill, double minded, backslidden, carnal, bound by unresolved past issues, dealing with strongholds to sexual sin, struggle in their identity, are physically ill and cycle in sicknesses, addicted to drugs, pain medicines, alcohol, pornography, food, etc., and to recognize that they need tools, skills, and a processing to wholeness. They need the Spirit of Counsel and they need you to implement it into the vision of your ministry. May an urgency to stop the perishing of your sheep and region over take you now in Jesus name! SHIFT!

COUNSELING VERSUS MENTORING

Chapter 17

I want to address some terms that are being used in this day and age that can give the impression that someone is receiving counseling, but this is not the case. This is important because of the rise of mentoring, coaching, and consulting work. All of these are beneficial and necessary ministries and businesses, but are not necessarily counseling. Each play a role in helping to equip people, ministries, and the world in being healthy and focused as they journey in destiny.

Counseling (Therapy)

In addition to the Spirit of Counseling, counselors are usually educated paid professionals that require ongoing training to keep them accountable and equipped in being able to service their clients. Counseling is an in-depth exploration of past and present unresolved experiences, and of personal and generational issues. Counseling addresses personal issues, generational strongholds, sin issues, character flaws, unresolved painful experiences, and etc. Counseling involves a process of sessions where the person is enlightened, delivered and healed, as they examine themselves, life role players, experiences, and how they need to proceed forward in being delivered and healed. Once a person has been healed or has required resolution regarding issues and experiences, they are then provided tools, skills, and guidance for personal empowerment and development, so they can maintain and sustain in their healing process. Many times we will provide exploration, wisdom, and direction to a person, and contend that is counseling. But counseling is a strategic set of committed sessions that are ongoing until goals have been achieved. Jesus had the "Spirit of Counsel" and was the "*Wonderful Counselor.*" He expected us to receive counseling with him for a lifetime as we journey in relationship with him. Counseling is not advice. It is a committed processing to wholeness.

In Christian Counseling a series of sessions of biblical truths are used to process a person, couple, family, business, community, government, or nation to healthiness and wholeness.

The counseling process may include:
- A succession of personal, couples, family, or group therapy
- Deliverance ministry
- Inner healing techniques
- Homework assignments
- Feedback, constructive criticism
- Tools and skills to help reshape behavior and transform lives

Though there are many professional counseling styles and techniques that can be used, each case is different. It is essential to rely on the Holy Spirit with:
- How the counseling process should unfold
- How many therapy sessions should take place
- What homework assignments are given
- Whether deliverance ministry is necessary
- What inner healing techniques should be utilized

Legally, most people who are seeking counseling are obligated to six to nine sessions. Anyone who is healed in less than three sessions probably just needed advice, guidance, or revelation to get over a blockage - a barrier that blocked healing or deliverance. God may have even graced them with a miracle concerning their situation.

It has been my professional opinion and experience that it takes at least three sessions to establish a comfortable relationship, where a person feels safe in disclosing. A person may initially expose deep painful issues, because they are elated to have someone to discuss them with. Then they may become withdrawn due to
- Shame, guilt, condemnation
- Fear of not being believed
- Fear of their information being shared with others

This is the reason it will generally take three sessions to establish a healthy atmosphere where the person feels safe in sharing. By the sixth session, a person is in the middle of deep exposure of issues. Thus at least three to six more sessions are needed to adequately explore root causes, pains and hurts, peace and forgiveness, etc., while processing a person to a place of sufficient healing that is sustained and maintained.

I personally believe anyone who contends they are a counselor, should be professionally educated with ongoing training, even if they have the Spirit of Counsel. We have to stop whipping people with scriptures without providing them with tools to adequately apply those biblical principles in a healthy manner. We also have to be aware that there are other factors that can impact someone's life (e.g. psychological, mental, financial, economical, educational, chemical, physical, social). Professional education and ongoing training will provide a balanced perspective of realism to the counseling ministry, as there are so many factors we need information on to assist us with adequately helping and transforming our clients.

Mentoring

Mentors may be educated in different areas, but there is not a professional degree specifically for mentoring. Many who are called to mentoring, believe they possess a level of expertise that can better someone else's life. There is no professional guidelines to mentoring as this is usually a self-promoted position. This means that even though people should be led God, people decide if they want to be a mentor or not.

Mentoring can be for a season or a lifetime. A mentor can also walk with you in different seasons, and be absent in other seasons. A person can have mentors based on the needs, desires, skills and development he or she needs at that particular season of life. Mentors generally provide wisdom, guidance, and instruction to someone that may be less experienced or just may need a safe place for self-examination, confirmation, support, empowerment, instruction and accountability. The mentor is usually older and wiser, and has personal experience or knowledge in the areas to which they are imparting. Life experiences can definitely be impacting as we can take keys that are shared and implement them in our lives, or we can use the wisdom to avoid life hardships and challenges. Moreover, shared commonality in experiences can serve as encouragement and empowerment to us overcoming life challenges. Mentors also help cover and pray for people while they are working on goals and life issues.

Though you may share painful experiences and explore unresolved challenges with a mentor, and even receive some processing of issues, mentoring is not counseling. Mentors are usually focused on how they can SHIFT a person to the present, and guide them into the future. They do not regard the past, but the present and future is their focus. Also, some mentors may not be equipped to help you explore past issues and present unresolved issues in-depth. This is where mentoring tends to cross boundaries that may not be beneficial to mentees, as many mentors can open up wounds and explore challenges, but because they are not equipped to really bring deliverance and healing in this area, the mentee is left exposed, vulnerable, and can even become unstable due to not being able to handle what has been unveiled and exposed.

When people come into my life that I am supposed to journey with, I examine if it is for a season or a lifetime. But I also examine if they need counseling or mentoring. Generally those that require mentoring have maintained a level of life stability and though they have some unresolved issues, these issues are not a detriment and hardship to their present and future life, where in-depth exploration is required to bring deliverance and healing. They can be delivered and healed through a few guided suggestions that they can usually implement independently, then report back to me for accountability, support and further direction. Those that I am to counsel, need in-depth exploration of past and present issues, and will require more personal time and one on one attention. Mentors must be able to discern the needs of those who come to them for guidance. If they require counseling, then they should be encouraged to pursue a professional Christian counselor. The mentor can still journey in life with them, and provide support, encouragement, and accountability. As the person is healed of unresolved issues, the mentor can further journey with the person, while instructing, developing, and providing further guidance as they mature in their destiny lifestyle.

Coaching

A coach focuses on unlocking a person's potential as it relates to their talents, gifts, and life's purpose. Coaches work to help people form goals and a vision plan for getting an idea or vision for a business, ministry, organization, product, etc., up and running successfully. They also work with the person to improve their personal and business performance. They provide support, critical thinking, constructive criticism, feedback, guidance, and accountability, as the person explores goals, ambitions, and desired achievements. Most coaches are not issue focused, and do not counsel. They will at times, assist with exploring a present life challenge that is hindering a person's development and progress. They do not perform in-depth counseling, and if they do explore past challenges, it is often related to responsibility, accountability, and consistency in implementing and working on a desired vision plan. Coaches are future focused and seek to strengthen their clients in the areas of wisdom, confidence, and perseverance, so they can operate in their full potential. If a person has more in-depth issues, a coach will refer them to a counselor who can address those issues, while they remain focused in working with the person on their coaching vision plan. In *Exodus 18*, we find Jethro operating in the gift of coaching and administration.

Consulting

A consultant provides expertise, advice, strategies, solutions, and vision plans to assist people and businesses with improving or succeeding in goals and endeavors. On my secular job, I work as a professional Behavioral Consultant. Though I perform some counseling and mentoring with clients and staff, my main job duties are to provide skills building, and wisdom and direction to help clients live the best life possible despite personal challenges and limitations. I also help organizations run successfully despite the challenges and limitations of their customers. I create a vision plan for peoples' lives, families, or companies, and then I train them on how to implement that plan successfully. I then monitor their progress and provide feedback as necessary, while making changes to the vision plan that can improve and stabilize their lives and organizations. I do not process personal issues with clients or organizations, and basically I am required to provide consultation and a business plan whether they deal with personal challenges or not. For the most part, I provide enablement using skills and resources to help them cope and progress regardless of limitation and life issues. The focus is more on providing the best course for achieving goals than to focusing on bringing deliverance, healing and breakthrough. The people and organizations survive not because they are delivered, but because they work the plan and consultations that are given to them. When we think of this spiritually, someone can go through their entire life bound and still be successful. The main purpose and foundation of salvation is for a person to be delivered, healed and set free. Though consultant work is very important, people, ministries, businesses, and organizations, need to be delivered and healed in their foundation. Otherwise the solutions and strategies provided by the consultant will enable them, but not bring true wholeness to the inner man or the inner workings of their life and destiny path.

Managing & Administrating

Managers and administrators achieve organizational tasks that help ministries, businesses, and organizations run successfully. Managers and administrators are focused on works. They believe issues will get resolved as duties are completed. They are focused on ensuring everyone and everything cooperates and works together despite differences and challenges. They may address small fires of conflict, but are not focused on past unresolved issues, or personal quirks and issues. Managers and administrators will complete evaluations to see how they can better improve the success of an operation in the future, but they will be more focused on implementing works, measures, and precautions to ensure that happens. And if that means a person or endeavor is not a part of the future event, then so be it. As a manager or administrator will operate in conflict resolution skills to implement the vision plan and to get the job done. Rarely is there any in-depth counseling or mentoring being implemented. They are solution and success focused, and solution and success driven. They will eliminate and replace in order to achieve their desired outcome.

> ***1Corinthians 12: 27-28 The Amplified Bible*** *Now you [collectively] are Christ's body and [individually] you are members of it, each part severally and distinct [each with his own place and function]. So God has appointed some in the church [for His own use]:first apostles (special messengers); second prophets (inspired preachers and expounders); third teachers; then wonder- workers; then those with ability to heal the sick; helpers; administrators; [speakers in] different (unknown) tongues.*

> ***1Corinthians 14:40 The Amplified Bible*** *But all things should be done with regard to decency and propriety and in an orderly fashion.*

Examples of the Gift of Administration in the Bible:
- Jesus organized his ministry by choosing his inner circle of three disciples (***Mark 9:2***), appointing the twelve (***Mark 3:13-14***), and sending out the seventy two by two (***Luke 10:1***)
- Joseph was positioned over the land to govern in a time of famine (***Genesis 41:41-57; 47:13-26***)
- Titus was positioned to govern the ministries in the region (***Titus 1:5***)

A Good Administrator Possesses The Following Characteristics:
- Excited about the vision and about fulfilling tasks and duties.
- Can hear God for strategies and consistent witty ideas that improve and advance the ministry.
- Able to use strategies and witty ideas to obtain favor, blessings, and save money.
- A people person, or at least open to engage with all types of people.
- Have great communication skills and can effectively communicate and give direction and guidance with clarity.
- Wise and mature, and lives a balanced and mature lifestyle.
- Able to empower others to fulfill tasks and carry the vision.
- A natural organizer - organized and able to organize people, projects, tasks, money, goals, and departments within the vision.
- A multi-tasker and can successfully administrate several projects at one time.
- Are able to solve problems and diffuse challenging conflicts and situations.

- See the future of the vision and can implement ideas, strategies, tools, etc., to progress the vision forward.
- Understands the importance of not just using people to complete tasks and fulfill roles, but are great motivators and personal esteemers of team members and workers.
- Humble, respectful, honoring, and careful not to bully, belittle and control and manipulate people.
- Willing to be hands on when necessary to complete tasks.
- Can recognize when he or she is overwhelmed, and needs to rest and refresh.
- Balanced in fasting, praying, and studying the word, while accomplishing administrative duties.
- Good decision maker, and able to step in and run and assist with the vision and overseeing parts of the vision when necessary.
- Operates in a spirit of excellence, and is willing to make personal improvements and improvements to the vision and team such that it produces excellent results.
- Possesses professional skills of an administrator or business to effectively assist with events, meetings, vision tasks.

Many leaders have great management and administrative skills, but these skills should not be mistaken for counseling. People will come into compliance for a while, but then their issues will start to manifest as they may not have the maturity to focus on works, and deal with their issues independently of task or assignment. Their unhealed issues will cause conflict among the team and stifle the progress of the vision.

We must recognize where people are in life and what their needs are. Our greatest passion as leaders should be to see ourselves and people whole, and walking in their God ordained destiny. SHIFT!

THE CHARACTERISTICS OF A HEALTHY LEADER

Chapter 18

A leader should possess God's nature and his character. I would define nature and character as follows:

- Nature is the reality and disposition of who God is; how God acts, thinks, or behaves. It is the essence of who He is.
- Character is the attributes that make up who He is. It is what makes up His nature.

The character of God is very complex, as just when we think we understand him, he presents another avenue of himself that lets us know we are yet learning his nature and his image. It is important for leaders to have God's character and nature so we can:
- Be restored into our original identity before the fall of man in the garden.
- Gain continual understanding of who God is and is not.
- Achieve evolving revelation of our identity – who we are and who we are not
- Discern what is of God and what is not of God – what is of the devil and the world.
- Think, act, and be the reflected image of God in the earth - be examples of his word and identity in flesh form.
- Draw and disciple souls for his glory.

God will allow situations to help instill and build his character and fruit in his leaders and saints in general. When God is building his character, he is exposing and maturing the image of himself that he created us to be and desires us to be.

> *Genesis 1:27 So God created man in his own image, in the image of God created he him; male and female created he them.*

Image is *selem* in Hebrew and means:
1. Illusion, resemblance, hence, a representative figure, especially an idol: — likeness
2. representation; counterpart

Synonyms of the word "*image*" from Dictionary.com

carbon copy	form	model	reflection
figure	icon	photocopy	replica
copy	illustration	photograph	reproduction
dead ringer	likeness	picture	spitting image
equal	match	portrait	statue

Character Traits Of God

Alert Mark 14:28
Attentive Hebrews 2:1
Available Philemon 2:20
Bold Acts 4:29
Chastens Hebrews 12:6, Psalms 94:12
Compassionate 1John 3:17
Confident 2Timothy 1:7
Convicting Romans 7:9 John 16:8
Content 1Timothy 6:8
Creative Ephesians 2:10, John 1:3
Dependable Isaiah 55:11
Determined 2Timothy 4:7-8
Diligent Colossians 3:23
Discerning 1Samuel 16:7
Discrete Proverbs 22:3
Empowering Philippians 4:13
Enduring Galatians 6:9
Enthusiastic 1Thessalonians 5-15-16
Fathering 1Corinthians 8:6
Faithful Hebrews 11:1
Flexible Colossians 3:2
Fierce Jeremiah 20:11
Forgiving Ephesians 4:32
Generous 2Corinthians 9:6
Gentle 1Thessalonians 2:7
Gracious Nehemiah 9:17
Grateful 1Corinthians 4:7
Good 2Chronicles 7:3
Holy 1Peter 1:16
Hospitable Hebrew 13:2
Humility James 4:6
Initiating Romans 12:21
Jealous Exodus 34:14
Judge James 5:12, Psalms 75:7
Joyful Proverbs 15:13
Just Micah 6:8
Kind Isaiah 54:8
Loving 1Corinthians 13
Loyal John 15:13
Meek Psalms 62:5
Merciful 2Samuel 24:14
Obedient 2Corinthians 10:5
Orderly 1Corinthians 14:40
Patient Romans 5:34

Persuasive 2Timothy 2:24
Punctual Ecclesiastes 3:1
Pure Titus 1:15
Rebuker Psalms 3:11, Job 5:17
Reconciler 2Corinthians 5:18
Redemptive Ephesians 1:7
Resourceful Luke 16:10
Responsible Romans 14:12
Rewarding Hebrews 6:10
Righteous Job 37:23
Secure John 6:27
Self-controlled Galatians 5:24-25
Sensitive Romans 12:15
Sincere 1Peter 1:22
Sovereign Isaiah 14:27
Truthful Ephesians 4:25
Wise Proverbs 9:10
Worshipper Zephaniah 3:17
Wrath & Anger Psalms 7:11
Vengeful Nahum 1:2, Romans 1:18
Virtuous 2Peter 1:3

We should live and lead through the nature and character of God.

Dictionary.com defines *lead* as:
1. to go before or with to show the way; conduct or escort
2. to conduct by holding and guiding
3. to influence or induce
4. to guide in direction, course, action, opinion, etc.
5. to conduct or bring (water, wire, etc.) in a particular course
6. a guiding or directing head, as of an army, movement, or political group.

> ***Romans 12:8 The Amplified Bible*** *He who exhorts (encourages), to his exhortation; he who contributes, let him do it in simplicity and liberality; he who gives aid and superintends, with zeal and singleness of mind; he who does acts of mercy, with genuine cheerfulness and joyful eagerness.*

> ***Matthew 20:25-28 The Amplified Bible*** *And Jesus called them to Him and said, You know that the rulers of the Gentiles lord it over them, and their great men hold them in subjection [tyrannizing over them]. Not so shall it be among you; but whoever wishes to be great among you must be your servant, And whoever desires to be first among you must be your slave – Just as the Son of Man came not to be waited on but to serve, and to give His life as a ransom for many [the price paid to set them free].*

Character Traits of a Healthy Leader
- Balanced
- Loving
- Compassionate/Careful
- Mature in God, Self-Controlled, Temperate
- Obedient to God & Submissive to Authority
- Humble/Kind/Gentle/Meek
- Joyful/Cheerful/Thankful
- Considerate/Thoughtful/Respectful
- Virtuous, Pure, Righteous, & Holy
- Healed & Whole, Especially of Past Issues & Generational Strongholds
- Repents Quickly
- Easily Forgiving of Self & Others
- Confidential
- Trustworthy/Dependable/Punctual
- Patient (Long Suffering) & Tolerant
- Fervent & Persevering
- Able to Release People & their Issues to God
- Prophetic/Has Foresight into the Vision & Lives of the People
- Has & Engages Through God's Eyes & Heart
- Discerning
- Operates in the Spirit of Knowledge, Wisdom, Understanding, Counsel, Revelation

- Operate in the Gifts of the Spirit
- Has Clarity about his or her Calling & Destiny
- Vision Carrier
- Intelligent
- Articulate & an Effective Communicator
- Good Listener/Attentive
- Trained, Teachable, Life Long Learners
- Confrontational & Can Ask the Hard Questions in Love
- Able to Give & Receive Constructive Criticism
- Self Confident/Healthy Identity
- Study of the word
- Rooted & grounded in biblical truths & live a lifestyle by God's truths
- Empowering
- Creative & Resourceful
- Has an Intimate Relationship with the Lord
- Intercessor & Prayer Warrior
- Holy Spirit Filled & has Holy Ghost conviction
- Praiser & Worshiper
- Has the gift of Faith & unwavering belief in the power & word of God

Role of A Healthy Leader:
- Exude and constantly strives to operate in the nature and character of God.
- Supreme motivator - able to esteem and encourage others in purity and without any hidden motives.
- Effectively communicate, inspire, motivate and give clear/sound direction or at least motivate and encourage others to invest in the vision even if the fullness of it has not been revealed.
- Pursues the eyes, ears and heart of Christ for the vision; sees a person and the vision beyond where they are and for who they are, and esteem, teach, impart, activate, and help process them and the vision to that place.
- Discerns and prays concerning the team members personal callings in Christ and provides avenues for them to operate in the calling.
- Lead and follow.
- Delegate duties based on callings and step back and allow the person/persons to operate in that assignment, while giving grace for mistakes to be made, and constructive criticism that helps them progress forward in healthiness.
- Shift team members from a mindset of not just being utilized in giftings and talents, but understanding and cultivating the calling and full destiny on the lives of team members.
- Effectively communicate with all types of people, able to explore difficult issues, even if it is issues the team/member has with the leader or a decision a leader makes.

- Sensitive to the personal issues of team members; can decipher when deliverance and healing issues are necessary for assisting that person is progressing towards healthy maturity in the Lord.
- Seeks to be spiritually and emotionally healthy by constantly striving to improve self, while creating avenues to improve others.
- Comfortable with making mistakes, while realigning self and the vision with correcting what has been wrong.
- Repents quickly, solves personal issues in a healthy and timely manner, and does not allow personal challenges to affect his or her communication with others or the ability to adequately lead the group.
- Maintain balance between the vision and personal life; discerns when to rest and refresh ones' self, the team, and the vision.
- Fears God not man. Allows God to be the source of his or her strength, success, and promotion.
- Is humble, confident, and mature in the things of the Lord.
- Has a sense of humor; can laugh at self, Satan, and in the face of adversity.
- Faithful to the services and visions of their covering, local assembly, and faithful in seeing the vision of God come to past within the group.
- Does not mind praying, fasting, and sacrificing time, self, and desires for the good of the vision.
- Creative, inventive, and ambitious; passionate for the things and people of God.
- Honest, fair in judgment, pursues the eyes and will of the Lord, so that His will can be established in people, situations, and the environment.
- Extends grace without holding grudges, or harboring resentment or unforgiveness.
- Assertive, competent, confident, courageous, bold when necessary, and forthright.
- Open to allowing God to be free to move without building high places on areas of success, yet trusting that God can do above and beyond one's last or previous success.
- Flexible, open to change, and operating in the timing and movement of the Lord.
- Remain rooted and grounded in the word, pursues and operates in the truth of the Lord.
- Pursues the fullness of the Holy Spirit. Has the gifts of the spirit operating in his or her life or ministry.

The healthy leader may experience wounds, but allows God to perfect those things which concerns them.

> ***Psalms 138:8*** *The Lord will perfect that which concerneth me: thy mercy, O Lord, endureth for ever: forsake not the works of thine own hands.*
>
> ***Psalms 119:73*** *Your hands made me and fashioned me; Give me understanding, that I may learn Your commandments.*

Though I give examples of healthy biblical leaders throughout this manual, I am going to share a few in this chapter.

- Nehemiah was a focused, fasting prayer warrior, who had a burden to rebuild the walls of Jerusalem. *Nehemiah 1:3-4 And they said to me, The remnant there in the province who escaped exile are in great trouble and reproach; the wall of Jerusalem is broken down, and its [fortified] gates are destroyed by fire. When I heard this, I sat down and wept and mourned for days and fasted and prayed [constantly] before the God of heaven. He was a cupbearer of the King Artaxerxes, which was a high position of authority.* Nehemiah endured all types of challenges and obstacles while rebuilding the wall. Nehemiah organized people who would build the wall, and an army of people who would keep watch in case of attack. But despite trials, ridicule, and death threats from his own nation and surrounding nations, he would not come down until the walls were complete. Through a courageous and persevering character, Nehemiah and his team built the wall in 52 days. Nehemiah understood the benefits of fortifying the walls and securing the gates so that people could be safe in the providence of the Lord.

- Daniel was a healthy governmental leader who prided himself on being obedient to God's word and standard in every area of his life. *Daniel 6:3 Then this Daniel was preferred above the presidents and princes, because an excellent spirit was in him; and the king thought to set him over the whole realm.* Daniel was strict about maintaining an intimate relationship with God where he abided "in Christ" and allowed everything in his life to filter through that relationship. No matter what trials occurred in Daniels life, he was not willing to sacrifice his personal times of prayer and communion with the Lord. Daniel was so focused on wellness that even his times of fasting was a healthy sacrifice unto the Lord (*Daniel 1:12*).

- Peter is an example of a wounded leader who operated through his wounds then was restored as a healthy leader. Peter did not know he was a wounded leader. Jesus informed him of the open doors he had in his soul, yet Peter was adamant that he was sold out for Christ and was equipped to go the distance with him. *Luke 22:31-33 And the Lord said, Simon, Simon, behold, Satan hath desired to have you, that he may sift you as wheat: But I have prayed for thee, that thy faith fail not: and when thou art converted, strengthen thy brethren. And he said unto him, Lord, I am ready to go with thee, both into prison, and to death.* Peter had encountered Jesus and even sat under his teachings, but he had not SHIFTED to abiding in Jesus where the principles he learned had become his identity and lifestyle. Peter ended up denying Jesus three times, while manifesting timidity, immaturity, a lying spirit, disloyalty, dishonor, and denial of Christ. He was not equipped to stand in the face of adversity and be a witness to who Jesus Christ was to the world. Peter was convicted by his actions where he wept bitterly (*Matthew 26:33-34*). After Jesus rose from the grave, he visited Peter. Jesus said to Peter, "That thou art Peter, and upon this rock I will build my church; and the gates of hell shall not prevail against it (*Matthew 16:18*). Peter SHIFTED in his soul as he gained awareness of his identity in the earth. He was instrumental in growing the church as he preached the gospel of Jesus Christ with unwavering faith and boldness.

Healthy Leadership Nuggets

Healthy leaders are careful about the things of God and his people as all they want is to please and represent him.

Healthy leaders value balance and personal wellness. Deliverance and healing is not just an emergency fix, but a part of their personal lifestyle.

Healthy leaders consistently self-evaluate, while seeking God's truth about how they are, who they are, and what needs to be changed within them such that they are more like him.

Healthy leaders are not just concerned about preaching the word, but being the word of God to the people and the world.

Healthy leaders pursue the conviction, voice, and heart of God. They just do not want his presence around, they want God's presence fully living and working in their lives.

Healthy leaders are not just role models of God's gifts and callings, but of his integrity, character, his nature, his deliverance, his healing, and his sustaining transformation.

Healthy leaders care about what they impart into those under them. They understand that whatever is in them as the head flows down is infection or purification to the body.

Healthy leaders do not feast on just what taste good. They feast on what is beneficial in making them healthy and whole. They seek the mature meat of the word of God.

Healthy leaders value counseling as they recognize it is the wisdom, knowledge, direction, and strategy of God. They are always seeking to hear God and empowering others to do the same. They understand that the pulpit and the altar reconcile people to Christ, but counseling processes people to wholeness.

Healthy leaders do not beat their members in the head with their pet peeves and ministry challenges over the pulpit. They take their sufferings and challenges to God and allow him to heal and refresh them.

Healthy leaders do not hold grudges when there are trials, conflicts, and challenges with those they oversee. They have the eyes of Christ and engage people from his eye view of who he desires them to be, despite what they are currently displaying in their present lifestyle. And even if the person is not ready to be processed to where God desires to take them, the leader is balanced and open to imparting what that person can handle at that present time.

Healthy leaders have healthy identities, and clear focused vision about what they are to do in the earth.

Healthy leaders do not lie and cover up their mistakes, character flaws, and sins. They admit them, apologize to God and those they oversee, and seek to live out that apology in a spirit of true repentance and conviction that demonstrates that they are seeking transformation.

LEADER! BE THOU MADE WHOLE!
Chapter 19

It is important to note that wholeness is intertwined within our salvation with God. The Greek word for wholeness is the same word for "*saved*, which is "*Sozo.*"

<u>*Sozo* in the Greek is defined as:</u>
1. to save, i.e. deliver or protect (literally or figuratively): — heal, preserve, save (self), do well, be (make) whole
2. to save, keep safe and sound, to rescue from danger or destruction
3. to deliver one from injury or peril
4. to save a suffering one (from perishing), i.e. one suffering from disease, to make well, heal, restore to health
5. to preserve one who is in danger of destruction, to save or rescue

<u>Dictionary.com defines *wholeness* as:</u>
1. comprising the full quantity, amount, extent, number, etc., without diminution or exception; entire, full, or total
2. containing all the elements properly belonging; complete
3. undivided; in one piece
4. Mathematics. integral, or not fractional
5. not broken, damaged, or impaired; intact
6. uninjured or unharmed; sound
7. pertaining to all aspects of human nature, especially one's physical, intellectual, and spiritual development
8. the whole assemblage of parts or elements belonging to a thing; the entire quantity, account, extent, or number
9. a thing complete in itself, or comprising all its parts or elements

Most people believe wholeness is difficult to achieve, as aside from believing God and accepting eternal life, we do not acknowledge, embrace or live the fullness of what it means to be saved. However, as Jesus becomes our personal savior, we must grasp the understanding that wholeness is the inheritance of accepting reconciliation, and entering restoration with him. I would say that many of us easily receive being rescued from eternal damnation, and coming under the covering of God. Yet, we do not grasp that we are and can be made whole.

> *Matthew 9:20-22 And, behold, a woman, which was diseased with an issue of blood twelve years, came behind him, and touched the hem of his garment: For she said within herself, If I may but touch his garment, I shall be whole. But Jesus turned him about, and when he saw her, he said, Daughter, be of good comfort; thy faith hath made thee whole. And the woman was made whole from that hour.*

In this passage of scripture Jesus tells the woman with the issue of blood that her faith made her whole. The woman believed that wholeness was possible - attainable - and therefore, it became her portion. *Comfort* in this scripture means *"to have courage, be of good courage, and to be of good cheer."* *Courage* is the ability to do a difficult task or face a difficult adversity. The woman had to face her sickness with the belief that she was made whole, and then she had to gladly encourage herself within it.

Courage is not something you strive for. It is something you have to be at that very moment of adversity, in order for it to be your posture and truth. We have to have belief and faith at the same time to manifest courage. Often we are striving for wholeness instead of believing and standing in faith that through Jesus, we are made whole. In this passage, Jesus had not died and rose again, so the woman initially pursued what she believed to be in Jesus. Jesus died and rose again for our wholeness, so it is not something we are striving for. It is something we have in our possession. It is something we are, and as we begin to courageously live from this revelation and posture, while encouraging ourselves in this truth, we will see wholeness manifest in our lives.

As one who has received prophecy that I would be a representation of total wholeness, I will admit that learning to live from the truth that I am whole is challenging. Especially when I have battled sickness, incurable diseases, and warfare throughout, my walk with the Lord. One of the things I have learned is that I have to embrace all of salvation. The fullness of *Sozo* must be my truth. And I must be fully converted into that truth to see the prophesy of being a representation of total wholeness manifest in my life.

Convert means *"to adopt, transform, or exchange one thing or function for another."*

> **Isaiah 53:5** *But he was wounded for our transgressions, he was bruised for our iniquities: the chastisement of our peace was upon him; and with his stripes we are healed.*

Jesus took my transgressions, iniquities, chastisement, and exchanged them for *Sozo*. I did not deserve wholeness, but was adopted into it through his grace, blood, and resurrection. And just as the woman had to operate in courage and cheer when God told her to go in comfort, for her faith had made her whole, I as well, have to accept and confidently journey in the transformation that has taken place on my behalf.

One of the reasons I believe Jesus told the woman with the issue of blood to cheer as she walked out and lived in wholeness is because cheerfulness produces joy, contentment, and fulfillment, while further breeding wellness and wholeness. Being waned in these areas causes us to pursue things, and make decisions that steal, or alter our wholeness. Many are saved or say they are saved, but dread their walk. They dread not being able to engage in behaviors they were delivered from, and still love the things of the world. We must joy in our salvation. We must be happy we are saved, and value all that it entails. We must develop a lifestyle of loving the things God loves, and hating the things he hates, while living from his delights.

Our conversion is tainted when we say we live for Jesus, but we lust for the world.

> ***1John 2:16*** *For all that is in the world – the lust of the flesh [craving for sensual gratification] and the lust of the eyes [greedy longings of the mind] and the pride of life [assurance in one's own resources or in the stability of earthly things] – these do not come from the Father but are from the world [itself].*

God is not of the world. We are trying to preach a gospel that is not the truth of us. We must embrace salvation as our life's foundation, such that we want to defy anything that would try to steal or alter our wholeness. We are not being strong armed or obligated to be saved, but we want to live for God and have all he entails for our lives. Cheer reveals a true heart. ***Proverbs 22:17*** contends, *"A merry heart does good like a medicine: but a broken spirit dries the bones."*

- Wholeness is about wanting to be who God saved you to be.
- Wholeness is about courageously empowering - comforting yourself - in who God saved you to be.
- Wholeness is about committing to be who God saved you to be.
- Wholeness is about contending to be who God saved you to be.
- Wholeness is about never wavering - holding steadfast - to who God saved you to be.
- Wholeness is about refusing to settle for anything less than who God saved you to be.

Healing Nuggets:

1. Spend time studying and familiarizing yourself with the fullness of salvation aka Sozo.
2. Make sure you have embraced all Sozo entails; ask God to show you areas where conversion is still needed. Come under subjection of Jesus' saving power in those areas.
3. Ask God to give you a love and lifestyle for the things he loves, and a hatred and lifestyle for the things he hates. Ask him to teach you how to live from a place of repentance and conviction in this area.
4. Consistently throughout your walk, spend time decreeing out your wholeness and the truth of Sozo governing your life.
5. Rid your life of anything that does not represent wholeness and the fullness of salvation.
6. Stand in belief and faith, courage and cheer, when the enemy, life, and people try to thwart your wholeness. Refuse to settle. Make whatever changes necessary to restore your truth, contend for your truth, be your truth!
7. Empower those under you to live a life of true conversion, where wholeness is their tangible inheritance.

8. SHIFT! BE THOU MADE WHOLE!

Wholeness Prayer
LEADER! I decree that you are sin free, curse free, demon free, sickness and disease free, lack free, poverty free, death free. I decree that by the works of Jesus Christ on the cross, you are delivered, healed, liberated and made whole. I decree that you are not pursuing these gifts. They are you inherited portion as a believer, daughter, son, and converted friend of Jesus Christ. I decree that as you journey in intimate communion and relationship with Jesus Christ, you are an example of true salvation, wellness, and a fruitful kingdom life. I DECREE YOU ARE SHIFTING FROM STRIVING IN SALVATION TO BEING SALVATION! SHIFT!

REVIVING THE WOUNDED LEADER

Chapter 20
(Written By: Nina Cook)

After experiencing wounds and brokenness, the leader has to be revived as a new healed and whole person, that God has processed to wholeness.

<u>Dictionary.com defines *revive* as:</u>
1. To activate, set in motion, or take up again; renew
2. To restore to life or consciousness
3. To put on or show again
4. To make operative or valid again
5. To bring back into notice, use, currency
6. To quicken or renew in the mind; bring back

As the wounded leader is revived they are activated, set in motion, made operative again, quickened, brought back into notice, and use from a renewed place. Renew is listed multiple times in this definition, and is key to the healthy revival of the wounded leader. Leaders must be revived as God renews his original design and image in them.

As God revives the leader, he revives them in his image. Quite often, we strive to revive ourselves in our own image, and in the image of what we know, want, desire, and think is best. Nonetheless, when God revives us he recreates us in his very likeness and glory. As the leader is being revived, they are SHIFTING into a former nature, however, it is not the former nature of the wounds, it is the former nature of God's primitive intent.

> ***Genesis 1:26-27*** *And God said, Let us make man in our image, after our likeness: and let them have dominion over the fish of the sea, and over the fowl of the air, and over the cattle, and over all the earth, and over every creeping thing that creepeth upon the earth. So God created man in his own image, in the image of God created he him; male and female created he them.*

> ***New International Bible*** *Then God said, "Let us make mankind in our image, in our likeness, so that they may rule over the fish in the sea and the birds in the sky, over the livestock and all the wild animals, and over all the creatures that move along the ground." So God created mankind in his own image, in the image of God he created them; male and female he created them.*

When God made mankind, he created them in his image and likeness. Directly proceeding that he says, *"and let them have dominion."* In the ***New International Bible*** it says *"Let us make mankind in our image, in our likeness, so that they may rule."* The level to which a leader embodies the image of God is in direct relation to their capacity to rule. The enmeshment of the image and likeness of God in a person precedes their ability to effectively rule as a leader. As God revives the wounded leader he revives them in his image, such that they can be restored to a place of genuine godly leadership. God has placed an innate ability in leaders to have dominion and rule, it is a part of the DNA of a leader. But when they are wounded, this distorts their image, thus effecting their leadership capabilities. As a result, the wounded leader has to undergo a process of being revived in the image of God, so that genuine healing can occur in the identity, personality, character, and nature of that leader. During the revival process the leader's full godly image is brought back to life and renewed to wholeness.

The reviving leader has to surrender to the process of being healed in the totality of God's image in them. Essentially, the leader is becoming a new person, and not the leader that they were in the past no matter how good their leadership may have been. This may seem hard because it feels like starting from scratch, and the leader has to learn and discover the new them, while allowing God to recreate them. Nevertheless, it is imperative that the leader be submitted to this process to obtain true and lasting revival as God's leader. This process is God doing a new thing. The leader must grant God the ability to do a new thing in them, and then be okay with re-learning themselves from this new place.

> ***Isaiah 43:19*** *Behold, I will do a new thing; now it shall spring forth; shall ye not know it? I will even make a way in the wilderness, and rivers in the desert.*

The wilderness and desert lands that are being spoken of in this passage of scripture are lands that are uninhabited, desolate, and uncultivated. A wounded leader in the state of being revived may feel uninhabited, desolate, and uncultivated as they have had to be gutted out of their former wounded state of being, and be emptied out in totality to be revived in the new. But God's word declares that he will do a new thing in those places that seem deserted and barren. It is in those areas that the leader allows God to establish his rivers of provision to revive them in the things that embody God's image for them. Discern, look for, behold the new that God molds and puts into course, as it is essential that the focus of the leader is on the new, so as to not risk harmful things of the old being revived.

It may be the leader's heart to want to revive the good things and good attributes of the past, but when God makes something new, ALL things become new! Whether the things of the past were good or bad, the past will bring the wounds of the leader back into recognition. Even though the leader would want to be able to choose what they want to resurrect, when a leader opens the door to the past, he or she gives way to any and everything being able to maneuver its way back into the present existence of the leader's life. The leader cannot be the reviver. I repeat – THE LEADER CANNOT BE THE REVIVER! The leader has to trust God with the reviving and resist the need to revive themselves, and to control the reviving process. God does not need to bring anything back from the old because he is God, and his creative powers are not limited. God is an original creator, and not a recycler. He does not run out of resources. If the leader allows God to revive them, what they thought was good in the past will be so much better in the present, and even in the future, as God does a new thing.

> ***2Corinthians 5:17*** Therefore if any man be in Christ, he is a new creature: old things are passed away; behold, all things are become new.

New in the Strong's in this scripture means:
1. New (especially in freshness)
2. As respects form; Recently made, fresh, recent, unused, unworn
3. As respects substance; Of a new kind, unprecedented, novel, uncommon, unheard of

Creature in the Strong's in this scripture means:
1. Original formation
2. The act of founding, establishing, building etc.
3. The act of creating, creation
4. Institution, ordinance

As God revives, he creates a new, unused, fresh kind of leader. Something that is uncommon, unheard of, unprecedented, which is another reason why the leader has to resist the temptation to revive themselves. As God does the reviving, he establishes things in the leader that they have never experienced before. God creates an entirely NEW creature; OLD things passing away are a key to this process. New and old cannot co-exist. The leader cannot be made new until they first have allowed the old to pass away. The need to be revived implies that a death must have occurred. To be revived, the leader must be surrendered to letting things die that are not a part of God's image for them.

Pass away in the Strong's of the scripture means:
1. Perish or neglect
2. To pass away, perish
3. To pass by, pass over, that is to neglect, omit (transgress)

Perish in Dictionary.com means:
1. To die or be destroyed through violence, privation, etc.
2. To pass away or disappear
3. To suffer destruction or ruin
4. To suffer spiritual death

As God revives the leader as a new creature in their original formation, the leader will undergo a spiritual death. All that is of the past must die so that they can live new. Before the leader can be effectively revived, the past must be utterly destroyed and ruined. The perishing of the past is so efficient that the definition says that it will disappear, making the past no longer a factor, concern, or challenge for the leader. The only time that the past can become a challenge is if the leader decides to go back and associate with the things of the past. In doing so, they are essentially keeping company with the dead, choosing death, and to be stagnated in the past. They are rejecting the new life and path that God is presenting before them. In being revived, the leader has to make the choice to continually behold the new things that God is doing in them. They must keep their focus on discovering and cultivating their new nature and character in God's image. The leader has to consciously put the attention on the creating, founding, establishing, and instituting that is occurring in them. As they immerse themselves in receiving insight and revelation from the Lord, the process will overwhelm them with the new to the degree that the past will have no room to remain. The reviving leader must commit to letting the past disappear, and make a vow to the Lord that they will not dwell amongst the dead. They must commit to abiding in the reviving spirit of the Lord, and choose life over death.

In this essence, the reviving leader gets the opportunity to be born again, because revival provides a new life. The level of submission to God and letting go of the previous life, will determine how that new life looks. The new life can be filled with the fullness of God's original created image, if the leader chooses to let the past perish. Jesus trusted God, and he knew that if he died in him, he would also be raised in him. As God revives you trust him with your life. He will not fail his chosen leaders. He created you in his perfect image once before, and he is able to do it again.

BALANCE! RESPITE FOR THE LEADER!

Chapter 21

It is very important for a leader to have balance. Otherwise, burnout and even crossing boundaries with people and ministry endeavors is inevitable. Self care is essential as a leader cannot be a role model or impart healthiness and wholeness into those they oversee if he or she is not healthy and whole.

> ***Matthew 10:8*** *Heal the sick, cleanse the lepers, raise the dead, cast out devils: freely ye have received, freely give.*

Received is lambano in the Greek and means:
1. to take (get a hold of, have offered to one, violently - to seize or remove)
2. attain, be amazed, assay, attain, when I call, to hold, catch

Though God gives us power to heal, cleanse, raise, and cast out, we also discern from the definition that a person can pursue what they desire or need from God with such focus, and even aggression of one taking or seizing it. As the person receives it, he or she is able to give it to others.

It is important to seek God for personal revelation and knowledge, so the leader can be delivered, healed, and equipped with the deliverance and healing tools and keys necessary for releasing breakthrough to a client.

> ***Psalms 42:7*** *Deep calleth unto deep at the noise of thy waterspouts: all thy waves and thy billows are gone over me.*

A leader cannot take a person in deep deliverance and healing if they:
- Have not received deep deliverance and healing for themselves.
- Do not consistently go deep in God's presence for answers and strategies for the people under them.
- Are not constantly refreshed and replenished in God's presence.
- Do not seek seasons of healing, refreshing, respite, counseling and consecration for themselves, where they are taken deep, purged of sins, soul challenges, war wounds, burdens, and challenges of helpings others.

Freely receiving from God provides respite and rejuvenation that enables a leader to give what they have received and have become. A leader must pursue deliverance and healing for themselves, so they can be a representative of wellness and, can give from a fruitful and replenished well.

Many leaders have trouble taking time to refresh. We tend to have a mindset that if we take time away:

- Things will not get done.
- People and duties will become stagnant or even regress.
- People and duties cannot survive and grow without us.
- We are failing or neglecting people or duties.
- We are failing God and our calling.
- We are failing the vision of our business, organization or ministry.
- We are not equipped as if we were we would not need respite.
- We are weak, as resting means we cannot handle what has been granted to our hands.

Most of our mindsets regarding resting is rooted in pride, as the focus is more about us and how our identity and self-worth, is rooted in what we do, rather than who God is and what he does through us. Such a disposition is error as we constantly need to do and help in order to have a sense of value or self importance. This is idolatry, because much of what we are doing is about building up our own kingdom, where we are glorified, rather than establishing God's kingdom where he is glorified. There is also a fear that someone will take what we have built, and even with blatant moral discrepancies, some feel they are above taking a sabbatical to be restored in God. This is pride at work as the focus is self. There is a false sense of security, and obligation in and to God, when really the person's trust and commitment is rooted in self, and in his or her accomplishments. This is a dangerous place to be in because the person operates as if God is with them, when really they have left the governing of God, and are now positioned for a great fall.

> ***Proverbs 16:18*** *Pride goeth before destruction, and an haughty spirit before a fall.*

Though we are called to watch over, journey with, mentor, equip, and build people up, while providing tools to sustaining in wellness, we should not use them for self-validation. Moreover, we are not called to micromanage people. If people can only sustain in their deliverance and healing when we are excessively pouring into them and managing them, then error and imbalance has occurred. We have either become the fixer, the rescuer, or God in their lives. We are playing roles that makes them dependent on us, rather than independent and accountable to God and their deliverance and healing process. This is idolatrous and unhealthy for us and those we are overseeing.

Jesus did not get his identity as savior from people, and he did not micromanage people. Jesus knew that some would fall. And though he equipped and prayed for them, he recognized that some would go to hell and some would yield to sin, error and backsliding no matter how much they knew him as savior. We see examples of this with Judas and Peter.

Judas was an apostle that was taught and equipped by Jesus. However, that did not stop him for betraying Jesus for money.

> *Matthew 26:21-25 And as they did eat, he said, Verily I say unto you, that one of you shall betray me. And they were exceeding sorrowful, and began every one of them to say unto him, Lord, is it I? And he answered and said, He that dippeth his hand with me in the dish, the same shall betray me. -- The Son of man goeth as it is written of him: but woe unto that man by whom the Son of man is betrayed! it had been good for that man if he had not been born. Then Judas, which betrayed him, answered and said, Master, is it I? He said unto him, Thou hast said.*

Peter was one of the first initial disciples of Jesus. He was also one of the first initial apostles. Jesus not only counseled and mentored him, he was also in Jesus inner circle and was chosen to be a fisherman of men by Jesus.

> *Mathew 26:31-35 Then saith Jesus unto them, All ye shall be offended because of me this night: for it is written, I will smite the shepherd, and the sheep of the flock shall be scattered abroad. But after I am risen again, I will go before you into Galilee. Peter answered and said unto him, Though all men shall be offended because of thee, yet will I never be offended. Jesus said unto him, Verily I say unto thee, That this night, before the cock crow, thou shalt deny me thrice. Peter said unto him, Though I should die with thee, yet will I not deny thee. Likewise also said all the disciples.*

- Jesus did not try to counsel or rescue them out of what would occur.
- Jesus did not stop his purpose and go out of his way to make sure they did not abort all he had poured into him.
- In *Matthew 26:36*, Jesus took time to pray and refresh with the Lord in the garden of Gethsemane. His focus was not on Judas or Peter, but on being further empowered in his purpose.

As leaders, we must trust what we have imparted into people. God made us watchman, self-validators, and not micromanagers.

> *Ezekiel 3:17-18 Son of man, I have made thee a watchman unto the house of Israel: therefore hear the word at my mouth, and give them warning from me. When I say unto the wicked, Thou shalt surely die; and thou givest him not warning, nor speakest to warn the wicked from his wicked way, to save his life; the same wicked man shall die in his iniquity; but his blood will I require at thine hand.*

> *Ezekiel 33:8 When I say unto the wicked, O wicked man, thou shalt surely die; if thou dost not speak to warn the wicked from his way, that wicked man shall die in his iniquity; but his blood will I require at thine hand.*

A watchman observes, covers, warns, and counsels. The watchman does not attend excessively to the person to make sure they do what God is requiring. The watchman does not do more than required for self-worth, or to prove his or her ability and success.

If we have been who God has directed us to be, and have imparted at his leading, then we have to respect that people still have choices. Ultimately, they have to make the decisions to live what they have received. No amount of micromanaging will stop a person from making poor or unhealthy decisions. If it is in the person to sin or error, they will find a way to do it whether we are Lording over them or not.

Often as leaders, we rate our success by a person's ability to successfully sustain in what we have invested. Jesus saved, delivered and healed people, but it was their responsibility to maintain their breakthrough. It was never his responsibility nor did he take ownership in the lives of mankind. Even as Jesus was on the cross and it appeared as if he was defeated, he was accomplished. This is the reason he could pray for forgiveness of his persecutors and declare in *John 19:30*, "*it is finished.*" He did his part, and now it was left in our hands to accept the gift of redemption he provided, and live our lives through it.

It is important for leaders to have a balanced lifestyle of resting and replenishing with the Lord, and to enter seasons of rest with the Lord. When we feel the need to steal away with God, and when God tells us to rest, he is preparing us for a greater purpose than what is currently going on around us. The enemy and people do not enter a place of rest just because we desire to, or are unction to by the Lord. The enemy continues to be his same old devouring self, and people continue onward with their lives and issues. During times of rest, we notice the enemy's workings and the needs of the people all the more, because our defenses are down due to a posture of rest. We are also on the outside looking in, so we are seeing what is occurring and as caregivers our life's purpose is to step in and save the day. However, when we continue to focus on the enemy and people's issues, rather than resting and seeking a refreshing in God, we are being disobedient, and we are uncovered from the protection of God. This gives the enemy a legal right to attack us, and people the right to weary and drain what little strength we have. We must be postured in a place of knowing that as we are obedient to God, he will fortify us from the lurking enemy, and take care of the people we are to help.

<u>One of the Greek words for *rest* is *anapausis* and means:</u>
1. intermission; by implication, recreation: — rest
2. cessation of any motion, business or labour

Rest is a literal putting to death of your works. The only way to enter true rest is to cease all works, and not be drawn into battles that are not God ordained.

> *Matthew 11:28-30* *Come unto me, all ye that labour and are heavy laden, and I will give you rest. Take my yoke upon you, and learn of me; for I am meek and lowly in heart: and ye shall find rest unto your souls. For my yoke is easy, and my burden is light.*

Moreover, there is a changing of guards in the place of rest. The leader exchanges his strength, and his workings for God's easy yoke and burden.

God promises refuge and lightheartedness when there is a true positioning of rest. At times we are not able to discern the refuge because resting usually manifests what is already unrested/disquieted within us. If we are anxious, agitated, murmuring, complaining, sick, tired of warring, overworked, over burdened, etc., it is usually an indication of the weariness that is already in us, and is the reason God required a time of rest in the first place.

We tend to see such irritations as being from the enemy and the enemy harassing us in our rest, but this is not the enemy, this is what needs to be cleansed out of us - exchanging our overburdened soul for a refreshing of our soul. We simply recognize these things now because we do not have people, the enemy, trials, war, duties and labor to distract us. If we really enter a place of rest these harassments manifesting from within us will dissolve, and then the enemy will not have a foothold in our time of rest to heighten, and take advantage of these open doors in our lives.

Rest is a fixed and stable place or position. In this place the leader is not wandering in and out of rest. The leader is submitted to being seated in God, and their work is centered on staying grounded and postured in this position.

> ***Psalms 91:1-2 The Amplified Bible*** *HE WHO dwells in the secret place of the Most High shall remain stable and fixed under the shadow of the Almighty [Whose power no foe can withstand]. I will say of the Lord, He is my Refuge and my Fortress, my God; on Him I lean and rely, and in Him I [confidently] trust!*
>
> ***The Message Bible*** *You who sit down in the High God's presence, spend the night in Shaddai's shadow, Say this:"God, you're my refuge. I trust in you and I'm safe!"*
>
> ***Hebrews 4:11*** *Let us labour therefore to enter into that rest, lest any man fall after the same example of unbelief.*
>
> ***The Amplified Bible*** *Let us therefore be zealous and exert ourselves and strive diligently to enter that rest [of God, to know and experience it for ourselves], that no one may fall or perish by the same kind of unbelief and disobedience [into which those in the wilderness fell].*

As we further consider ***Mathew 11:28***,

<u>Labour is *spoudazo* in the Greek and means:</u>
1. seed (used in sowing): to use speed, i. e. to make effort, be prompt or earnest: — do
2. (give) diligence, be diligent (forward), endeavor, labour, study
3. do diligence, be diligent, give diligence, be forward, labour, study
4. to hasten, make haste, to exert one's self

The Greek word for labor denotes that when we are diligent to enter a place of rest in God, it is seed used for sowing. We sow into being diligent to rest and God rewards us by doing or leading us in doing all the work that needs to be done in us and for us. We are totally submitted to His strength and His spirit, and do nothing of and in our own accord.

It is therefore, important to have a passion in staying in this place when God is requiring it of you. Pursue it with passion like you would pursue anything that you deem important and be okay with ceasing from works, personal pulls and pulls of people or obligations and responsibilities that will only drain you and steal your time of renewal in God.

Another Greek words for *rest* is *katapausis* and means:
1. reposing down, i. e. (by Hebraism) abode
2. a putting to rest calming of the winds, a resting place
3. metaph. the heavenly blessedness in which God dwells, and of which he has promised to make persevering believers in Christ partakers after the toils and trials of life on earth are ended

Dictionary.com defines *repose* as:
1. to lie at rest
2. to lie dead
3. to remain still or concealed
4. to take a rest
5. to rest for support: lie

As we are diligent in pursuing such a place of rest and calmness, our spiritual and natural posture should literally appear as dead. Also, unhealthy things should die in us just because we have been obedient to resting in God.

Repose suggests that this rest should be as a death. The quietness we enter should be in such submission that we appear dead from doing works. We should be totally submitted and focused on being humbled, bowed and prostrate before Jesus.

> ***Hebrews 4::12 New Living Bible** says: For the word of God is living and active and sharper than any double- edged sword, piercing even to the point of dividing soul from spirit, and joints from marrow; it is able to judge the desires and thoughts of the heart. And no creature is hidden from God, a but everything is naked and exposed to the eyes of him to whom we must render an account.*

This asserts that we are not trying to hide our sins, faults, weariness, but are taking them to him - before him. As we are diligent in resting, his word goes in and surgically removes everything that is not like him. It divides the good from the bad and cleanse us (our souls), then renew and reconnects us (our spirits) in places that were disconnected from him.

> ***The Message Bible*** *God means what he says. What he says goes. His powerful Word is sharp as a surgeon's scalpel, cutting through everything, whether doubt or defense, laying us open to listen and obey. Nothing and no one is impervious to God's Word. We can't get away from it--no matter what.*
>
> ***The Amplified Bible*** *Let us therefore be zealous and exert ourselves and strive diligently to enter that rest [of God, to know and experience it for ourselves], that no one may fall or perish by the same kind of unbelief and disobedience [into which those in the wilderness fell]. For the Word that God speaks is alive and full of power [making it active, operative, energizing, and effective]; it is sharper than any two-edged sword, penetrating to the dividing line of the breath of life (soul) and [the immortal] spirit, and of joints and marrow [of the deepest parts of our nature], exposing and sifting and analyzing and judging the very thoughts and purposes of the heart.*

<u>*Sharper*</u> is <u>*tomoteros*</u> in the Greek and means:
1. to cut; more comprehensive or decisive than, as if by a single stroke; whereas that implies repeated blows, like hacking
2. more keen: — sharper

Sidebar Prayer:

Ohhhh we diligently seek to rest in you Jesus. We repent for anyway we have not rested when you required it, and we shift to diligently pursuing a resting place of refuge in you. As we rest Lord, let your word take refuge in us. Go deep in releasing your word in us Lord.

Let the sharp scalpel of your word surgically work in us Jesus! We willingly come to the operation table of rest to be judged by your word, to be delivered by your word, to be healed by your word, to be revived by your word, to be renewed by your word, to be refreshed by your word, and to be further directed by your word. Lord divide and separate us from everything that is not like you. Disconnect and gut out everything that is not like you. Penetrate deeply - pierce deeply where we are gutted out all the way back to Adam and Eve.

Everything that cannot got into the next season of our lives, scalpel it out. Let the sword be keen in discerning and removing all evil, all the demonic, every crevice and fashion of the devil and his existence. And as you do a complete work in us....as we die in you. Conceal your likeness in us Jesus. Reconnect us to you in places we have been detached. Reconnect us in places where we have been damaged due to past warfare, sin, or illegal violations of the enemy.

Ohhhhh we die in you and rise in you Jesus. We die on your operation table of rest and rise into resurrection newness in you Jesus. Yes! Yes! Yes! We take our rest and let you do you in us Jesus. We submit to the work that only you can do in this time of dying in your secret place of rest.

Jesus often took moments of respite. It was a part of his lifestyle and enabled him to balance his ministry and calling and his personal wellness.

Luke 5:16 And he withdrew himself into the wilderness, and prayed.

Matthew 14:23 And when he had sent the multitudes away, he went up into a mountain apart to pray: and when the evening was come, he was there alone.

Luke 6:12 And it came to pass in those days, that he went out into a mountain to pray, and continued all night in prayer to God.

Luke 9:28 And it came to pass about an eight days after these sayings, he took Peter and John and James, and went up into a mountain to pray.

Mark 6:30-34 And the apostles gathered themselves together unto Jesus, and told him all things, both what they had done, and what they had taught. And he said unto them, Come ye yourselves apart into a desert place, and rest a while: for there were many coming and going, and they had no leisure so much as to eat. And they departed into a desert place by ship privately. And Jesus, when he came out, saw much people, and was moved with compassion toward them, because they were as sheep not having a shepherd: and he began to teach them many things.

In this last scripture Jesus and the disciples went to a secluded place to rest and refresh. The people spotted them coming from their place of leisure and came after them. Jesus was moved with compassion because the people were like a sheep having no shepherd so he began teaching them. There are a few keys here that we can glean from.

- Compassion is a fruit of the Holy Spirit, which is the character and nature of God. So compassion enabled Jesus to minister through the heart and love of God, and not through his own strength.
- The people were without teaching and shepherding. They needed equipping. They needed teaching to sustain in their Christian walk. In the era to which Jesus was ministering, he stated in **Matthew 9:37**, *"The harvest truly is plenteous, but the labourers are few."* Often those we are counseling or ministering to have other leaders, mentors, and supports that can empower and guide them during our time of rest. Moreover, in this day and age, we have sufficient labourers, programs, and organizations where people can receive assistance if they have a crisis. And if we have been giving them what God has required, many of those we lead have been provided with the tools necessary for sustaining in their lives. We have to trust the support systems that are available to intervene during our time of rest. We must trust what we have imparted, and more importantly we must trust God with people.

- A shepherd pastors, cares for, oversees, covers, teaches, guides, trains, equips, heals, and protects the sheep. If it is not compassion drawing us out of a time of rest, then:
    - We risk teaching people things they do not need, is not of God, are already equipped with, or cannot handle at the time.
    - We risk guiding them in a direction that is not of God, or not the correct timing.
    - We risk attack from the enemy by trying to cover and protect them in a season where we are not fortified or have the grace to fight and shield them from the enemy.

Mark 7:24 And from thence he arose, and went into the borders of Tyre and Sidon, and entered into an house, and would have no man know it: but he could not be hid.

When you need rest you must take it, and when God calls you to a season of rest you must be obedient to it. If you have to hide to seek respite, do it. If people in desperate need find you like they did Jesus, then Holy Spirit will grace you to minister to them. But this is very different than knowing you need rest from those you are consistently pouring into. God will provide a shepherd for a lost sheep. Yet, he will make the equipped accountable to walking out what the shepherd has imparted. As a leader, we must have balance and make sure we are taking care of our needs with just as much efficiency and care as we do those we counsel and minister to.

SUGGESTIONS FOR TAKING REST TIME
Chapter 22

In addition to daily prayer and study, a leader should be taking weekly time to just replenish before the Lord, and just for leisure purposes. Jesus encouraged the disciples in this area:

> *Mark 6:30-32 reads: And he said unto them, Come ye yourselves apart into a desert place, and rest a while: for there were many coming and going, and they had no leisure so much as to eat.*

These wisdom keys can be implemented for short and long term times of respite.

- Decide how much time you are going to take and stick to your regimen (e.g. A few hours, one day, three days, seven days, twenty one days, forty days).

- If it is for a few hours, give yourself that time without feeling like you have to share it with anyone. Just take it. God knows what can occur during that time and if something happens that you need to be a part of, he will unction you. Moses was experiencing the weighty glory and instruction of the Lord and God said to him "*Go, get thee down; for thy people, which thou broughtest out of the land of Egypt, have corrupted themselves*" (***Exodus 32:7***). If you are needed, God will make sure you know.

- Establish a day just for you during the week so people will know you are off limits for that day. If your respite is for a longer period of time, let those close to you know that you will not be available for those amount of days, and to only contact you in case of emergency. If you have a ministry, let those who you oversee know you will not be available, and put someone in charge that can oversee the ministry while you are resting.

- If you are married and have children, tell your spouse of your respite plans and ask him or her to come into agreement with giving you this time of refreshing. Let the children know as well, and have them go to your spouse for whatever they need. Depending on your home environment, you may have to take respite outside of the home. Be okay with doing this. You cannot adequately be there for your family if you have nothing to give. Your family can also leave the home and give you time at home with Jesus. Some leaders have time during the day for respite, while everyone is away. It is important to schedule that time in a few days a week, where it is just you and Jesus. Be disciplined in your other duties and responsibilities, while making this a balanced priority in your life.

- Log off of all social media and messenger sites. These are an asset not a priority. If you have built a ministry through these sites, and they are rooted in the Lord, then they will keep. You do not have to operate in fear where you are deceived into believing that if you do not feed people everyday, they will not follow you. They should not be drawn to you, but to the God in you. This is another avenue the enemy is draining people and leaders, and they do not recognize it. Many social media people are fickle and flighty. They feed on the next catchy word or trend, but rarely are they implementing what is spoken in their lives to produce real change. Jesus is not about tickling people's fancies. He is about saving and transforming lives. Be focused on transforming people rather than gorging them with revelation that their lives and spiritual walks cannot digest. Delete the apps off your devises if you have to. Do whatever you need to do to close in with Jesus.

- If your rest time is longer than three days then commit to checking emails, texts, and phone call messages once a day. Only respond to what is important and immediately requires attention. Put a 30 minute time limit on this so that you are not being drawn back into works when you should be resting. Unless it is a life or death situation, delegate any other emergency and duties to a responsible party, and return to communion with the Lord. And even with life and death situations, you must recognize that all things are in God's hands. Jesus was about his father's business when Lazarus died, and some of it included him resting and refreshing before the Lord. Jesus was challenged by Lazarus' death, how others responded to Lazarus' death, had compassion for their grief, and he also was grieved to the point of weeping. However, Jesus did not feel guilty because Lazarus died, nor did he take on the guilt others tried to put upon him. He also raised Lazarus from the dead. You have the power to resurrect anything that dies once you return from your time of rest and being about your father's business of getting what you need from him so you can walk in pure power and authority (***Read John 11:32-45***).

- This time of rest is for you. You are not praying for anyone else, praying for the ministry, interceding, etc., unless God leads you to do so. Otherwise, it is time for you to take yourself before God, so he can replenish and renew you.

- You may have to spend the first few minutes, hours, or days of your rest time releasing people and duties to JESUS and breaking soulties to them. ***Matthew 11:28-30*** says *Come unto me, all ye that labour and are heavy laden, and I will give you rest. Take my yoke upon you, and learn of me; for I am meek and lowly in heart: and ye shall find rest unto your souls. For my yoke is easy, and my burden is light.*
You will have to release the yoke of people, ministry, and life, and anyway you are tied and obligated to them and take on the yoke of the Lord. You will know there is a unhealthy yoke when you are trying to pray for yourself and press into Jesus, but that person, situation, concern, or duty keeps coming into your mind/heart, and drawing your attention away from you and God. Break ties

with it, and surrender it to the greatest hands it could be in which is Jesus. If this does not work, then search if it belongs in this time of prayer with you and Jesus. If Jesus says it does, then allow Jesus to direct you in how to pray, journal, or approach it.

- As you surrender matters to God, pursue God, repent for sin issues and character flaws, etc., and also take time to receive. So often we are talking and pressing in through a hunger and desire for a great encounter with God, until we do not realize God is with us, and is pouring himself into us. Take time in silence while just resting in the presence of the Lord. Just wait in the Lord. If he talks that is okay. If he does not talk, that is okay too. He is your friend. You do not talk to your friend the entire time you are hanging out. Sometimes you are quiet and just resting and being together. Be okay with doing this with the Lord. You do not have to gimmick and perform for God, and please do not require him to gimmick and perform for you. Wait in courage that he is with you and is enjoying rest time with you. ***Psalms 27:14*** *Wait on the Lord: be of good courage, and he shall strengthen thine heart: wait, I say, on the Lord.*

- Be okay with falling asleep. Some of you need to sleep. Sleep is spiritual, healthy, and brings healing and direction. ***Psalms 63:6*** *When I remember thee upon my bed, and meditate on thee in the night watches.* ***Psalms 4:4*** *Stand in awe, and sin not: commune with your own heart upon your bed, and be still. Selah.* ***Psalms 16:7*** *I will bless the LORD, who hath given me counsel: my reins also instruct me in the night seasons.* ***Isaiah 26:11*** *With my soul have I desired thee in the night; yea, with my spirit within me will I seek thee early: for when thy judgments are in the earth, the inhabitants of the world will learn righteousness.* At the moment you SHIFT into personal rest, you are deciding to enter a night season. You have blacked the rest of the world out and you are in a time of communion with the Lord. The only light you should be seeing is his glory light. God releases dreams, visions, instructions, and strategies while we sleep. I often hear God talking to me in my sleep. He will have me get up and journal things he shares and then I will return to sleep where I am communing with him. ***Proverbs 3:24*** *When thou liest down, thou shalt not be afraid: yea, thou shalt lie down, and thy sleep shall be sweet.* When something is sweet it is pleasant, delightful, refreshing, enjoyable, joyful. This is one way God cleanses heaviness, depression, stress, and frustration. He does it with good sleep. Sometimes you can feel the Holy Spirit healing and refreshing you as you sleep. Sometimes you are just experiencing good sound sleep. If you get sleepy, go to sleep and trust that because you took time with God, he knows what you have need of. ***Psalms 3:5*** *I lay down and slept; I awoke, for the LORD sustains me.*

- Sometimes we lie down in prayer with God and we are so engulfed in his presence that we go into a trancelike state where we feel like we cannot move. We feel like we are in between being sleep and awake. Be okay when experiencing this. God does some of his best healing and communing in this state. He is satiating and replenishing you. Satiate means "to bathe, to satisfy, to soak, and to fill you up." ***Jeremiah 31:25-26*** *For I have satiated the weary soul, and I have replenished every sorrowful soul. Upon this I awaked, and beheld; and my sleep was sweet unto me.* ***The Amplified Bible*** *For I will [fully] satisfy the weary soul, and I will replenish every languishing and sorrowful person. Thereupon I [Jeremiah] awoke and looked, and my [trancelike] sleep was sweet [in the assurance it gave] to me.*

- Have a journal, pin, and bible handy so you can scribe whatever God shares and study scripture as God leads. A recorder can also be beneficial if you want to record any words of prophecy, knowledge, strategy, and counsel that the Lord gives. These words will still need to be written so the vision can be engraved (imparted and established) into the earth realm, where you and others can read and utilize it. ***Isaiah 30:8*** *Now go, write it before them in a table, and note it in a man, that it may be for the time to come for ever and ever.* ***Habakkuk 2:2*** *And the LORD answered me, and said, Write the vision, and make it plain upon tables, that he may run that readeth it.*

BALANCING FAMILY AND MINISTRY
Chapter 23

Balancing Dating & Engaged Relationships:

- If you are dating or engaged, be honest about your ministry schedule and your times of prayer and study with the Lord. Role model your schedule, rather than giving the impression that you have free time that you do not really have. Let the person know the reason God has required the specific disciplines for you so they can pray concerning what you are sharing, and have a clear vision of who you are in God.

- Seek the Lord together for any changes you each need to make in each of your spiritual walks to make time for one another.

- Create a vision plan for cultivating your relationship and commit to working it.

- Schedule prayer and study time together. This will help with your transition if you have been single for a while, and are used to spending a lot of time praying, studying and doing ministry. This will also help you build one another up in the Lord.

- Have a balance between attending ministering activities and leisure time. Be cognizant of not just spending time together at ministry events. Schedule leisure events that you both may enjoy, but do not hinder or jeopardize your walk with the Lord.

- Communicate when you feel neglected or torn between the relationship and ministry. Encourage the other person to do the same. Commit to not holding back your thoughts and feelings in this area as it will cause an open door to division and strife. Communication is key to giving your thoughts and feelings a voice in the relationship, and to getting your needs and desires met. You must be able to communicate, because the Lord will not tell you every single thing no matter how anointed you are. This will cause you to grow in being honest and vulnerable with one another in your desires, needs, and standards.

- If you are dating or engaged, the Lord will give you grace to sustain the relationship. In busy seasons time will be stretched. You must set aside special time for one another knowing God has given you the grace to walk in the relationship. He released the relationship in due time knowing you could balance ministry, work life, and personal relationship. Therefore be okay with working through these seasons.
- Be able to celebrate one another. You are not in competition with one another but there to support, strengthen, and esteem each other greater than yourselves as you move forward in unity. No one wants to date or become engaged with someone who cannot genuinely celebrate their success. You must be willing to gut out any

subtle jealousy, inadequacy, or revenge of wanting to perform better than your potential spouse.

- Please know that whatever you root in your foundation will be difficult to gut out in the future. It is important to have a balanced healthy foundation that your relationship can stand on.

Balancing Marriage and Family Relationships:

- Make weekly time for your marriage and family. Schedule it on your calendar and make it a priority. Ensure you schedule time for just your spouse alone, as well as the entire family. Remember to never stop dating your spouse! It is also important to confirm on a regular frequency that the scheduled time is a time that works for the family and change it as needed, but do all you can to not cancel it.

- Resist adding events to your calendar that are not a part of what God is requiring of you in the present season you are in. Make sure you communicate and share your calendar with your spouse and family, to ensure that their needs are covered during these times and/or adjustments can be made.

- Resist enabling people and having meetings where people just want to waste time, but are not about true change.

- Trust your team and promote accountability. If they cannot be accountable then replace them with someone who can. A lot of times, we keep people in positions to avoid conflict, but this is at the expense of you having to step in and do it. Replace them with someone that can be accountable, so you do not have to spend your time fulfilling duties that others can do.

- Pace yourself in your ministry vision. Be cognizant to hearing God concerning what you need to be working on at any given season so you will not stretch yourself too thin.

- Be disciplined in scheduling meetings and completing ministry duties when other family members are busy so you all can be working at the same time, as opposed to hitting and missing one another. If there is a time that this cannot be accomplished, it is important that you communicate this to your family and be disciplined with the scheduled time.

- Invite and implement your family into your ministry endeavors and what God is doing in your life. Often we are selfish and protective in this area without realizing that it can cause family members to be jealous of your relationship with God and your ministry. It can also cause wounds and conflicts where there are demands to choose between the two. Ask your family for feedback on your ministry endeavors and be open to hearing them. This will help them feel a part of this portion of your life verses separating the two. Remember your family is your primary ministry!

- Every marriage and family is different. It is okay to consider suggestions from others, but it is best to search God for a vision plan for your marriage and family. What works for others may not work for your marriage and family. Consult with your spouse and family concerning the plan, and give them the opportunity to change and add to the plan. The vision plan can include how you desire your relationships to be, desires of spending time together, commitments to supporting one another's life events, activities and outings you all can plan and do together, and etc. Revisit the plan every few months to make sure it still works for your current family dynamics and adjust it accordingly.

- Do not try to fit ministry duties and obligations that may arise in particular seasons, inside the dynamics of your marriage and family. Take time to evaluate what season you are in with God, and share what God has said with your spouse and family. Then together you all explore with God, what standards will be needed to complete the will of God, while also remaining committed to the family needs and desires.

- Text, call, and email to express affirmations of love, appreciation, support, and encouragement. Ensure that you are communicating in a fashion that fits each family members needs. While your child may receive from a text message, your spouse may prefer you call, so they can hear your voice. Know what each family member needs and desires, and engage them accordingly. Also, make sure they are aware of your needs and desires so they can bring fulfillment to your life.

- Consistently check on your spouse and families' well-being. Show concern for their soul with such fervor as you would those under your ministry. At no point should your family feel as if they lack priority in your life.

- Plan family vacations that are not centered around ministry. It is important that you spend time connecting and making memories with your family to ensure continued balance for both you and your family. It can be as simple as a weekend trip, or a 7-day trip. The key is you are making time to focus on them. Consider and plan separate trips for just you and your spouse, and then one with the entire family at least once a year.

- Speak into your family and make sure their spiritual needs are met. They need to see and know that you care about their spiritual growth just as much and more than those you are assigned to in the Kingdom.

DEALING WITH SIN STRUGGLES AS THEY SURFACE
Chapter 24

When sin struggles arise, we must immediately take them to the Lord. Dealing with them speedily will help avoid public exposure. It will also prevent you from having to sit out of ministry for a long period of time, where personal restoration and faith restoration with those you oversee and conduct ministry with is needed.

1Corinthians 9:27 But I keep under my body, and bring it into subjection: lest that by any means, when I have preached to others, I myself should be a castaway.

New International Bible No, I strike a blow to my body and make it my slave so that after I have preached to others, I myself will not be disqualified for the prize.

New Living Bible I discipline my body like an athlete, training it to do what it should. Otherwise, I fear that after preaching to others I myself might be disqualified.

Wisdom Keys For Conquering Sinful Desires:
- When you begin to have sinful thoughts, do not let them linger. Also do not feed them with filth from TV, music, social media, internet, novels, activities, and etc. Immediately begin to guard your gates so that the thoughts will not cause you to transgress between you and God.
- Shut in with the Lord and even take a few days to fast and consecrate.
- Spend time praying, repenting, and closing any doors you may have opened, or the enemy is trying to open.
- Build yourself up in the word to counter attack whatever it is you are struggling with.
- Spend time studying your standards, and adding new principles that will further sustain you in your destiny journey.
- Search God for what it is in you that needs to be fulfilled spiritually, and that may be manifesting through flesh and soul issues. Spend time letting him fill you in these areas, or spend time receiving patience and contentment, as you wait on his promises to be fulfilled in your life.
- Acquire a couple of accountability partners. Do not confide in people who are going to take advantage of your weak state or feed your struggle. Steer clear of these type of people. Confide in a leader, counselor, mentor, or friend, who is serious about you walking in destiny, and being all God desires you to be.
- Do not let the enemy isolate you where you are simply spending idle time, while being tormented and drawn away by your thoughts and feelings. Go around healthy people who can empower you, and build you up as you conquer this struggle.
- Seek prayer from your accountability partners. It is important to seek prayer immediately and continually as many people like to wait until their desires have

pushed out the voice, presence, and conviction of God in their life. By this time, many are more apt to yield to the sin for relief than to seek prayer and counsel.
- Build a strong support system with your overseer, a counselor, and a couple of mature friends so you feel comfortable with immediately inquiring support and prayer when struggles arise.

DEALING WITH WOUNDS AS THEY SURFACE
Chapter 25

When wounds arise, we must immediately take them to the Lord. Dealing with them speedily will help avoid public exposure. It will also prevent you from having to sit down for a long period of time, where personal restoration and faith restoration with those you oversee and conduct ministry with is needed.

> **Hebrews 4:15** *For we have not an high priest which cannot be touched with the feeling of our infirmities; but was in all points tempted like as we are, yet without sin.*

Touch insinuates that there is a connection, contact, or an identification of something. When a touch occurs, there is an impact depending on its force. If God is touched by what we feel, then of course we are impacted by them.

Thoughts and feelings help you to identify what is in you, upon you, or around you that is healthy or that needs deliverance and healing. If your thoughts and feelings are negative, impure, sinful, perverted, lustful, demonic, overwhelming, unhealthy, then it is an indication that something in, upon, or around you is challenging the God in you.

It is important to be able to identify your thoughts and feelings, and to put words to them. Many people are not in tune with their thoughts and feelings or deem it weak to acknowledge their thoughts and feelings. Knowing how to recognize and express your thoughts and feelings is vital to being able to deal with wounds when they surface.

If you cannot be true to what you think or feel, then you will be prone to:
- Stuffing your pain, stress, and challenges
- Presenting as if all is well when you are really wounded
- Delaying in dealing with your wounds

Each one of these are learned unhealthy coping mechanisms that we most often learn from childhood. We are taught to suck it up, keep it moving, get over it, be a big boy or girl, cowards cry, and on and on. And once saved, we are taught that thoughts and feelings do not matter; only our spirit man matters.

But we are made up of three parts:
1. Body
2. Spirit
3. Soul (mind, heart, emotions)

They each help to shape our identity in God.

Using biblical principles and tools from counseling, it is essential for all leaders to learn the following skills, and to teach them to their congregation:

- Communication Skills
- Anger Management Skills
- Coping Skills
- Interpersonal Relationship Skills
- Social Skills
- Leadership Skills
- Coping with Trauma
- Coping with Grief and Loss

You can go on the internet and learn these skills, intertwine them with biblical principles, practice them as a lifestyle, and teach them to your congregation, so they can have the skills they need to have healthy dialog, fellowship and relationships. We are doing ourselves and people an injustice by slinging scriptures at them, but not equipping them with tools that can really transform their lives, and breed a healthy home, community, and ministry environment.

Wisdom Keys For Immediately Conquering Wounds:

- When wounding situations arise, acknowledge your challenges concerning them.

- Spend time quietly identifying and acknowledging the thoughts and feelings you are experiencing. Journal them if necessary.

- As you are searching out your thoughts and feelings, identify if they are coming from:
  - Within you (your soul, heart, perception, memories)
  - From around you (from the situation itself, other people, your environment, atmosphere, frequencies and airwaves)
  - The demonic realm (demons sending the thoughts or demons talking to you)

Knowing where they are coming from will help you in being able to dismantle them if they are outside of you, and release them if they are coming from within you.

Exploring Your Thoughts & Feelings
Proverbs 4:2 Keep thy heart with all diligence; for out of it are the issues of life.

If the thoughts or feelings are coming from within you, identify if they are coming from a current situation or past situations. If they are coming from past situations, cleanse out roots, while receiving deliverance and healing from those situations, and the current situation.

If time is a factor, then separate your current thoughts and feelings from past thoughts and feelings, and ask the Holy Spirit to give you sufficient grace to deal with the current situation in a healthy manner. As he leads you, acquire deliverance and healing from the current challenges, and then address the issue with people if this is necessary, and as God leads.

In your private prayer time, spend the next few days dealing with past thoughts and feelings that have surfaced from unhealed wounds.

With current and past experiences, be sure to cast out and break any demonic spirits, demonic strongholds and curses that may be operating in your soul, heart, mind, thoughts, emotions, and body.

People & Environments
The situations we experience have a voice and feelings. They take on a personality based on what they are about, and as we are a part of them or around them they interject those thoughts and feelings onto us. We therefore, have to break ties with the situation itself, and every way it has taken claim to our soul. This will enable us to separate our thoughts and feelings from that of the situation. It is also important to shield yourself from anyway the situation is trying to take over your identity, where you cannot have a clear or Godly focus on handling the situation. That way, as you are before God, receive cleansing and healing from your thoughts and feelings, and Godly direction on how to resolve the matter.

Sometimes we take on the thoughts and feelings of others. Remember thoughts and feelings "*touch*" so they have an impact. What someone says to us and around us impacts us. It is our responsibility to make sure that impact does not yield us to transgression. And if they wounded us with their thoughts and feelings, we must rebuke and cleanse out what was spoken, forgive and release offense, and cleanse out anyway we were affected by what they spoke or felt. Often we do not deal with this quickly, and people's thoughts and feelings end up negatively impacting our position and character when it was either not our issue, or when it was not a challenge for us.

Thoughts and emotions can linger in the environment, atmosphere, on frequencies, and airwaves. This can be one of the ways we can be continuously impacted by an experience long after it is over and/or resolved. It is important to pray cleansing prayers over environments and atmospheres when challenging situations occur, and when they are resolved. You should also do this when you pray for people in your home or office, as their emotions and thoughts can still linger on frequencies and cause idle chatter in the spirit realm around you; or cause you to still be challenged by their issues, or a situation when it is resolved. This is one of the ways the enemy keeps us bound to offense and unforgiveness when we have sought deliverance and healing. Remember the devil is the prince of the power of the air so he does not play fair (*Ephesians 2:2*).

Demonic Influences

Ephesians 6:12 *For we wrestle not against flesh and blood, but against principalities, against powers, against the rulers of the darkness of this world, against spiritual wickedness in high places. Some thoughts and feelings maybe coming from territorial spirits and principalities or sent from witches and warlocks to torment you, bind, hinder, oppress, depress and seize you.*

These spirits take advantage of situations that occur in your life by infiltrating and tormenting you with floods of thoughts and feelings, so that you cannot deal with the situation in a Godly manner. These spirits will also use unresolved wounds inside of you as doorways and portals, to send negative thoughts, feelings, and curses to attack you.

You can discern these thoughts and feelings, because they will feel as if they are pressing upon you or around you. You may also feel like a knife or piercing on the temple, forehead, back of the head, top of head, brain, chest, heart, or stomach. You may experience cloudiness, confusion, blackness, or darkness in your thoughts and feelings, scatteredness, thought racing, restlessness, dizziness, migraines, or pressure in and around the head, heaviness, depression, instability, raucousness, sickness, burning lust, as these thoughts and feelings plague you. They will be trying to get you to agree with them so they can bind, oppress, depress, further wound you, and etc.

Know that you have power over all the power of the enemy (**Luke 10:19**).
- Rebuke these thoughts and feelings.
- Break their powers over you.
- Cast out spirits that are being used if necessary.
- Cut off alliances between you and principalities and territorial spirits.
- Close up portals and doorways they are using to attack you.
- Deal with witches and warlocks or wicked people who are sending curses and spells if necessary, and close up gateways they are using to attack you.
- Deal with your wounds so their legal right is cut off; release them to the covering of the Lord, so that they cannot be manipulated as you are processing to wholeness.

Quickly deal with and release all offense and unforgiveness.

Deal with the thoughts and feelings you are experiencing.

Be resolution focused. This means you are open to surrendering pride, righteous justification, anger, and resentment for the good of being healed and the situation having a Godly outcome.

Be conscious of the words you speak. We tend to speak vows that are curses when we are angry. Then we forget to cancel them in the spirit realm. So even as we may have received deliverance and healing regarding a matter, the vow inflicts an additional wound. And if we do not deal with it, then it is on our soul as a door opener to further wounding.

Use your skills (e.g. conflict resolution skills, communication skills, etc.) when resolving conflict, as they will help you avoid further wounding of yourself and others.

Be okay with taking a couple of days to fast, pray and heal before the Lord to deal with more painful situations that require more attention for healing to occur. The quicker you deal with wounds, the quicker you heal, or at least receive direction from the Lord on how to proceed in processing to healing and wholeness.

WRITING SUCCESSFUL VISION PLANS

Chapter 26

Isaiah 30:8 Now go, write it before them in a table, and note it in a book, that it may be for the time to come for ever and ever.

Written vision plans take what is spiritually stated, and physically engraves (imparts and establishes) it into the earth realm. It solidifies what God has spoken about you and that vision such that what he has already imparted in the earth about you connects with what he is further releasing about you in the spirit. As they meet, manifestation occurs, and evolves in helping your destiny to unfold in the earth. The Ten Commandments are a prime example of a Godly vision plan.

The Ten Commandments provided a clear written vision of how God wanted the Israelites to live (*See Exodus 20*). It was God's way of establishing a covenant bond with Israel as their Lord and savior, who delivered them from Egypt, and desired them to further live in redemption with him. They were engraved on tablets so the Israelites could have the vision plan before them, while being physically established (engraved) in the earth.

Sampson

Sampson was given a vision plan for his life before he was conceived. This was a clear vision for keeping Sampson safe, blessed, anointed, strong, and powerful. If followed correctly, this plan would have enabled Sampson to successfully sustain in his destiny task as a deliverer of Israel.

Judges 13:3-5 And the angel of the Lord appeared unto the woman, and said unto her, Behold now, thou art barren, and bearest not: but thou shalt conceive, and bear a son. Now therefore beware, I pray thee, and drink not wine nor strong drink, and eat not any unclean thing: For, lo, thou shalt conceive, and bear a son; and no razor shall come on his head: for the child shall be a Nazarite unto God from the womb: and he shall begin to deliver Israel out of the hand of the Philistines.

Timothy

Timothy was provided a vision plan for his ministry. It was tailored to issues that were occurring in his congregation, and to the lives and marriages of the saints at that time. It was an example of how we are to have a specific vision plan that fit the needs, challenges, training, and development of our ministries.

1Timothy 1-4 I exhort therefore, that, first of all, supplications, prayers, intercessions, and giving of thanks, be made for all men; For kings, and for all that are in authority; that we may lead a quiet and peaceable life in all godliness and honesty. For this is good and acceptable in the sight of God our Saviour; Who will have all men to be saved, and to come unto the knowledge of the truth.

Verse 8-15 *I will therefore that men pray every where, lifting up holy hands, without wrath and doubting. In like manner also, that women adorn themselves in modest apparel, with shamefacedness and sobriety; not with broided hair, or gold, or pearls, or costly array; But (which becometh women professing godliness) with good works. Let the woman learn in silence with all subjection. But I suffer not a woman to teach, nor to usurp authority over the man, but to be in silence. For Adam was first formed, then Eve. And Adam was not deceived, but the woman being deceived was in the transgression. Notwithstanding she shall be saved in childbearing, if they continue in faith and charity and holiness with sobriety.*

John
John wrote a vision plan to prevent sin from occurring in the lives of the people he oversaw. He was making sure they knew how to avoid sin, and deal with sin should they fall.

1John 2:1-2 *My little children, these things write I unto you, that ye sin not. And if any man sin, we have an advocate with the Father, Jesus Christ the righteous: And he is the propitiation for our sins: and not for ours only, but also for the sins of the whole world.*

Peter
Peter provided a vision plan for walking in wellness and sustaining maturity of the Lord.

1Peter 1-25 *So put away all malice and all deceit and hypocrisy and envy and all slander. Like newborn infants, long for the pure spiritual milk, that by it you may grow up into salvation – if indeed you have tasted that the Lord is good. As you come to him, a living stone rejected by men but in the sight of God chosen and precious, you yourselves like living stones are being built up as a spiritual house, to be a holy priesthood, to offer spiritual sacrifices acceptable to God through Jesus Christ....*

Nicodemus
Jesus gave Nicodemus a personal vision plan for being born again.

John 3:1-21 *There was a man of the Pharisees, named Nicodemus, a ruler of the Jews: The same came to Jesus by night, and said unto him, Rabbi, we know that thou art a teacher come from God: for no man can do these miracles that thou doest, except God be with him. Jesus answered and said unto him, Verily, verily, I say unto thee, Except a man be born again, he cannot see the kingdom of God. Nicodemus saith unto him, How can a man be born when he is old? can he enter the second time into his mother's womb, and be born? Jesus answered, Verily, verily, I say unto thee, Except a man be born of water and of the Spirit, he cannot enter into the kingdom of God. That which is born of the flesh is flesh; and that which is born of the Spirit is spirit. Marvel not that I said unto thee, Ye must be born again.....*

We are to write the vision and make it plain:

> ***Habakkuk 2:1-4*** *I will stand upon my watch, and set me upon the tower, and will watch to see what he will say unto me, and what I shall answer when I am reproved. And the Lord answered me, and said, Write the vision, and make it plain upon tables, that he may run that readeth it. For the vision is yet for an appointed time, but at the end it shall speak, and not lie: though it tarry, wait for it; because it will surely come, it will not tarry. Behold, his soul which is lifted up is not upright in him: but the just shall live by his faith.*

Calendar & Journals are Accountability Plans

It is essential that leaders have calendars and journals. Trying to keep everything in your head causes stress, burnout, and memory loss. It also opens the door for you to appear inconsistent, immature, and unreliable due to missed appointments, and not being accountable to plans that you make vows to keep. Write everything down and keep dates and times of even small commitments so you can stick to working your vision plans, and being responsible and balanced in scheduling and attending appointments

Even schedule your time with the Lord and other goals you are working on. God must be a priority. He must come first and everything else flows through him. Also, after your immediate family that lives in the house with you, what he requires of you comes next. So schedule that in as well. As you take care of God's work, he will exceedingly take care of your work.

> ***Matthew 19:29*** *And every one that hath forsaken houses, or brethren, or sisters, or father, or mother, or wife, or children, or lands, for my name's sake, shall receive an hundredfold, and shall inherit everlasting life.*

> ***Matthew 6:33*** *But seek first the kingdom of God and His righteousness, and all these things will be added unto you.*

<u>Vision Plans Can:</u>

- Be Seasonal (specifically and strategically focused on where you are in your life and ministry)

- Specific in Assignment (strategic to a goal you and/or God wants you to obtain)

- Personal or Ministerial (tailored to your personal life or ministry - both are needed as a leader)

- Specific to Deliverance and Healing or Personal Growth and Development (tailored to current sin issues, character flaws, generational strongholds, cycles and habits, training and development needed to mature in one's gifts and callings, ministerial and personal growth, etc.)

- Strategic to Walking in Sustaining Destiny
    - What is your purpose and calling?

    - What is God revealing concerning your purpose and calling?

    - What is God requiring of you at this season of your destiny?

    - What character traits, connections, disciplines, and accountability measures do you need to fulfill what God is requiring in this current season?

    - What type of relationships, acquaintanceships, connections, covering, mentorship is beneficial to your destiny walk (e.g. What do you need from a spouse, what type of friends, acquaintances, connections do you need, what is your standard for marriage, friendships, acquaintances, connections; what type of covering/mentorship do you need, what is your standard for a healthy covering and/or mentoring relationship?

    - What is God requiring from you daily, weekly, seasonally as it relates to respite, personal prayer, and study time that is specifically focused on you, respite, lifestyle and seasons of fasting and consecration (e.g. Take Monday's for personal time, every two months take a vacation, fast two days a week, every quarter do a 21 day fast, take time off from all ministry the entire month of December).

    - Standards are not just morals and values, as morals and values can be good, decent, and respectful, but lack Godly principles and standards. Though Jesus fulfilled the law, there are still statutes we have to abide by that demonstrate that we belong to God and his kingdom (*read Matthew 5:16-21*). Now that we have our own personal relationship with God through the works of Jesus Christ, what God may require of you may be different than what God is requiring of someone else. Standards are tailor made biblical principles that align with the word of God, while enabling us to hold fast the profession of our faith. Standards keep you from transgressing against the character, nature, virtue, maturity, discipline, faith and steadfastness God is requiring for your life. What are the standards God is requiring of you, such that you sustain your journey in a successful destiny lifestyle with the Lord.

    Hebrews 4:14-16 *Seeing then that we have a great high priest, that is passed into the heavens, Jesus the Son of God, let us hold fast our profession. For we have not an high priest which cannot be touched with the feeling of our infirmities; but was in all points tempted like as we are, yet without sin. Let us therefore come boldly unto the throne of grace, that we may obtain mercy, and find grace to help in time of need.*

Wisdom Keys for Accountability to Vision Plans:
- Plans should be consistently revisited and reevaluated before the Lord, and only changed or demolished at his leading.
- Plans should be consistently worked and invested into before totally revamping a plan. Give God your best effort at working a plan so even if it needs changing, you are being accountable to what he is requiring of you.
- If the Lord tells you to get rid of a plan, scrap it immediately. He will give you a more efficient plan that is in line with where you are and what he is doing, or he may have you return to that plan at a later time in your destiny journey.
- Consider an accountability partner to help you remained disciplined in working your vision plan. This person should be invested in your personal and spiritual walk, and able to intercede and carry you in the spirit.
- Even if you and God decide to totally revamp a vision plan, spend time self-evaluating before the Lord. Examine what was good and bad about the vision, successful and unsuccessful about the vision, areas you did or did not follow through, disciplines needed to fulfill the plan, the reason you are revamping, what you will do differently with your new plan. Repent for any areas of sin, disobedience, failures, and where you dropped the ball. Spend time fasting, consecrating ,and spiritually building yourself up in the character, integrity, accountability and disciplines you need before starting your new vision plan (e.g. Standing on scriptures and decrees that build your confidence and identity, praying and fasting against personal and generational curses, strongholds, cycles and habits, receiving training in areas related to the success of the vision).

EXAMPLES OF VISION PLANS:

Personal Wellness
Block these times out on your calendar so you will not give this time away to anything else, and so you can be accountable to your personal wellness plan.
- Take a personal leisure day every Monday.
- Pray at 5am to 7am Tuesday - Friday (An hour of that is just you and Jesus and the other is for people and ministry).
- Saturday is flexible and Sunday, and Monday pray 7am to 9am (An hour of that is just you and Jesus and the other is for people and ministry).
- Fast Tuesdays and Thursdays until 6pm water only.
- Work on sermons and teachings 12pm to 2pm on Tuesdays and Thursdays
- Exercise Wednesday, Thursday, Friday at 9am for 45 minutes.
- Counseling and mentoring hours Wednesday and Saturday from 9am to 12pm and from 2pm to 5pm.
- Take a quarterly three day personal fast and consecration sabbatical where it is just time with God (March, June, September).
- Take a sabbatical the second week of November to the first week of January of the next year.

New Year Exploration Vision Plan
Every year around November, I use this plan as a time of reflection and exploration. I also give this plan to my leaders, close spiritual children and mentees that I do life with. I give them a month to complete it, and I individually meet with each of them and share successes, constructive criticism, and direction and prophecies God has given me concerning them for the upcoming year.

1. What has your spiritual progress and challenges been like for 2016?
2. What has been the most enjoyable time of this year? Explain your answer.
3. What has been the most challenging time of this year? Explain your answer.
4. Did you achieve your goals and what God desired of you personally and spiritually? Explain your progress or lack there of in detail. What would you do differently? What would you do better?
5. How did KSM impact your growth and/or lack there of?
6. What is God saying for you personally for 2017?
7. What is God saying for you as it relates to KSM for 2017? As it relates to Taquetta and leadership in general?
8. What disciplines do you need to achieve your goals?
9. What do you desire and feel you need from me and/or KSM in order to achieve your goals?
10. What do you need from God to achieve your goals?
11. List three goals you are committed to working on to achieve the things God is requiring of you.
12. List three goals you are committed to work on to grow in your gifts and callings. Write a vision plan for how you will achieve these goals.
13. Share anything else that would benefit what God is asking of you for 2017, and as it relates to you being apart of my life and KSM.

Ministry Vision Plan
You can have a broad ministry plan that require years to achieve, and that even generations ahead will have to fulfill. You can also have a short term ministry plan that will enable you to work on your broad ministry plan without becoming burnout, or releasing and doing things out of the timing of the Lord.

Your short term plan can be for a year, two years, five years, etc. The Lord will lead you in what is realistic and obtainable for you. I have a broad vision plan of all God desires me to fulfill, then I seek God for what I am to work on in my current season of life. I usually consistently work on my short term vision for a year -January through December. In November of each year, I take a sabbatical and examine, re-evaluate, add, and take away from the plan as I prepare for the next year. My sabbatical is included in my plan, so I am able to rest while continuing to complete any last minute things related to my plan. This enables me to keep balanced in all God has granted to my hands, and not get overburdened by my life's vision and destiny. Remember destiny is a lifestyle walk with God.

Long-term Vision Plan:
- Plant a church
- Open a shelter for homeless women
- Write a book on healing the abusive woman

Short-term Vision Plan:
January 2017-November 2017
- Seek God for a leadership team
- Begin having church services in my home twice a month
- Set up trainings for my team in leadership, eldership, evangelism
- Have weekly 5am prayer via conference call with my team every Saturday at 7am
- Have weekly bible study via conference call with my team every Thursday at 8pm
- Meet with each team member monthly for a mentoring session and to build them up in their personal walk with Jesus, and personal gifts and calling
- Explore information on how to open a shelter
- Volunteer at a women's shelter twice a month to learn the dynamics of operating a shelter
- Write vision, missions statement, policies and procedures, and laws for shelter
- Explore grants and funding for women's shelter. Narrow down at least three grants that are in line with our vision. Have a clear understanding of their operations so I can begin writing on the grant and funding requirements in January 2018
- Spend time before the Lord on Wednesday and Friday from 12pm to 2pm writing a book. Be okay if God does not give you anything. There is an anointing to scribe that will come upon you and even wake you up to write, or draw you away to scribe. If God is not leading you to write in your scheduled time, use it to do research on your book topic; also use it to cleanse any unhealed areas in you or challenges that is blocking the scribe anointing on your life; use it to just be before the Lord and rest while he downloads revelation into your spirit. When it is time for you to begin scribing, he will awaken it in you, and unction you to write. ***Psalms 45:1*** *My heart is inditing a good matter: I speak of the things which I have made touching the king: my tongue is the pen of a ready writer.* ***The Message Bible*** *My heart bursts its banks, spilling beauty and goodness. I pour it out in a poem to the king, shaping the river into words. Inditing* means "*to gush, flow, to stir.*" It is an anointing that overtakes you and you begin to spill out the heart of God through words.
- Take a sabbatical in November to reevaluate, reflect, revive, refresh, and plan for next year.

Example of a Vision Plan Regarding Personal Standards for Sustaining in One's Destiny Journey

This is an example of my plan. It is very strict, but tailored to me.

Vision for Standards: You are my representation of unwavering faith and wholeness. Pursue and strive to live a lifestyle of holiness, righteousness, purity and virtue. This is essential for operating in the raw power and strong anointing of God, and for keeping doors closed to sin, unnecessary drama, and hardship.

- Only date for marriage. Seek me for the standard of mate you are to marry and a standard for dating. Never settle from this standard.
- Seek me for the standard of personal friends you should have; keep your personal life guarded from people that may not value and operate in this same standard.
- Seek me for a heart to hate the things I hate and love the things I love.
- Do not watch movies, listen to music, attend events, or entertain conversations that entails perversion, gossip/slander of others, witchcraft, and blaspheme or dishonor God.
- Be a life long learner and pursuer of being trained and equipped in your destiny and calling, but be spirit lead in what and who you receive from.
- Seek me before attending any church events, trainings, conferences, etc. This will assist with not opening the doors to tainted impartations that can cause defilement.
- Maintain a consistently weekly fasting regimen and seek me for quarterly personal fasts and consecrations (March, June, September). This is in addition to ministry fasts and consecrations, and seasons of strategic fasting and consecrations.
- Guard your mouth and be quick to repent, as what you speak could release word curses.
- Guard your eye and ear gates as they can be door openers to demonic dreams and ungodly dream impartations.
- Repent quickly and consistently check in with the Holy Spirit to make sure you have his conviction.
- Check yourself for humility such that how I use you will not become a stumbling post for pride.
- Forgive quickly and seek to resolve conflict quickly. Bring me your true feelings. Be open to releasing them to me so you can heal and resolve matters in a Godly manner.
- Be a life pursuer of personal deliverance and healing. Know that it is apart of your destiny walk with me.
- Do not participate in pagan holidays. Remember, this is just an example however, God will tailor your standards in what is best for you. e.g. Sampson could not cut his hair as it cut off his strength. Pagan holidays are rooted in idolatry. Idolatry breeds defilement, and paganism opens the door to idolatry and sin.

- Do not take risks that will lend to sin and transgressions. Know what you can and cannot handle and be okay with not being able to handle or do things others do. Understand your risks based on your background and the generational strongholds in your family line. For example: You were a heavy drinker in the world and come from a line of alcoholics; so even social drinking is a risk you do not need to take as it could lend to drinking when stressed, overburdened, or to being addicted to alcohol.
- Eat healthy and exercise three times a week - Explore the generational health challenges in your family line, and seek me for a personal health plan to break curses. Minimize your pork and dairy intake and consume lots of fruits and veggies. This will help you sustain in strength, vitality, and wellness, while avoiding generational sicknesses that cut off the life span.

VISION PLAN FOR THE WOUNDED LEADER

Chapter 27

We do not know how much personal time biblical characters took to be restored when they sinned, or to heal from personal hurts and pains. We can tell that some did not take any time at all, and operated through their wounds.

Examples:
- Tamar being raped and never getting over it.
- Saul having mental illness.
- David who was a man after God's own heart, but continuously sinned, repented, and whose life and generations suffered them consequences of his actions.

Wisdom would say that God would never want us to continue ministering when we are living in blatant willful sin, or when we are in a season in our lives where a process of strategic deliverance and healing is necessary. Love covers a multitude of sins (**Read 1Peter 4:8**). However, love does not forfeit our accountability to those sins, nor lend an opening for continual sining. We cannot be an adequate representation of God and his word when we are in blatant sin, or in instances where we require personal attention regarding character challenges and unresolved issues. And grace - well grace yields a sufficiency that does not give us a hall pass to sin.

> **2Corinthians 12:9** *And he said unto me, My grace is sufficient for thee: for my strength is made perfect in weakness.*

<u>Sufficiency</u> in the Greek is *arkeō* and means:
1. raising a barrier; properly, to ward off, i.e. (by implication) to avail (figuratively, be satisfactory)
2. be content, be enough, suffice, be sufficient
3. to be possessed of unfailing strength
4. to be strong, to suffice, to be enough
5. to defend, ward off, to be satisfied, to be contented

Grace provides a supernatural power and equipping beyond our human limitations. In addition, grace is a gift that we did not earn. It is freely given through our belief and relationship with the Lord. Therefore, grace should breed a conviction where we want to do right. And because grace is an unfailing strength, it should empower us to do right. We must also literally receive the gift of grace for it to work in our lives.

> **2Corinthians 12:10** *Most gladly therefore will I rather glory in my infirmities, that the power of Christ may rest upon me. Therefore I take pleasure in infirmities, in reproaches, in necessities, in persecutions, in distresses for Christ's sake: for when I am weak, then am I strong.*

You have to actually take the gift of grace that is being given and operate in the gift - take it on as a blessing that can keep and sustain you. When considering this revelation, I would say that if you are in a place of willful sin, you are not operating under/through grace. You have either put the gift down or not taken it at all. Grace will provide you with the desire to pursue deliverance and healing, and power to endure, while you are being delivered and healed. We have to want to be free of sin to experience the sufficiency of grace.

I would further contend that if God wanted us to minister wounded he would tell us. Our woundedness would have purpose. That purpose would not

- Bring reproach to God or negate his word
- Cause others to stumble or think it is alright to sin
- Infect/affect other people
- Bring confusion to God's word

People would also clearly see God's sufficiency of grace upon us, as it would be a testament of his supernatural power. In this fashion, the wound would not get the glory, the person would not get the glory, the devil would not get the glory, God would get the glory.

> ***2Corinthians 12:9-10*** *And he said unto me, My grace is sufficient for thee: for my strength is made perfect in weakness. Most gladly therefore will I rather glory in my infirmities, that the power of Christ may rest upon me. Therefore I take pleasure in infirmities, in reproaches, in necessities, in persecutions, in distresses for Christ's sake: for when I am weak, then am I strong.*

We have a lot of sinful and wounded leaders ministering, and what is being exalted is sin, their pride, and the devil. They are saying it is God's will, but his grace is not in it, nor is it covering it.

Jesus told those he healed to "take up their bed and walk," "*go and sin no more,*" "*go in comfort thy faith has made the whole.*" The bible does not reveal what their progress to sustaining in healing and living a life of wholeness entailed. But we know from these statements that a vision plan for maintaining wellness was sparked in their life. Now whether they acquired the details from the priest, the disciples, or from further walking with Jesus, I am sure a personal time of reflection, self-exploration, and equipping with skills, tools, and changes were essential for sustaining in their vision plan.

As leaders, we have to want deliverance and healing as much as we want to conduct ministry. We have to want Jesus for ourselves just as much as we want him for the people, and for the calling that is on our lives. We have to value the power, blessings, and need for restoration just as we valued salvation and reconciliation.

Restoration Scriptures:
- ➤ ***Jeremiah 30:17*** *For I will restore health unto thee, and I will heal thee of thy wounds, saith the LORD; because they called thee an Outcast, [saying], This [is] Zion, whom no man seeketh after.*

- ➤ ***Joel 2:25-26*** *And I will restore to you the years that the locust hath eaten, the cankerworm, and the caterpiller, and the palmerworm, my great army which I sent among you. And ye shall eat in plenty, and be satisfied, and praise the name of the Lord your God, that hath dealt wondrously with you: and my people shall never be ashamed.*

- ➤ ***Psalms 51:12*** *Restore unto me the joy of thy salvation; and uphold me [with thy] free spirit.*

- ➤ ***Acts 3:19-21*** *Repent ye therefore, and be converted, that your sins may be blotted out, when the times of refreshing shall come from the presence of the Lord. And he shall send Jesus Christ, which before was preached unto you.*

- ➤ ***Isaiah 61:7*** *For your shame [ye shall have] double; and [for] confusion they shall rejoice in their portion: therefore in their land they shall possess the double: everlasting joy shall be unto them.*

- ➤ ***Job 42:10*** *And the LORD turned the captivity of Job, when he prayed for his friends: also the LORD gave Job twice as much as he had before.*

- ➤ ***Jeremiah 29:11*** *For I know the thoughts that I think toward you, saith the LORD, thoughts of peace, and not of evil, to give you an expected end.*

- ➤ ***Galatians 6:1*** *Brethren, if a man be overtaken in a fault, ye which are spiritual, restore such an one in the spirit of meekness; considering thyself, lest thou also be tempted.*

- ➤ ***Zechariah 9:12*** *Turn you to the strong hold, ye prisoners of hope: even to day do I declare [that] I will render double unto thee;*

- ➤ ***Matthew 6:33*** *But seek ye first the kingdom of God, and his righteousness; and all these things shall be added unto you.*

In the counseling field, people are encouraged to commit to six to nine sessions before being considered as having really searched out a matter, and acquired the necessary healing and skills to independently journey further in their healing process. Even then, most commit to more sessions depending on the depth of their issues and challenges. It takes about three months to complete six to nine consistent sessions and if counseling ends, then the person is placed on a follow up plan where they visit the counselor every two to three months for a maintenance session. Many people receive about three maintenance sessions, and some even continue on years later for accountability purposes and to have a safe place to explore life stressors that may manifest in their lives. Now if the world deems this as a sufficient plan for processing to wellness, then why does the church shun process. It is not of matter of God delivering and healing as that is a given. God can and does do quick workings. The process is for us to live out and sustain in what he does in and through us. Be willing to work a restoration plan when you have yielded to sin and wounds. You are worth every minute it requires to process you to sustaining wholeness.

The Lord Knows:
- How much time you need from ministry to be restored (e.g. month, three months, six months).
- What you need deliverance and healing in (e.g unresolved issues, generational issues, curses, bewitchment, besetting sins, addictions, root causes, identity restoration, forgiveness issues, betrayal, rejection, rebellion, etc.).
- What path you need to take to acquire deliverance and healing (e.g. ongoing counseling, fasting, prayer, scripture study focus, deliverance sessions, commitment regimen concerning church services, etc.).
- Who needs to assist you in your deliverance process (e.g. your overseer, Christian counselor or both, close friend that can help maintain accountability, etc., community services or ministries that may provide support, knowledge, and training regarding your issue).
- The skills you need to sustain in to maintain your wellness (e.g. communication skills, anger managements skills, social skills, interpersonal relationship skills, leadership training, assertiveness training, training in your gifting and calling, etc.).
- The skills, responsibilities, accountabilities, and vision plan needed to further journey in wholeness after you have been restored.

You and your overseer should search out a personal vision plan for you with Lord. If your overseer is too busy to walk with you through your restoration process, then allow them to be an accountability partner while pursuing a Christian counselor. I actually recommend a Christian counselor rather than another leader, as counselors are called to set time aside to deal with your personal issues. They will be balanced in their interactions with you, and they are qualified to seek God for what needs to be restored in your destiny lifestyle. Ministries truly need to establish Christian counseling in their churches to effectively minister to those in the church and community who need processing to wholeness, and to provide skills and sufficient support systems that prevent a yielding to sin, succumbing to woundedness, and backsliding.

If you need deliverance from sin and/or unresolved issues that you had before you were saved and you never dealt with them, you may need a longer time of processing to wholeness than if this had just become an issue for you. I assert this because the sin or wound has now become apart of your identity, personality, ministry, and lifestyle. It will take time to cleanse every avenue, provide you with tools to walk in healing, and for you to practice your new identity and skills as a lifestyle. I will use homosexuality for example. We have a lot of people, even leaders getting healed one day, and wanting to evangelize to others the next day. The passion and drive to deliver others is great, but what people are looking at is your lifestyle. Are you a living example of what you are preaching? Do you have a heathy identity and the tools to sustain so that you can really draw people into deliverance and healing? Or are you just drawing people into yourself, where they are gossiping about your life and passing word lots on whether you are truly delivered or not?

Let's consider another example. You live in California where marijuana is legal. You were a bud head in the world, and had an encounter at the altar one Sunday where you were delivered from addiction. A week later you start to struggle and succumb to smoking again. But now you are the substance abuse mentor at your church. And since it is legal you still smoke and justify your hidden addiction. However, the addiction starts to overtake your life and ministry, and you decide to go through a restoration process. Marijuana is your leaning post, your God, your coping mechanism, your recreational friend, your stress reliever, among other things. You may need more time to journey to a process of wholeness and practice deliverance from addiction as a lifestyle.

I do not want to give too many examples as I do not want the focus of time of recover to override the quality of processing to wellness with God. As I stated before, God will give you a time frame. And you will know if you are really healed or not. Be honest with yourself so a do over will not be necessary. How you use your time of restoration, and how you commit to your process, will factor into when God releases you back into your ministry duties. He sets the time and you determine if it is a wilderness or promise land experience.

Example of a Restoration Plan:

Deliverance from Fornication
- Step down from ministry for a specific time as the Lord leads.
- Commit to six sessions of counseling to explore underlying issues regarding fornication. At the fifth session determine if more counseling is needed. If not, commit to maintenance sessions every two months for accountability purposes.
- Complete a 21 day veggie, fruit, and water fast and consecration for personal cleansing and purification. Seek God and consult with your counselor on how to spend your time during your consecration (e.g. no tv, social media, all idle time spent consecrating with the Lord, attend church prayer services and bible study, and Sunday service).
- After three counseling sessions, attend a deliverance session to deal with root issues, generational cycles and patterns, curses and demonic strongholds.
- Pray Monday through Saturday from 6am to 7am. Spend time repenting, cleansing, completing counseling and deliverance assignments, and praying as the Holy Spirit leads

- Complete daily scriptural study in topics that will build you up in sustaining your deliverance (e.g. purification, holiness, integrity of a leader, etc.).
- Seek God for a vision plan to maintain your the standards needed to walk in deliverance and healing as a lifestyle. Begin practicing this plan in your everyday life.

Deliverance from Ministry Warfare and Hardships
- Step down from ministry for a specific time as the Lord leads.
- Commit to six sessions of counseling to explore wounds from warfare and other areas were deliverance and healing is essential. At the fifth session determine if more counseling is needed. If not, commit to maintenance sessions every two months for accountability purposes.
- Take a three day water only fast and consecration just to be before the Lord (use this time to release the ministry, the people, and your destiny to the Lord and to allow him to refresh and revive you).
- Pray Monday through Saturday from 5am to 7am. Spend time cleansing out warfare from previous seasons, hurts, hope deferred, oppressions, anger, frustration, stress, failures, trauma, from the warfare; cleanse out any demonic weapons that may be lodged in your soul, heart, mind, and body due to warfare, break curses you may have picked up from warfare, repent for any offense and sins you committed or forgive others of offenses and sins towards you, release anger and unforgiveness issues you may have towards God due to warfare, spend time renewing your love for God, ministry, people, and living in his will, complete counseling and deliverance assignments, and pray as the Holy Spirit leads.
- Build yourself up in tools, skills, and fruit needed to renew your authority, faith, and confidence in God.
- Build yourself up in your gifts and calling, attending trainings and workshops if possible or acquire some teachings in this area.
- Spend time away from the ministry. Do not attend any events or church services with your ministry.
- Delegate your responsibilities to capable leaders and trust them to handle ministry endeavors.
- Seek God about attending other events and church services where you can relax, refresh, and receive from him. Make sure you do not go to a ministry event that will try to get you to minister. Only go where you can receive.
- After the third counseling session, attend a deliverance session to deal with root issues and strongholds related to warfare.
- Attend a healing soaking room once a week if possible or create a healing soaking room in your home and soak in it once a week for two hours.
- Spend time doing leisure activities with family and friends to replenish, and help restore joy and love for life and ministry.

- Seek God for a ministry plan for when you return to ministry, and the standards you need for maintaining and sustaining in achieving your ministry goals and successfully walking in destiny with the Lord.

PRAYER FOR BREAKING RELIGIOUS FEARS & CONTROL

Chapter 28

In your matchless name Jesus, I fall out of agreement with the lie that sold out means neglecting myself, my family, my health, and personal responsibilities, for the sake of ministry. I break the stronghold of fear and control entered in through religion, where I can only feel I am pleasing you if I am killing myself with ministry duties and obligations.

I am not you Lord. I am not the savior. I am a vessel used for your glory. I break the power of idolatry and being an idol God to religion, ministry, and people. I repent for stepping into a dimension only you can fill by allowing religion, ministry, people, misinterpretation of scripture, works, and my own drive for success and validation provoke me to play roles you did not ordain.

I become clear that balance is essential for a healthy kingdom lifestyle. I become transparent that though I am a supernatural being operating in your strength, might and power, leisure and respite is essential to my healthy kingdom walk. I need rest! I need deliverance! I need healing! I need refreshing! I need empowerment! I need you leading me! I need you guiding me! I need you directing me! I need you living inside of me - working through me. I do not ever want to loose your presence, your conviction, a heart of repentance - intimacy of a covenant relationship with you!

I therefore humble myself under your mighty hand Jesus, and declare that I will forever live and abide inside of you! Abide in the literal essence of you! I will be an example of living inside Jesus Christ! Where everything I do and say is filtered through your character, your nature - my identity in you!

I decree that through abiding in you, my identity is healthy! I know who I am! I know whose I am! I know the calling and destiny for my life! I receive continual supernatural downloads that define my existence. Society does not define me! Fads do not define me! Movements do not define me! Ministry does not define me! Religion does not define me! People do not define me! Relationships do not define me! Money does not define me! Positions do not define me! Platforms do not define me! And the stupid devil shooooooole do not define me! Some of these matters are a sub factor of who I am, but are not the identity of me! You define me Jesus! And you do not make mistakes. You are clear on who I am and your biblical word helps confirm your truth concerning me.

I will never alter my identity to meet fleshly desires, to people please or gain favor with people, to acquire platforms and positions, to advance in ministry or my personal life, or for monetary reward. I will not prostitute my gifts, sell my birthright and calling, or alter or kill my destiny. I declare that I will live inside of you, where religion and the devil will find none of them in me.

I say Lord chasten me, correct me, rebuke me, instruct me, align me, qualify me, approve me. Release constructive criticism and revelation that constantly transforms me from level to level and glory to glory. For I shall be an example of a healthy leader who reproduces healthy leaders. I rebuke cloning! I rebuke making people work my vision with positioning for destiny! I rebuke groupies! I rebuke the Jr. Holy Spirit! I rebuke the false Holy Spirit! I rebuke delusional moves of God that do not produce kingdom fruit! I REBUKE IT!

I want the real deal Jesus! I want unadulterated -limitless - boundary-less - raw - supernatural - power of the Holy Ghost. If you are not in it, then I do not want it! If you did not design it, then I want no parts of it! If it is mixed then I'll pass on that Jesus! Let me be bold in standing for truth, purity, and righteousness! And by all means, transform me in an example of the stance to which I am contending!

Thank you Lord for making this prayer my lifestyle. I appreciate you Jesus, and the joy and fulfillment I have of journeying in destiny with you! SHIFT!

DELIVERANCE FROM THE FALSE GOSPEL

Chapter 29

There are many wounded people who are angry and rebelling against the church for being promised a Christ that they have yet to experience.

Many of these people have been prophesied too, but were never given the tools and instruction to activate the prophecy, and bring it to pass.

Many have watched the church receive countless prophecies that have never come to pass. There has been constant warfare and struggle, while prosperity, increase, and fruitfulness has been prophesied. Many churches continue to cycle with no clear vision to rectify this and align the church with the prophecies, or admit the prophecies are a lie or error.

Many have been a part of churches where the church has grown, but personal growth has been minimal. People are encouraged through self-help messages. They are given just enough God to get through the week, but not enough to transform their lives.

Many have been a part of churches where the leaders have become richer, and those in the pews remain poorer and stagnant.

Many were raised in church under strict religious rules and laws, but these rules and laws did not prevent them from yielding to sin or experiencing hardship.

Many have been raised in the church under strict rules and laws, but have seen leaders succumb to sin with little to no consequences.

Many have gone to their leaders for help, only for the leaders to take advantage of their struggle for their own personal gain and pleasure.

Many have spent years working positions and visions within the church, while being prophesied release. Yet, their gifts and callings lay dormant within them with no opportunity or avenue for training or alignment with destiny.

Many have been spent years trying to prove they are worthy to walk in the call on their lives. They are seen as rebellious and renegades if they attempt to express their desire to be taught and aligned with destiny. The measures given to prove readiness are often rooted in attending unfruitful services, and completing duties that the leaders do not want to perform themselves. Though it is important to learn to follow before one can lead, and being a servant is a part of ministry and a Christ like nature, many of these people have been abused and/or taken advantaged of in these positions and left in these positions too long. Sometimes these positions are used to keep a person under the leader's rule of thumb, where they cannot go forward in ministry. Their calling is stifled by doing works and not being aligned with destiny.

Many have attended churches and they have relationship with the church and relationship with God through church works and experiences, but not a personal relationship with God. People end up confused about God, and realize they do not know him, or see him working in their life.

Many have been in church for years and have never come into true identity or fulfillment. They become angry and leave because the Santa Clause God they have been sold on makes everybody happy but them. They spend years wandering in the world striving to find identity and fulfillment that only comes with relationship with God.

Many have spent years under motivational preaching that has provided religious formulas void of the true gospel and the anointing of Jesus Christ. The principles may work to bring prosperity and success, but not personal healing. The people are angry because no matter how much STUFF they have, they are still unfulfilled, unhappy, and void of true relationship with the Lord.

Many have spent years under hype theatrical preaching that tickles the emotions, and stirs up soulish praise, but does not transform the souls and lives of the people. After realizing they have not changed, they leave feeling betrayed for yielding to a gospel with form and no power.

Many are stuck in the bondage of some churches because the leader has drawn them and fed them just enough to keep them wrapped up in receiving from them. There is a inner entangling, and soul tie that has been formed. They have been groomed to the liking and character of that leader, church, and style. Whether intentionally or unintentionally, the people have been groomed, essentially bewitched by that leader. They therefore, stay imprisoned to the bondage of their false gospel. The leader preaches and shares just enough word to keep the people to where no one will notice and become suspicious of them, their lifestyle, and their tactics. They preach with enough charisma, force, and strength that entices the flesh, and forms emotional and soulish ties with the inner man of those who are receiving of that leader. The people become settled in this and desensitized to the truth. They begin to accept the false as truth, and since the leader is speaking some of what is true enmeshing it in with the falsehoods, the people become not only bound, but also advocates of the false gospel. Becoming professors, supporters, and defenders of the abuse themselves. This is like the abused becoming abusers.

Many are stuck because the leaders that they are under do not teach them how to identify Godly fruit, character, maturity, and truth. The leaders are unable to do this because these things are not in them, and so they cannot teach and impart something that they do not have. Since the people under them are not equipped and taught how to identify fruit, they are trapped in the example of the fruit that is presented before them, and this becomes their truth. This is sad because they are setup for failure, and to be drawn into the false, because they have never experienced the truth.

There may be those who are taught about identifying fruit and trying the spirits of others, while being simultaneously taught that it is out of order to discern the spirit, and check the fruit of their leaders. This is being used as a means of manipulation and control to keep the people bound to them. As the people are taught to try the spirit of others, but not their leaders, it plants a seed that prompts them to try the spirits of those who are preaching things that challenge and go against their leader. As a result, the leader and not the spirit of God becomes the example, and the measuring rod for truth.

The leaders of the false gospel whether they know it or not are like the ravening wolves clothed in sheep's clothing as they have no fruit of the gospel. Their ministry is clothed and covered from the outside with what should be safe and harmless, but behind that, the wolf is lashing out on the people showing its true self from time to time. We have to be willing to look beyond the outside, and go deeper to checking the fruit that is developed from what is preached and shared. As this will be the true evidence.

Scripture References for the False Gospel
Matthew 7:-15-20 *Beware of false prophets who come disguised as harmless sheep but are really vicious wolves. You can identify them by their fruit, that is, by the way they act. Can you pick grapes from thornbushes, or figs from thistles? A good tree produces good fruit, and a bad tree produces bad fruit. A good tree can't produce bad fruit, and a bad tree can't produce good fruit. So every tree that does not produce good fruit is chopped down and thrown into the fire. Yes, just as you can identify a tree by its fruit, so you can identify people by their actions.*

1John 4:1 *Beloved, believe not every spirit, but try the spirits whether they are of God: because many false prophets are gone out into the world.*

Romans 16:17-18 *Now I beseech you, brethren, mark them which cause divisions and offences contrary to the doctrine which ye have learned; and avoid them. For they that are such serve not our Lord Jesus Christ, but their own belly; and by good words and fair speeches deceive the hearts of the simple.*

Hebrews 13:9 The Amplified Bible *Do not be carried about by different and varied and alien teachings; for it is good for the heart to be established and ennobled and strengthened by means of grace (God's favor and spiritual blessing) and not [to be devoted to] foods [rules of diet and ritualistic meals], which bring no [spiritual] benefit or profit to those who observe them.*

2Peter 3:17 The Amplified Bible *Let me warn you therefore, beloved, that knowing these things beforehand, you should be on your guard, lest you be carried away by the error of lawless and wicked [persons and] fall from your own [present] firm condition [your own steadfastness of mind]. But grow in grace (undeserved favor, spiritual strength) and recognition and knowledge and understanding of our Lord and Savior Jesus Christ (the Messiah). To Him [be] glory (honor, majesty, and splendor) both now and to the day of eternity. Amen (so be it)!*

1Timothy 1:3-6 As I urged you when I was on my way to Macedonia, stay on where you are at Ephesus in order that you may warn and admonish and charge certain individuals not to teach any different doctrine, Nor to give importance to or occupy themselves with legends (fables, myths) and endless genealogies, which foster and promote useless speculations and questionings rather than acceptance in faith of God's administration and the divine training that is in faith (in that leaning of the entire human personality on God in absolute trust and confidence) — Whereas the object and purpose of our instruction and charge is love, which springs from a pure heart and a good (clear) conscience and sincere (unfeigned) faith.
But certain individuals have missed the mark on this very matter [and] have wandered away into vain arguments and discussions and purposeless talk.

Characteristics of Wounded People:
It is important for healthy leaders to recognize wounded people in their ministry, and be open to bringing healing to them. These people maybe:

- Untrusting
- Angry
- Resentful
- Bitter and operate through a negative, pessimistic/condescending well
- Unforgiving
- Bound by shock and trauma
- Prideful and resistant to correction
- Fear being hurt again by leaders and people in general
- Guarded in their heart to protect themselves from potential re-victimization
- Resistant to deliverance and healing of their wounds
- In denial about their pain and how their experience impacted them; they may not even know they are wounded, or fear receiving ministry from leaders and churches
- Mad at the church
- Mad at God
- Lash out at their present leader for things their past leader did to them
- Rebellious towards God, leadership, the church, his or her calling and responsibilities
- Anti-church and sometimes anti-Christ
- Unable to discern a healthy leader from an unhealthy leader due to filtering everything through their wounds
- Rejecting of their purpose and calling
- Difficult to empower, disciple, and mature due to unresolved hurt
- Continuously testing of their new leader and requiring proof that the new leader will not hurt them
- Easily let down and have minimal to no room for allowing a leader to error
- Slanderous towards leaders, the church, and God
- Bitter crusaders for exposing the flaws of leaders and the church

- Confused and challenged with separating their experience from the truth about God, his word, and his true church
- Bound in an all inclusive mentality concerning leaders and the church, even though there are some great leaders in the body of Christ
- Attempting to use the word to justify their hurts and remain stuck in their pain
- Contending that they will never be like the leader that wounded them, but without deliverance they become that leader, and sometimes worse than that leader
- Religious in their ideology due to being wounded and expecting others to follow biblical laws and principles perfectly to prove their salvation, and that they are not false
- Untrustworthy and open doors to be used by the enemy to betray leaders, the church, and God due to being unhealed from their experience
- Bent on seeking out and connecting to other wounded people for the purposes of strengthening their theory and slander towards leaders, the church, and God
- Breeders for imparting bitterness towards leaders, the church, and God in others

These Wounded People will Need:
- Relationship with a healthy leader that can show and speak truth to them, as they will not heal from just being in the pews or among a ministry.
- Grace, as they will test the healthy leaders' patience, character, compassion, and ability to love unconditionally.
- Counseling so they can explore their hurtful experience, and separate the truth of their pain from the generalizations that have been made, due to being hurt in the church.
- Counseling to be delivered and healed of their experience.
- Deliverance from the wounded spirit and the spirit of religion; they will be religious in the unhealthy doctrine they formed within themselves, due to being wounded.
- Delivered and healed from shock and trauma, bitterness, anger, unforgiveness, hatred of church and leaders, fear, etc., and other spirits that entered their lives through their experience.
- Deliverance from shame, guilt, and condemnation, and feeling responsible for letting themselves be victimized, or for staying so long in a unhealthy relationship and/or ministry.
- A processing to wholeness where they practice living from the new healed place, such that the negative characteristics from wounding are weeded out of their character, personality, thought processing, and behaviors.
- Continual intercession, esteeming, and encouragement as they process to wholeness.
- Given minimal ministry duties until they are totally cleansed of the wounded breeder anointing.

Wisdom Nuggets:
- Each person will be different, so their pains and process to wholeness will be based on their identity and experience.
- Let God lead you in whether you as the main leader are to walk with them in their healing process, or another healthy leader in your ministry.
- Even if you are not walking with them, check in with them from time to time so they know you care, and that they are under a safe, respectable covering and ministry.
- Remain alert and discerning in your interactions so you will know who is really striving to be healed, and who is an open door for drama and/or the spirit of betrayal due to being unhealed.
- Maintain healthy boundaries, for even as the wounded person can be resistant to relationship, they may be clingy, covetousness, sensual, and inordinate in their interactions. The healthy leader needs to be responsible for maintaining appropriate boundaries, and role modeling boundaries and Godly character to the wounded person.
- Some wounded people have transgressed to reprobate, or may not be ready to be healed. Be discerning so you will not become drained by those who are more interested in proving all leaders are bad than healing and embracing a healthy leader.

LEAVING & CLEAVING MINISTRIES

Chapter 30

I want to speak on leaders and church members SHIFTING to blessing people when they leave their church. Though some leave messy, everyone that leaves is not caught up in drama or is against the leader and ministry. Yet, because of those who do leave messy, the wounded leader, and even members view every person leaving as:

- Betrayers who are against the leader and ministry.
- Abandoning the ministry and/God.
- Competition and church splitters, as they feel other members will follow that person.
- Out of God's will, because they may not want the person to leave, understand the reason for the SHIFT, or agree with the person leaving.
- Cursed because they do not want the person to leave, or feel it is not the person's time to leave.

I do want to note that most often people will know when God is leading them to leave a ministry. Often the person will feel obligated to stay due to familiarity, and usually drama ensues, which pushes the person out the door. This can become messy because things are then said and done by the person leaving, and the leaders and members. Such actions are done through the well of emotions and flesh, that incite confusion and conflict. People need to understand that if you stay longer than God is requiring, you are out of God's will, and when you are out of God's will, you are uncovered. Being uncovered opens the door for the enemy to come in and wreak havoc. Even if the leader and people are not messy, there can be unnecessary warfare in your personal and ministry life, because you are toiling a ground that God has released you from.

Reasons God will have a person leave a ministry:
- The person has received all they can under that ministry.
- The person needs to connect or be under the covering of another ministry to further align with God, and the calling and destiny on his or her life.
- The person needs to receive greater training and equipping.
- The person has a specific assignment somewhere else; some people are sent into ministries to raise up or cover a specific remnant within that ministry, or to impart or govern a specific area of that ministry, community, region, nation.
- It is time for the person to independently focus on their own life and ministry vision.
- The leader and/or church is operating in somethings contrary to God, and he is requiring the person to separate themselves from the reproach, consequences, and judgment that may come upon that ministry.
- The person was only to be there for a season, a particular work, or for specific training. Some ministries are not your lifetime. God is a SHIFTING God. He

never plateaus. He is always focused on upward mobility and success. He is always seeking to do the exceeding, abundant, and beyond. What we deem as success could be just the beginning for God. He may be elevating you or allowing you to experience different facets of his glory and kingdom. Remain a life learner so you can SHIFT with God.

It is important to understand that:
- We are not one church, but a body of believers.
- We are one kingdom under God.
- We are not in competition with one another.
- We are all ONE church with different assignments and functions.
- If someone leaves and goes to another church or starts a ministry, they are still your brother and sister in Christ. They are an extension of God's work through you, and of the body of Christ as a whole.

Romans 12:4 For just as each of us has one body with many members, and these members do not all have the same function.

1Corinthians 12:12 For as the body is one, and hath many members, and all the members of that one body, being many, are one body: so also is Christ.

If someone decides to leave your church and go to a false church, church full of hype, mixture or witchcraft, or leave to start a ministry out of God's timing, you still have to respect their decision. Slandering and betraying them is not going to change their mind. It is only going to strengthen the sin and rebellion that is already in them. Now they feel justified all the more in their actions of leaving, and it will take longer for them to realize their error, repent, and realign with God.

Reasons people do not leave when God says:
- False loyalty
- False obligation
- Fear of being betrayed or being viewed as a renegade
- Fear of not being supported
- Fear of being abandoned and ostracized
- Fear of leaving the familiar
- Fear of going alone
- Fear of failing
- Fear that there is no one to step in and do their work, or the lack of raising up a successor
- Feeling like they are letting down the leaders or ministry
- Bound by ungodly or unhealthy soulties with the leader, people, and the ministry
- Bound in religion and tradition
- Rebellious; self-focused rather than God focused

Many people will ask God for elevation, and when he releases it, they do not want it because they did not know it would require leaving a ministry. People will prolong the SHIFT by contending they are waiting on confirmation from God. Yet, God has gone silent because he is not into constantly repeating himself. People then become intertwined with all kinds of drama and church warfare, because they are waiting for God to speak on a matter that is speaking for itself in every facet of their soul and lives. Some even become complacent with the church drama, and they take that on as an assignment they need to fix before they can leave.

Many people do not leave immediately when God requires because they are plagued with thoughts and emotions that their current leader and ministry should be willing to equip, develop, mature, and release them into what God is saying for them. After years of services to a ministry, we tend to have expectations of the leader and the ministry that really only God can fulfill. We expect that leader and/or ministry to:

- Know who we are in the spirit, know our gifting and calling
- Further train us beyond what the ministry is capable of giving us
- Further train and equip us personally for destiny, and birth us into deeper levels of destiny
- Position us for destiny and to be used of God
- Provide platforms for us to be used
- Ordain us and release us in our calling and destiny

Though only God can fulfill this role and these expectations in our lives, it is not unrealistic to believe God would use our leader and present ministry. However, many leaders:
- Do not have, do not grasp, or do not want ministry vision to this magnitude.
- Are too overwhelmed with their own vision to equip, position, ordain, and release people.
- Are not walking in the fullness of their own destiny and life vision, so how can they give you something they do not have.
- Fear losing people if they ordain and release them.
- Tend to keep people working in positions generally based on need, what they do well, or talent, rather than having a vision for aligning people to serve in the ministry where their calling and destiny can flourish.
- Keep people serving in their ministry so they can have help, even at the expense of their destiny.
- Are insecure and bound by emotional competition and jealousy; they may appear to be for you in their actions, but in their thoughts and emotions, they are inadequate. They are not emotionally capable of sharing their platform with you, ordaining you, or releasing you.
- Actually believe they are doing what God is requiring them to do. We tend to judge leaders and ministries by their potential, but all ministries have the

potential to be more. But many may not be designed by God to do more. Many may not have the vision or courage to do more.
- Actually believe you working in their ministry is equipping and aligning you in your destiny.
- Will contend those under them do not need a title and ordination though they have one. Maybe after they received theirs they realized it was not that important. I am laughing right now, because it is important, but some leaders do feel this way, and even preach this as if it is a fair truth. .
- May not be the ones God has chosen to further develop, mature, ordain, release, and cover you in ministry.

We assume that these leaders are the chosen vessels for governing our lives, but that is more of a displaced expectation than a realistic one. Truthfully, this place belongs to God only. We have to become realistic about those that are overseeing us when it comes to our gifting and calling. A lot of times, we remain under a leader because:

- We idolize them, and we want them to be the ones to validate who God is and what he is saying in us. We want them to be the ones to ordain, release and cover us. But if this is not God's will, then it will not happen no matter how much hocus pocus optimism and wishful thinking you operate in. And if it does happen without God's blessings, it will offset your destiny. Though you may have what you want, you will not have what God has designed to fulfill your life, while bringing glory to his life.
- We are bewitched and soultied in confusion and delusion, as sometimes a leader will provide a measure of training and promises of ordination and release, but never follow through with it. We are angry, baffled, hurt, and disappointed, because we desire this and have experienced a measure, so we remain hoping they will fully follow through with their promises. But again, sometimes leaders get sidetracked, are inconsistent, are taking on more than God said, or simply cannot release you into something God is not allowing.
- We do not recognize that for what God is striving to do, and is going to do, our present leader has taken us as far as they can. The leader is not equipped to cover our "next," or is not God's choice in covering and equipping us in our "next." Indignation and deception has us so self-focused in what we want, we cannot see and receive truth.
- That leader may have the gifts and anointing, but not the character sufficient enough to cultivate you in ordination or destiny. God has designed a leader that can cover you in your calling, and impart his character and nature in you, so you can sustain in destiny.

We tend to chose leaders because of commonality, personality and idolization, but God chooses leaders because of destiny. He knows what each one of us need to be adequately equipped in destiny. The longer you remain, while agonizing over what the leader and ministry will not give you, the longer you are prolonging your growth and destiny.

If you have been in a ministry for five, ten, twenty years, and your main focus for being under a leader or a part of a ministry, is still on what you can get from the leader and the ministry, then whether it is your own doing or a lack of full discipleship, you have not been adequately equipped in the gospel of Jesus Christ. By now you should have been efficiently discipled, where your focus should have SHIFTED on how God can further develop you to build up his church.

> *Ephesians 4:1-12 And His gifts were [varied; He Himself appointed and gave men to us] some to be apostles (special messengers), some prophets (inspired preachers and expounders), some evangelists (preachers of the Gospel, traveling missionaries), some pastors (shepherds of His flock) and teachers. His intention was the perfecting and the full equipping of the saints (His consecrated people), [that they should do] the work of ministering toward building up Christ's body (the church).*

Often we want to remain in a church because we like what we are getting from the leader and the ministry.
- We are selfish. We are focused on what we can get, rather than what we can give.
- We are cycling in being fed the same ole stuff to tickle our flesh, while draining our leader. We do not use what was imparted to win souls and advance the kingdom of God.
- We are lazy. We want to receive of the work of the Lord, and do our Sunday and Wednesday works, but do not position ourselves to effectively advance God's kingdom.
- We want a title and platform in the comfort of our church, but do not want to take the gospel to the world.
- We want what our leader has, but have not considered or have rejected what God has for us.

Many people do not leave as God unctions, because they have difficulty dealing with the grief and loss of leaving. Sometimes just the thought of leaving causes an influx of emotions.

Anytime you leave or lose something, whether good or bad, there are emotions to process through. Loss creates a void in our soul and lives. We have to now learn to live without that person, place, or thing.

> *2Corinthians 5:17 Therefore if any man be in Christ, he is a new creature: old things are passed away; behold, all things are become new.*

The "new" can be exciting, but it also can be scary. It is an unfamiliar place where we have to trust and learn God, and ourselves at a new dimension. What we learned in previous seasons has prepared us for the new, but may not necessarily be our survival mechanism, spiritual tools, and supports, for sustaining in the new place. Our focus should be on this truth of *Ephesians 3:20*, *"Now unto him that is able to do exceeding abundantly above all that we ask or think, according to the power that worketh in us."* God has greater for you in the new place. SHALL YOU NOT KNOW IT?

Isaiah 43:19 Behold, I will do a new thing; now it shall spring forth; shall ye not know it?

When God is requiring a person to leave a ministry, we must view this as elevation for the entire body of Christ. We must bless and support people, so they can be obedient to the will of God, and transition in the healthiest manner possible.

If people do not support your transition, you must SHIFT with God regardless of ill treatment. Some people either are not meant to go with you to your "next" or abort their position in your "next." You must take on the mindset that you are going to be exactly where God wants you to be and do whatever he is requiring, no matter who likes it or not; no matter who joins you on your journey or not.

Today I encourage you to:

- Let the familiarity with your leader, the people, your positions, and the ministry go!
- Let the false expectations you have for your leader and the ministry go!
- Let the anger, hurt, disappointment, and resentment of not being ordained and released go!
- Let the fear of the unknown go!
- Let the excuses, laziness, disobedience and rebellion go!
- Let the lie that you waiting on God and to hear from God go!
- Let the unhealthiness and drama go!

Stop toiling a ground that is bringing death to your destiny. God is waiting to further align you with the "new!" SHIFT!

Wisdom Keys for Shifting with God!

Leave Honorably
Schedule a meeting with your leader/s and share with them what God has spoken to you. Be respectful and honoring no matter how they respond. Let them know that you are simply being obedient to God, but do not defend what God has led you to do. Speak honestly, and do not add more to what God has said. If you do not know all of what God has prepared, be honest in sharing that, and let them know you are open to sharing as God further reveals information to you. Give a date of departure, and tie up any ministry duties, etc., say your goodbyes to those you have done ministry with, bless them in their continued endeavors, and move forward with God.

It is always good to equip successors while you are in a leadership position. However, if you did not do this, seek God on what day you are to leave, then share this with your overseer, and encourage them to find a replacement for you. If you know of those within the ministry that are equipped to replace you, then recommend them to your leader. If the leader is in agreement in them replacing you, ask them if they are open to taking your place. If they accept the position, pray a blessing impartation over them, release all duties to them, and encourage them and those under them in being able to carry the vision further. Share any revelation and duties that will enable their transition to be smooth and successful. If there is no one to take your place, then move forward, while trusting God to provide for the ministry.

Avoid Gossip
If people become messy and gossipy regarding your transition, do not get into this type of conversation with them. Do not have conversations about flaws and issues regarding the leader and the ministry. Simply focus on the fact that it is your time to go and SHIFT. Shut down all conversations that will try to draw you into dishonor as even if it is true, when you yield to gossip and slander, it is dishonor to God, and to the fact that he SHIFTED and separated you to steer you away from mess. Tell the gossipers you have nothing to say, and if you have to cut ties with them then do that. When I left my previous church, I shut the gossipers down by blessing the leadership and the ministry, and simply contending that it was just time for me to transition and therefore, I was being obedient to God. There was no room to entangle me in their gossip, so they hushed with trying to engage me in conversation.

If you are being slandered by gossip and betrayal due to the leader and/or the ministry due to leaving, do not seek to defend yourself, and do not try to have others within that ministry to comfort and support you in your time of transition. Those that would try to comfort and support you from that ministry are going to be torn between you and that ministry. Any assistance they give you will be mixed with confusion and turmoil, and will still connect you to something God has brought you out of. You can be cordial and friends, but receive your support and healing from people who are not attached to the situation, and that can focus you on healing and SHIFTING with God. When I left my previous ministry, my God sister and brother still attended that ministry. They are like blood family to me, and my God sister is one of my main life supports. But for this situation, I did not go to her to help me with this transition. I did not want to put her in a position to choose, be torn, or draw her from what God was still requiring her to do in the ministry. I also did not want her to feel like she had to fix or defend how others were responding to my transition. That was not her responsibility as I simply was doing what God was leading me to do. So though she and I remained close, and she was in my everyday life, I went to my overseer, my mentor, and two close friends who lived in other states, to help me process through my thoughts, feelings, and experiences with the SHIFT that had taken place in my life.

Avoid The Victim Mentality
Do not go to broken saints and saints who are still wounded by church hurt for support and counsel when you are transitioning out of a church. I mention this because even if you do not seek them out, they will find you. I do not know if the devil sends them or if it is because you are in a vulnerable place, and possibly even wounded that they smell the blood of your wounds and flock to you. But whatever the case, when they come, do not rely on them for support. Give up your need to have people understand you for the sake of just healing in a healthy manner, and SHIFTING with God. You do not need a support group of wounded folks who only want to drown in their pain, and validate that leaders and the church are a farce. Such people are out for revenge, and to tear down leaders and the church, thus becoming an enemy of God and his will to advance his kingdom in the earth. Your focus should be to build up the kingdom, so do not attach to this crowd.

Do not get stuck in rehearsing your pain that it drowns out your ability to be healed and to hear God for the next revelation and moves he has for your life. When you constantly rehearse your pain, you are stuck in a victim mentality. You have become your own offender, because you are now the one continuing to reopen and inflict pain upon wounds that God has healed or wants to heal.

You do not need to talk to 700,894,842 folks about what has happened to you. Especially when all they are doing is agreeing with you, and validating that it should not have occurred. True encouragers sympathize with you, while seeking to bring healing so your pain will end. They do not feed into your pain where it continues or deepens. If you continuously need attention and validation for your wounds, then you are bound by a victim mentality and have become your own offender. Get a few accountable, mature, healthy people that can be sympathetic to you, yet SHIFT you to being delivered, healed, and advancing forward with God.

Draw Nigh Unto God
Though it is important to have a few mature supports who can encourage you, support you, provide deliverance, healing, and wise counsel, everyone is not going to understand your transition. Even people that support you and provide guidance, will not fully understand your SHIFT. Transitions are supernatural. They are a time of really treading in the truth, power, faith, and encouragement of God. He is the only one who can FULLY comfort, support, instruct, guide, and help you comprehend what is happening to you and for you. Transition is a time of drawing near to him. Often those who are supports will confirm what he personally does in, through, and for you. Study the story of Jesus as he transitioned from leading the disciples to dying on the cross. It will provide significant keys and revelation of how to draw near to God and transition with him.

Break Soulties
Break soulties with anything that will try to keep you stuck or focused on your past ministry season, where it is a hinderance to you being focused on the "new." Lots wife

looked back because her soul was still tied to Sodom and Gomorrah (Genesis 19:26).

You may have to break soulties with:
- Your leader/s.
- The people in the ministry. You may have to break soulties with friends and acquaintances. Sometimes it is difficult to leave when we are tied to people we love. The soultie is unhealthy if it is hindering or causing a struggle where we cannot SHIFT with God. The soultie may need to be broken and then re-established in the new place you are in.
- The ministry itself.
- Prophecies or promises you think you have aborted due to leaving. Declare they will come to pass in your future seasons.
- Drama and messiness that you were a part of or that was present within the ministry.
- False promises and promotions that never came to pass or that was only given in measure. Declare they will come to pass in your future seasons.
- The potential you saw in the ministry and hoped would manifest.
- Disappointments, pains, and hurts that you endured from the leader, the ministry, and during your transition.
- The community and region if you were shifted to a new community and region to minister in.
- Ministry positions and platforms you held that may be pulling on your heart and soul.

Deliverance and Healing:
See the chapter on betrayal if that is your experience when transitioning out of a ministry. It will provide further detail for being delivered and healed in this area.
If you are going to be a progressive person you have to be focused forward. That means anything that is going to keep you stuck or bound in the past has to be removed. As much as you will be justified and want to hold on to your emotions, do not do it. Give them up to be delivered and healed. SHIFTING comes with its own set of emotions that you have to conquer. Do not confound your transition by holding onto unhealthy or challenging emotions that will keep you bound and stifled. Remember when a SHIFT has occurred, the foundation has been cracked. When your emotions are driving you, you are subject to fall into one, rather than having the focus to jump over hurdles and obstacles. Transitions display your maturity and faith in God. You will learn where your character is strong, and where you need improvement and further development.

> **2Timothy 2:3-4** *Take [with me] your share of the hardships and suffering [which you are called to endure] as a good (first-class) soldier of Christ Jesus. No soldier when in service gets entangled in the enterprises of [civilian] life; his aim is to satisfy and please the one who enlisted him.*

Endure the trials of SHIFTING with integrity and character, while taking your pains and hurts to God so he can deliver and heal you. Seek your close support system for further deliverance and healing of areas that may be difficult to heal or be free from. Some areas will require a continual battering and release unto God before breakthrough occurs. This is a transition, so it is a process that is occurring. Therefore you will have to be processed to wholeness even as you are being processed to your "next." God is also doing some new things in your mind, heart, and soul to build you in your "new." Some things will happen quickly and some will happen over time. Let God lead you in the process of transitioning into the "new" with him. As you surrender your process to God, receive deliverance, and healing in the following areas:

- Forgive anyone who hurts you, does not understand you, or betrays you.
- Cleanse and heal from all bitterness, anger, rage, resentment, retaliation, murder, slander, and gossip.
- Release all expectations and hurt from not being supported, being overlooked, not being understood, and being betrayed.
- Break powers of shame, guilt, condemnation, accuser of the brethren, gossip, slander, and word curses against your "next".
- Cast out and break powers of fear, inadequacy, insecurity, and feeling unworthy of what God has for you. Consistently declare out who you are, and what God is requiring of you. Command the earth, region, and new place to receive you as God's chosen vessel (*See Romans 8:22*). Refuse to be denied, and know that you deserve to be where God is taking you.
- Have your personal confidants praying and covering you as you SHIFT. Be specific in what they should pray for, so they can be in agreement with what God is saying.
- Deal with the grief and loss of your transition. Do not stuff your grief, ignore it, or wallow in it. Typically the stages of grief are denial, anger, bargaining, depression, and acceptance. It is very easy to get stuck in one of these stages during transition. The main reason is because we expect everything about the new to be glorious and easy. We assume that there will not be challenges, hardship, new things to learn and conquer, etc. We quote *"new level - new devils,"* but we expect blessings and overflow. We become challenged and fixated on all that we loss and have given up. Such a focus plagues us with grief. Your feelings are real and understandable, and God cares about how you feel. Tell the Lord exactly how it hurts and sucks, but be willing to let the feelings go. Receive his deliverance and healing when he strives to exchange your grief for comfort, peace, joy, love, and healing.
- Immediately complete and implement whatever God tells you. Some of it will sound far fetched. Remember that God uses the foolish to confound the wise. His methods are not of this world. They are conventional. Some matters you will not understand until you implement them, or until future seasons of your life. I am still learning and understanding things that God had me do in a major SHIFT that occurred years ago. I had to give up my need to understand so I could flow with God. It was totally worth it. You will not regret trusting God.

- Embrace your new relationships and connections. They will be different and some will not be what you are used to and expected. But God is not trying to establish the old, he is about the "new." You have to trust who he has put in your life, and not make them be responsible for what others have done and have not done in your life. Just because they are new, it does not guarantee that you will not be hurt again. Neither does you putting up walls and being resist to embracing these relationships. God does not control our freewill to be messy. But as you go through this transition, it is important to accept people for exactly who they are, flaws and all. Learn to engage people from the truth of who they are, as then you will be able to accept and heal from challenges you will encounter in your relationships. This helps in discerning drama and challenges before they occur, and dealing with them quickly so you can keep it moving with God.

Addressing the Congregation During Transitions
A lot of times we move forward and act like it is ministry business, however, as leaders, we need to address the challenges that occur when people transition out of the ministry. We must be open and available to discussing, and bringing healing to the people and the ministry organizations, as regardless to whether people leave in a healthy or unhealthy manner, it is still loss. Addressing the loss especially needs to be done if the person was a major leader within the ministry. Be open to the following:

- Meet with the congregation, and or members of specific ministries, and deal with feelings and issues of abandonment, grief, and loss. Many people will feel abandoned because of unresolved issues of abandonment in their personal lives. Many will not even know that these unresolved issues are there, and will feel voided and hurt due to the person's transition. A lot of slander and gossip can be avoided simply by dealing with this area, and helping people to process their feelings. As I transitioned out of my previous church, I had several meetings with my leaders before leaving. I believe people would have handled my transition better if this information was shared with them by leadership.
- Pray for the congregation as a whole and for people who may need more personal processing in the areas of abandonment, grief, and loss, and provide people with healthy tools and supports to process their thoughts and feelings.
- Demonstrating genuine support of the person that is leaving is key to helping members transition in a healthy manner. If leaders are silent regarding a transition, it leaves room for the enemy to cause division and confusion, and for people to form their own interpretation about that person's transition. When people see leaders giving genuine blessings despite challenges of losing that person, they are apt to deal with their feelings in a healthy manner.
- Do not preach about the issue over the pulpit, or make public remarks regarding your challenges with the person's transition. This provokes gossip and slander, and causes people to take sides.

- Do not lend to gossip and slander, and discourage people from engaging in such negativity. Promote unity and respect of the person's right to make their own decisions.
- Provide people with wise counsel regarding their own thoughts and feelings concerning being challenged by the person leaving, or them feeling they should leave.
- Be kingdom minded and not church focused. Kingdom minded leaders recognize that we are all one body advancing the kingdom of God, church minded leaders are focused on building their own little kingdom, and gathering people unto themselves.

Decreeing leaders and ministries bless people as they transition to new places within the body of Christ. Decreeing that transitions will be smoother, as people learn to respect God's will and flow in the process of SHIFTING with him.

DELIVERANCE FROM THE WOUNDED LEADER

Chapter 31

Contrary to what we may believe, and the importance of obeying those who have rule over us, God does not tolerate or honor the wounding of sheep by wounded leaders.

> **Hebrews 13:17** *Obey your leaders and submit to them, for they keep watch over your souls as those who will give an account. Let them do this with joy and not with grief, for this would be unprofitable for you.*

> **The Amplified Bible** *Obey your spiritual leaders and submit to them [continually recognizing their authority over you], for they are constantly keeping watch over your souls and guarding your spiritual welfare, as men who will have to render an account [of their trust]. [Do your part to] let them do this with gladness and not with sighing and groaning, for that would not be profitable to you [either].*

Leaders have the responsibility to make sure they are living an adequate lifestyle to be able to lead and watch over those under them. They must give an account for the proper governing of those under them. When we think of someone who is "*on watch*," we expect them to be alert, observant, and positioned to see what is occurring now, and what is on the horizon. We are expecting that person to be on guard, cautious and discerning, careful of what is happening and what will happen, such that we are void of attack, danger, or unexpected challenges. The watchmen is essentially a protector who willingly resists sleep so that the flock is kept safe.

A wounded watchman tends to be impaired, damaged, marred, defaced, disfigured, or scared. They are not operating at full strength and capacity due to their injuries, and have the propensity to be focused on themselves and their wounds and pains, rather than the assignment at hand. Therefore, the wounded watchman is a danger to himself, and to those he or she is guarding and protecting.

Watching over someone's soul is a very intimate responsibility. We cannot see the soul with the natural eye. Therefore, it requires spiritual sight to watch over someone's soul. And in order to operate in spiritual sight, the leader must have natural relationship and interaction, but also operate inside the spirit realm of the congregation, or within a specific person's life. When the watchman is operating inside the spirit realm, he or she is using the portals of prayer, intercession, and discernment to peer into the distance of the congregation or of one's life, such that he or she can counsel, instruct, teach, train, warn, correct, encourage, and guide the person properly in avoiding danger and challenges. Here are some biblical examples of Paul being a watchman over the souls under his ministry.

Paul Praying for the Congregation

Romans 1:8-12 New International Bible First, I thank my God through Jesus Christ for all of you, because your faith is being reported all over the world. God, whom I serve in my spirit in preaching the gospel of his Son, is my witness how constantly I remember you in my prayers at all times; and I pray that now at last by God's will the way may be opened for me to come to you. I long to see you so that I may impart to you some spiritual gift to make you strong — that is, that you and I may be mutually encouraged by each other's faith.

Ephesians 3:14-21 New International Bible For this reason, I kneel before the Father, from whom his whole family in heaven and on earth derives its name. I pray that out of his glorious riches he may strengthen you with power through his Spirit in your inner being, so that Christ may dwell in your hearts through faith. And I pray that you, being rooted and established in love, may have power, together with all the saints, to grasp how wide and long and high and deep is the love of Christ, and to know this love that surpasses knowledge — that you may be filled to the measure of all the fullness of God. Now to him who is able to do immeasurably more than all we ask or imagine, according to his power that is at work within us, to him be glory in the church and in Christ Jesus throughout all generations, for ever and ever! Amen.

Paul Praying for Timothy

2Timothy 1:1-5 New International Bible Paul, an apostle of Christ Jesus by the will of God, in keeping with the promise of life that is in Christ Jesus, To Timothy, my dear son: Grace, mercy and peace from God the Father and Christ Jesus our Lord. I thank God, whom I serve, as my ancestors did, with a clear conscience, as night and day I constantly remember you in my prayers. Recalling your tears, I long to see you, so that I may be filled with joy. I am reminded of your sincere faith, which first lived in your grandmother Lois and in your mother Eunice and, I am persuaded, now lives in you also.

Paul was able to sufficiently watch over his congregation and speak instruction and encouragement into their lives because he was healthy in his soul. This was key because Paul was in prison and was suffering much persecution when writing some of these letters to his congregation. He also had a buffeting thorn in his side to keep him humble due to all the revelations he received from God. He was able to keep watch over their souls because he was cognizant of his own soul. Paul knew what was in his soul, and was submissive to God dealing with his soul issues.

2Corinthians 12:7-10 And to keep me from being puffed up and too much elated by the exceeding greatness (preeminence) of these revelations, there was given me a thorn (a splinter) in the flesh, a messenger of Satan, to rack and buffet and harass me, to keep me from being excessively exalted. Three times I called upon the Lord and besought [Him] about this and begged that it might depart from me; But He said to me, My grace (My favor and loving-kindness and mercy) is enough for you [sufficient against any danger and enables you to bear the trouble manfully]; for My strength and power are made perfect (fulfilled and completed) and show themselves most effective in [your] weakness. Therefore, I will all the more gladly glory in my weaknesses and infirmities, that the

> *strength and power of Christ (the Messiah) may rest (yes, may pitch a tent over and dwell) upon me!*

In Paul's case, God did not remove the wound, yet gave him supernatural power to deal with it. Paul accepted the process of healing God gave him and was able to remain balanced in his life and ministry responsibilities.

Unless a wounded leader is abiding in God, and is submitting his own soul issues to God, there is no way for him or her to give an adequate account for your soul and to properly govern your soul. You are uncovered and run the risk of impending danger due to being unprotected. Moreover, the leader's spiritual sight is impaired because of soul wounding. The leader may not be able to adequately discern who is a threat and who is not a threat. The leader then is likely to fire on whoever approaches or who they foresee as potential danger, which could be you.

Since the leader is in charge of your soul, a knitting of souls has taken place. This is intended to be a healthy Godly soultie. But because the leader is wounded, and is not dealing with his or her wounds, it has potentially become an unhealthy soultie. This is the reason a person may have difficulty making a decision to leave from under an unhealthy leader - their soul is tied to that person. You essentially love them as you love yourself, and so you feel empathy, loyalty and obligation to them. In **2Timothy 1**, Paul expressed his love for Timothy and how he longed to see him.

> **2Timothy 1:1-4** *Paul, an apostle of Jesus Christ by the will of God, according to the promise of life which is in Christ Jesus, To Timothy, my dearly beloved son: Grace, mercy, and peace, from God the Father and Christ Jesus our Lord. I thank God, whom I serve from my forefathers with pure conscience, that without ceasing I have remembrance of thee in my prayers night and day; Greatly desiring to see thee, being mindful of thy tears, that I may be filled with joy.*

This was a healthy loving relationship between a leader and a spiritual son, so had Paul succumb to soul wounding, Timothy would have found it difficult to leave the ministry, as it was evident that their soul was knitted together.

> **The Message Bible** *I, Paul, am on special assignment for Christ, carrying out God's plan laid out in the Message of Life by Jesus. I write this to you, Timothy, the son I love so much. All the best from our God and Christ be yours! To Be Bold with God's Gifts. Every time I say your name in prayer – which is practically all the time – I thank God for you, the God I worship with my whole life in the tradition of my ancestors. I miss you a lot, especially when I remember that last tearful good-bye, and I look forward to a joy-packed reunion.*

Paul and Timothy loved one another as they loved their own soul, and it was evident in their conversation and relationship with one another.

Because of the knitting of souls, you may have to break soulties with the leader that wounded you before you can
- Wholeheartedly forgive them, break free from false loyalties and obligations you have with them.
- Heal your gifts and calling of wounds inflicted by them.
- Intercede for their healing.
- Proceed in following God's leading of removing yourself from under their ministry.

Even as soulties bind you to their soul, they can also bind your wounds to their wounds. Soulties are rooted in needs and desires, emotions, and actions, so there is a literal impartation of who the leader is instilled in you that binds you through that tie and vice versa.

Depending on the circumstances and experiences you have with your wounded leader, your unhealthy relationship can be abusive. Whether abusive or unhealthy, initially one feels like a failure and wants to fix the relationship. Unhealthy and abusive ties cannot be fixed. They must be broken and then a new healthy knitting of souls must occur. This is the reason it can be difficult to restore relationships. People are still tied to the old residue and impartations of the previous relationship connection.

When you fear acknowledging, conversing about, admitting you need help or that things in the relationship with a leader who is wounding you needs to change, you have SHIFTED from this just being a unhealthy dynamic. You have taken on the mentality of a victim of abuse. Even if the leader is not physically or sexually abusing you, your actions have gone into survival and self protection mode. You are operating in a victim mentality such that you become a protector of the person that is wounding you.

Soulties are broken in personal prayer time spent with the Lord. This prayer time is specific and intimate as you are:

- Being honest with the Lord about your thoughts and feelings, and what you have experienced.

- Acknowledging and forgiving those you have soulties and an unhealthy relationship with.

- Forgiving yourself for engaging and remaining in the relationship. Many people have guilt, shame, and condemnation regarding staying tied to a relationship, and allowing themselves to engage in that relationship.

- Soulties have to be verbally renounced and broken as they operate like vows and ropes that knit and bind you to that person or thing. They also are alive as your life is tied to that person's life if that makes sense. So you have to let them know that you no longer want them in your life by verbally renouncing them and breaking them so they will loose your life.

- Using the authority of Jesus name to renounce and break ties with that person and any way they are connected to your soul, heart, mind, behaviors, life, etc.

- Sometimes it can be one tie but depending on the relationships and the interactions, their can be numerous times. I personally believe soulties operate as a parasite, as whether the tie is healthy or unhealthy, it initially connects as a life source and then it feeds off and imparts into the person. ***Ecclesiastes 12:6-7** [Remember your Creator earnestly now] before the silver cord [of life] is snapped apart, or the golden bowl is broken, or the pitcher is broken at the fountain, or the wheel broken at the cistern [and the whole circulatory system of the blood ceases to function]; Then shall the dust [out of which God made man's body] return to the earth as it was, and the spirit shall return to God Who gave it.*

- You may have to throw things away that may also be apart of the soultie and inordinate relations you have with that person.

- Then time should be spent cleansing and healing from the impact of those ties on your life.

Below are some suggestions for praying concerning soulties with the wounded leader.

You break soulties by spending focused prayer time:

- Break vows, covenants, commitments, and agreements you made with the leader.

- Break any false honor, false loyalties, and false obligations you have with the leader.

- Break any words spoken over you by the leader that were presented as words of prophecy, knowledge, and direction from God, but was really manipulation, seduction, and witchcraft.

- If prophecies, words of knowledge, direction, etc., was from God, cleanse them of wounds and impurities and declare out they will come to pass even as your life takes on a new path. You may also want to seek God for whether these words were for then, and whether God has new words of prophecy and direction for you. Remember God is a restorer and always does exceedingly. If he said it and/or if it is still his will for you, he will bring it to pass regardless to who is or is not in your life.

- Use the blood of Jesus and the fire of God to cleanse your soul of any impartation and deposits that were imparted into you by the leader and that you imparted into the leader. Ask the Holy Spirit to reveal what this may be. In a sexual soultie, part of your soul, personality and even body matter enters the other person and vice versa. In this wounded soultie, things like attitudes, behaviors, mindsets/ideologies, characteristics flaws, personality traits, tainted anointings, sin issues, demonic transfers, spirits, and strongholds are exchanged. These things must be cleaned or cast out.

- Break ties with any wounding experiences or commonalities that bind you to the leader where you should be healed, yet it keeps each of you dependent, and in pity of one another or you tied to the leader.

- Break soulties where you feel obligated to bring deliverance and healing to the leader, yet your interactions only bring more drama and wounding.

- Break soulties where you personally benefit/ed from the relationship, and therefore have a difficult time giving it up.

- Using the blood of Jesus, spend time cleansing out pains and hurts caused by the leader.

- Repent for any hurt you have caused, for putting the leader in the place of God, and for allowing the leader to be more in your life than God may have said.

- Repent, cleanse, and break any ties that drew you to the leader that may not have been God's will. Some relationships start out healthy and then take a turn. Some may not have been God's will, so we have to acknowledge and repent for instances where we are drawn away by our own lust.

- Ask God to heal every wound you incurred from the relationship. Spend time forgiving and releasing your pain, fears, insecurities, anger, resentment, etc., to God and allow him to heal your wounds. Some wounds heal instantly, while some require continual prayer to heal. You can also spend intimate time soaking wounds in the healing power of God. Be okay with God using your time of healing to restore your intimacy and dependency in him.

- Break soulties with the victim mentality if necessary. Use the blood of Jesus to cleanse out any mindsets and character traits you have in this area.

- Bind and cast out the destiny killing spirit if necessary. Use the fire of God to burn out any fiery darts, demonic weapons, and venom that was sent to you by the wounded leader. Sometimes the destiny killing spirit operates generationally, so break curses where this spirit passes down through your generations.

- Spend time healing and restoring your gifts and calling and anyway they incurred wounds from the leader. Rededicate your gifts to God, while breaking any soulties and ownership the wounded leader has claimed, or you have given in relations to your giftings and calling.

- Spend time healing your identity and building your identity in who God says you are and who he has called you to be. Cancel and cast down any distortions and lies you have with thinking you cannot be or achieve who God has called you to be without the wounded leader.

- Be honest with things you refused to acknowledge and discern regarding the unhealthy relationship. This is vital to breaking cycles of entering future unhealthy relationships. Explore what causes you to yield or remain in the relationship, and choices and characteristics you need, so that you do not succumb to such relationships in the future.

- Ask God to reveal to you what a healthy leader is. Begin to become that yourself, while allowing this revelation to guide you in future relationships.

- Seek God for a standard concerning your worth and never settle or allow yourself to be treated less than, regardless of the position or stature of the person.

- If God tells you to no longer be under the wounded leader, leave the relationship and/or ministry.

- If God tells you to stay, ask for direction and purpose, and operate accordingly, while maintaining your standard. This is rare, as God will usually place people in this type of situation who are mature and are on assignment for this specific purpose. That person infiltrates a body of people for the purpose of intercession and being a mentor, voice, and healer to the people being wounded. If the wounded leader is not seeking personal deliverance and healing or in a process of healing, God may not require you to stay. *James 1:13 Let no man say when he is tempted, I am tempted of God: for God cannot be tempted with evil, neither tempteth he any man.* If you feel God is telling you to stay seek confirmation in making sure you are not staying out of familiarity, fear, out of an inordinate need to rescue or fix the leader, or because you are not healed. Should God require you stay, continually keep yourself before God in dealing with any new wounding that may occur, and to fortify your identity against settling in your relationship standards.

- If God tells you to pray for the wounded leader, pray. If he does not give you this assignment, then move forward with your life and trust that he knows what is best for the leader.

RESTORING RELATIONSHIPS AFTER BEING DELIVERED

Chapter 32

After being delivered from a wounded spirit that has impacted the people you oversee, leaders must be open to rebuilding trust and restoring relationships. This is very important as many leaders just want to return to their position and relationship interactions, while expecting the same honor, loyalty, and respect they had before their fall. There is minimal to no regard for the fact that people are hurt, fearful, baffled, and torn. Moreover, scriptures are sometimes used to spiritually manipulate and silence people into being accepting of leaders, yet no reconciliation or healing has been bestowed upon the people, and no accountability has been taken for the breech in the relationship. This is not fair to the people as they should be given ample opportunity to ask questions, explore their hurts, receive healing, and time to try the leaders' spirit to ensure adequate transformation has occurred before they fully reenter relationship (*1John 4:1*).

When leaders wound members, the members often feel betrayed even though this may not always be the case. But as the leader, you have destroyed their perception of spirituality, and even of what a Godly person should be like. And for some, a fallen leader has destroyed the person's perception of God, and his ability to choose healthy leaders to advance his kingdom and to keep that person free of sin and issues.

As I shared in the chapter on betrayal, when a relationship is breeched, it has to be restored from the new resurrected place. You cannot return to the way things were. And though somethings may be similar to the past, the posture of restoration has to be from the new place of reconciliation. For this reason, the leader will have to walk with people through a process of restoring the relationship. It will take a series of steps, patience, and demonstrating of change to restore trust and rebuild relationships with the congregation and personally.

Below are some suggestions for restoring relationships after being healed from the wounded spirit:
- Publicly apologize if the entire ministry and/or body of Christ was impacted by your actions.
- Privately apologize to specific people who were wounded.
- Do not make excuses for your actions or use wounded or fallen bible characters to justify your actions. Do not play the "I am human" card. There is a higher standard for leaders, so accept responsibility when you fall short of them.
- Allow people a time of processing the apology.
- After processing, allow people to ask questions and answer them with honesty and humility. It is okay if you do not have an answer to a question. Do not make up something to look favorable or mislead the people. Be honest if you cannot commit to something they may ask you to do, as sometimes people will be so

hurt they will want you to prove you are changing. Demonstrate sincere change to those you need to, as you do not want to get into people pleasing.
- Share at least three tangible areas with the people that you will be working on so they can see your transformation.
- Be more specific in what you can work on with those you have relationship with. Depending on the depth of the relationship, ask them what they need from you to aide in restoring the relationship. Tell them what you need. Commit to working on two things every two weeks until all the request are actively restored to the relationship.
- Apologize quickly if you slack or error so that people will know you are serious about your process to wholeness.
- Do not use the bible scriptures or your position to manipulate people to honor and obey you. Let the process work for you such that it restores a healthy relationship.
- Do not use your platform to voice frustrations regarding your process and how people are responding. People will realign with the ministry vision as they see you realign with the ministry vision. Also, some people will forgive quickly and others will need time to trust again.
- Have a counselor or healthy leader come in and counsel, pray, and provide counsel for people who have been wounded by your actions. Corporate prayer is important to bring healing and unity to the congregation. However, personal counsel and prayer should be offered as well. The guest counselor and/or leader should not make excuses for your actions or reprimand people for being hurt and not easily forgiving. They should be open to and available to process people to wholeness. Only use guest counselors and/or leaders who can commit to yielding their time for at least a month. As those who cannot commit risk further wounding the people due to being inconsistent and unavailable.
- Commit to monthly evaluation meetings with the congregation, and personally for six months as people recommit to a trusting relationship with you, and the ministry vision. Make changes and adjustments as necessary to ensure healthy restoration.

HEALTHY RELATIONSHIP NUGGETS

Chapter 33

Boundaries
Boundaries are vital for a leader/member relationship. Boundaries must be clear and explicit. They should not cross sexual lines. Neither person should get needs and desires met that are beyond the scope of the covenant God is requiring for the relationship.

People can only fulfill the rolls in your life that God designed. Moreover, people have choices, so they can decide of what role they will play in your life. Fulfilling roles that God did not ordain provokes expectations that will breech boundaries, thus causing wounds and drama in the relationship and ministry.

No matter how much you try to make a person be more and try to acquire more from them, God's will and their choice will override your desires. As a result, you will be left wanting, longing, frustrated, in drama, spewing drama, and feeling rejected.

Seek healing when you find yourself wanting and pursuing more from someone than God, or the person is willing to give.

Instead of seeking people and trying to receive fulfillment from them, seek God as he can be everything you need. He can also connect you in the right timing to balanced relationships that can bring fulfillment to your life.

Anytime you are so focused on what people cannot and will not be to you, you miss the value of what they can be. You also miss the revelation that they were not meant to fulfill that need or desire in your life.

It is important to let people know what your needs, desires, and expectations are. Otherwise, you are having one relationship with the person in your head, in your fantasies, and a whole other one in real life. When you do this, it causes drama, conflict, discouragement, and can wreck the relationship you are to have with the person. It is usually you who is behaving this way, while blaming your broken heart on the person, rather than on your inability to effectively communicate your needs, desires, and expectations.

Healthy Communication
Learn healthy communication and conflict resolution skills, and role model and teach others how to communicate and resolve conflict.
1. Stay focused and listen attentively.
2. Ask open ended questions rather than closed ended questions that put people on the defense.

3. Do not attack. Express that these are your thoughts and feelings and allow the person a chance to explain themselves. Encourage them to give you the same opportunity. "I" statements are good because you are expressing how you perceived the situation without outright attacking or blaming. This is beneficial in instances where misperceptions have occurred.
4. Repeat what you need clarity on so the person can correct or elaborate on what they said. Remember, clarity brings knowledge and knowledge is power.
5. Be okay with conflict and disagreement; it is what makes us unique. When you embrace conflict as part of healthy communication, you will resolve conflict quicker and easier.
6. Stay focused on resolving the matter and not allowing challenging thoughts and emotions to shut down the conversation.
7. Emotions and challenging thoughts are going to arise. But they should not rule you ability to be tempered, meek, and articulate. Focus on communicating through your spirit and the character of God rather than your emotions.
8. Be conscious with talking to God in your mind. Ask him to speak through you and to guided you in your responses.
9. Be honest and express your thoughts, feelings, concerns and disagreements in a calm and respectful manner.
10. Pay attention to nonverbal communication and undertones. Be open to addressing these forms of communications.
11. Be discerning when the conversation stops being about you and the person and SHIFTS to exposing unresolved issues. This happens a lot in leader/member relationships. Leaders are often a catalyst for healing mother, father, teacher, and authority figure wounds.
12. After resolving challenging situations, engage in small talk to restore joy, peace, and ease within the relationship interactions.
13. Start and end meetings and conflicts with prayer. Forgive where necessary, cleanse out hurtful feelings and thoughts; restore trust, honor, love, and validation one to another.
14. Do not take phone calls or texts unless it is an emergency.

The inability to communicate your needs, thoughts, desires and motives, is the result of a deeper issue. Even if you were not taught or role modeled healthy and effective communication, you are mature enough to stop using your upbringing and past as an excuse. Deal with your underlying root issues while receiving deliverance and healing. You are also mature enough to learn the tools needed to communicate your thoughts, feelings, and motives in a healthy manner.

Stop engaging in the generational and relational cycle that makes you broken and unhealthy. Do not let people draw you into generational and relational cycles that God has delivered you from.

The only person that can bring value to your words, thoughts, and feelings are you. If you cannot express them, do not expect anyone else to give them a voice or value them.

Check Your Desires
If you are driven by your need for love and belonging, where our desires are not put in check/right perspective, please know they will show in your interactions with your friends, acquaintances, and members. You will be possessive, jealous, comparing your interactions with that person to what they do with others, resentful, self-rejecting, then sulking when someone inquires as to the reason you have isolated yourself. And even when you try to physically get close to that person, they will feel uncomfortable because though it should be a hug, holding of the hand, laying on the shoulder or lap, etc., they can feel your inappropriate desires in what should be a genuine interaction.

When we are getting our need for love and belonging met outside of God's presence, it generally leaves us wanting, longing and broken. Seek God to heal areas of inadequacy, worth, identity, and unresolved relationship issues, while letting him bring and guide you to fulfillment to these areas of your life.

We all have an innate need for love and belonging, but when we are driven by it, it is lust that is guiding us.

When people cannot, will not, or should not fulfill needs, desires, and expectations that you have, respect these boundaries and choices. Ask God to cleanse you of any unhealthy or imbalanced soulties or emotions you have for the person. This is important because it does not matter if you stalk people in your mind or in real life; they have a choice to connect with you. We set ourselves up for self-rejection when we try to make people be what they are not to be or do not want to be in our lives.

Members will want to be close to you because you are the leader. It is important to have your desires in check so you will not overstep boundaries and engage in interactions that could lend you and others to sin.

Mind Stalking
Mind stalking is when you have an entire relationship in your mind with someone and in reality it is totally different. This is just as dangerous and scary as physically stalking someone, and even more so because usually stalkers are not allowed in a person's vicinity or personal space yet desires to be. A mind stalker is usually in the person's circle, but desires to be more to the person than what they are. They can be a friend, acquaintance, companion, or team member who wants to be closer to you than what they are.

Unbeknown to the person, the mind stalker is usually engaging with the person through his or her desires and motives, or through jealousy, anger, rejection, and resentment due to not being able to have what they want from that person. By the time the person figures it out, they are caught up in drama, confusion, and no longer trusting their judgment of people.

Leaders will have a few encounters with mind stalkers. Boundaries are essential with mind stalkers. The minute you make them more or give them more information about you than you should have, you have fed their desire and made them think they are important to you. As you balance this, they may become blatantly aggressive or passive aggressive, but they will make sure you know they are offended. It is best to have meetings with them with third parties present. And to have public conversations where others can be witnesses of the interactions. Many mind stalkers are unstable and unpredictable, so it is always better to keep yourself safe and accountable regardless to what they are thinking, may say, or may do.

Self-Rejection
Self-rejection will have you pushing people away and calling it the Lord. You will have a plethora of reasons as to why they cannot be in your life. Much of it is because people cannot be what you want, or you lack being able to truly connect to who they can be to you. And some of it is because you want people to be perfect cause you fear being hurt, so your focus is on who they are not, rather than who they can be.

Some self-rejection is because we want people to be God. We are looking for a redeemer, a healer, and someone who can fulfill our every need. Only God can do that sir/mam! Interestingly, the self-rejector rejects God, even when he is beckoning to be what they need.

Some members will reject your fellowship and leadership, then contend you are not adequately governing their soul. They need deliverance from self-rejection, and until they are delivered, they will not be able to receive from you or any other leader. Be cognizant of not getting so caught up in validating these people that it drains you. Instead, spend time interceding for them and assign them a counselor or mentor that can walk with them to wholeness. As they are healed, they will begin to engage you, and then you can begin investing time into developing a healthy relationship with them.

Foolish Relationships
> **Proverbs 13:20** *He that walketh with wise men shall be wise: but a companion of fools shall be destroyed.*

A fool is a stupid, insensitive, arrogant person, a silly person; a person who lacks judgment or sense. A fool is an ardent enthusiast who cannot resist an opportunity to indulge in enthusiasm. That means they will spend and sell your heart at the expense of their own self indulgence. While you are hurting, they will think it is funny, or find it pleasing to have gotten over on you.

A fool is also a weak-minded or idiotic person. So when you befriend or remain in relationship with a fool, you are setting yourself up to be deteriorated as a person, and to even be destroyed by their ignorance and folly. Stop blaming them. You have choices. Cut ties, heal, and move on.

Foolish relationships are draining, drama filled, and can destroy whatever joy or focus you have at the time. As a leader you are not obligated to entertain such relationships. Do not be someone else's emotional roller coaster as this is not Godly, or a requirement as a soul watcher. Lead the person from the context of a congregational relationship and let that be that. You are giving them what they can handle at the time, and until they are willing to learn by practicing healthy relationship dynamics, then you are not obligated by God to waste your time.

Foolish Relationships Cause Eternal Scars
> **Proverbs 13:20** *He that walketh with wise men shall be wise: but a companion of fools shall be destroyed.*

Destroyed in the Hebrew is *mar* and means:
1. especially by breaking; figuratively, to split the ears (with sound), i.e. Shout (for alarm or joy)
2. blow an alarm, cry (alarm, aloud, out), destroy
3. make a joyful noise, smart, shout (for joy), sound an alarm, triumph

There is indeed an alarm going off when we are engaged in relationships with unhealthy people. These people are seeking to triumph over us. Our destruction is their victory, as all kinds of alarms are going off within the relationship to let us know they are not healthy for us. Mar actually means to disfigure, scar, deface, render less perfect. A stripping of our identity occurs when we are in relationships with foolish people. We become unrecognizable at the expense of their personal gain. They truly turn us into people that we were never meant to be, and cause us to settle for less than what we should have in life.

When a disfiguring occurs, it is difficult to get back to your original self without having a scar or something to remind you that a change occurred. Even as you heal, your heart, soul, and physical disposition will never be the same. Foolish relationships are not worth such scars. Get out while you can, and be wise not to enter into them altogether.

Some Relationships Cannot be Fixed
> **Proverbs 13:20** *He that walketh with wise men shall be wise: but a companion of fools shall be destroyed.*

God calls relationships with fools unwise. That means no matter how much you try to stay and fix the relationship or the person, you are fooling yourself because the only wise thing to do is to get out of the relationship altogether. You cannot fix what was never meant to be - what was doomed for destruction from the beginning. Some people will come under your ministry, and relationships will either never gel or will be breeched such that they are unfixable. God will give you peace and clarity when such relationships surface. Follow his leading and trust what he is saying. He is saving you from unnecessary drama and wounds.

Unhealthy Relationships Imprison the Soul
Sometimes we are not willing or do not have the strength to release unhealthy relationships because of soulties that attach us to the person. Our soul could also be imprisoned to the person. **Proverbs 22:24-25** speaks of the snared soul. It reads, "Make no friendship with an angry man; and with a furious man thou shalt not go: Lest thou learn his ways, and get a snare to thy soul."

Though this scripture uses the word angry, that word angry also means a person who causes long suffering or an ire person. So if you are in a relationship with a person that causes you suffering or ire which means an unhealthy intense passion where there is always drama, chaos, wrath or conflict, and you are having a difficult time releasing this relationship, it could be because your soul is snared.

Snare means *"to trap, hook, capture, entangled."*

As you remain in an unhealthy relationship, your soul becomes a prisoner of that person. You are striving to learn their ways so you will not set them off, but your soul is already ensnared by their wrath, because they are dictating and controlling your life with their moods, drama, unhealthy entanglements and actions.

To be free, you have to break soulties with these people, and command your soul to be free from their imprisonment. Bondages of fear, control, confusion, bewitchment, and word curses also have to be broken off your life, and any deposits of them need to be cleansed out of your soul. Fall out agreement with feeling like you need this person and cannot live without them, are obligated to have relationship with them, and break any words and deeds that have been released over you in this manner.

A lot of times we do not want to let relationships go because we feel like a failure, feel rejected, stuck in familiarity, or have some type of false loyalty or obligation to the person we are holding on to, or to our position as a leader. Yet no one should be abusing you and in no way should you feel ensnared where you are having to dictate and maneuver around people's actions. **Proverbs 27:17** tells us that *"Iron sharpens iron, so a man sharpeneth the countenance of his friend."*

Even though you are the leader, those under you should still be sharpening you in some measure. When being sharpened you are being empowered to be the best you that you can be. If there is a cutting away of who you are, it is only to perfect the essence of who you are in a greater measure. You should always become a better you through those you are in relationship with. If you become less and even stagnant where you are no longer growing and being empower to grow, then the relationship should be reevaluated. Either you all are not being who you are to be to one another, or you are holding on to the relationship for other reasons that have no true defined divine purpose. Be okay with letting go and allowing God to connect you in relationships that can sharpen you.

The Message Bible *You use steel to sharpen steel, and one friend sharpens another.*

Relationship Empowerment
Proverbs 27:17 *tells us that "Iron sharpens iron, so a man sharpeneth the countenance of his friend." Iron is sharpened by rubbing it against another piece of sharp iron. When two pieces of iron, especially iron blades rub together, both become sharper. Also an equipping is occurring as both are empowering the other through the connection they have with one another. Both begin to change and transform while becoming more refined. Each are then more efficient for use.*

Sharp means "to become keen, acute, alert, watchful, defined, cutting edge, swift, tapered, fierce."

When people do not sharpen one another, the relationship becomes dull, slow, lazy, un-useful, and blurred in vision. Feelings are easily hurt due to unspoken and unmet expectations flaring. These expectations tend to out way the level of iron production manifesting in the relationship. If the relationship is unfruitful or not beneficial, check the iron production. For whatever reason, either you or the other person is not investing in the relationship. Someone has to start sharpening the other for production to manifest, so if you are waiting on the other person, then you are already demonstrating that you have some issues with investing in relationships or in that person.

Examine yourself and that relationship, and be okay with releasing it if necessary or doing what is necessary to sharpen it so it can produce what God has required of it.

If people are not growing under your ministry, connect them with ministries that can sharpen them. Give them your blessing if they feel they have received all they can from your ministry and desire to move on where they can be sharpened. If it was not time for them to go, God will deal with them and even have them return to further be sharpened under your ministry.

THE ART OF TRUE ACCOUNTABILITY
Chapter 34

This chapter is to help leaders discern the people who really want to change, and are ready to change. And to stop leaders from wasting time with those who are not ready to change or do not want to change.

Accountability Versus Consensus
A lot of times we will wait until we have made a decision about a matter then present it to our leadership, spiritual parent/children, friend, spouse, God, etc., as us desiring accountability to the decision we have made. What we fail to realize is no one can make a true account for something they did not initially know about or agree to.

When I go to the bank, I have to put my money in the account FIRST before there can be an account for my money, and before the bank can be accountable for my money. If I have $500 but go to Walmart and spend $300. I cannot then go to the bank and say I am depositing $500 when I only have $200. I have already made a decision and came into agreement with Walmart about the money I spent. The bank cannot give an account or be accountable to funds I have already spent and made a decision about. They can only respect, give an opinion, or come into consensus on the decision that I chose to make. They however, are not accountable for it, and cannot give an account for it. They can only hope I remain accountable to the consensus I made with them.

This is the reason most decisions made in this manner fail. There is consensus but not true weight where both parties are responsible for the outcome. The other person has no real investment, as they did not partake in the decision making process.

Also because both parties were not initially consulted in the decision making process, the decision maker tends to feel entitled to make adjustments to the agreement at will without any accountability to what was initially consented upon. The person then avoids being accountable as they keep changing the agreement, while never really reaching their goal, or self-evaluating the reason their agreement is not achieved. Though it is never actually spoken or acknowledged, the prideful truth is there is no real accountability when one person is the main and "only" shareholder in the decision making.

Sidebar Wisdom: Both leaders and members engage in this misperception of accountability. We must recognize that is not true accountability, and thus it produces little to no results in meeting goals, maintaining standards, and maturing in the Lord.

Accountability Gives an Account
Many times a person will take a matter to their leader, spiritual parent/child, friend, spouse, and/or God, and will make accountability agreements with them, but will not

want to take blame when he or she is not accountable to the vows and covenants that were made. Accountability is all about blame. It is all about giving an account for the agreement at hand.

Dictionary.com defines *accountability* as:
1. subject to the obligation to report, explain, or justify something; responsible; answerable.
2. capable of being explained; explicable; explainable.
3. synonyms are as followed: answerability, blameworthiness, liability, responsibility, burden, fault, guilt, incrimination, liability

When we enter an accountability agreement, we are obligated to:
- Report on our progress or lack there of.
- Clearly explain the reason we have or have not progressed.
- Attempt to justify our actions without using poor excuses or divert from our irresponsibility.
- Answer questions and concerns that surface regarding our actions or lack of.
- Take responsibility and blame for the progress or lack of progress.
- Be open to constructive criticism and hearing truth about the changes and improvements needed to ensure accountability.
- Repent to God and the person as necessary.
- Examine if cycles of sabotage and destiny killing spirits are at work.
- Examine strongholds such as spirits of laziness, sluggardness, irresponsibility, disobedience, anti-submissiveness, rebellion, lawlessness, etc., are at work; break their powers off your life and implement practices to rid yourself of anyway they have embedded their fruit in your personality and character.
- Encourage one another in each of your abilities and capabilities to fulfill the agreement.
- Re-evaluate the agreement, and be honest about whether we are capable of achieving it or not, or whether we are willing to invest the time to achieve it or not. This is important because we do not want to waste the other person's time investing in an agreement that we are not willing or not ready to be accountable to.
- If we are ready, then make any necessary changes and begin again. If we are not ready, then move on and let that be that.

Accountability Requires Discipline
Often we enter accountability agreements from the potential of the person, but not the reality of where they are in life. Though we are striving to achieve the potential, the foundation of accountability is based on that which can be clearly identified. Therefore, true accountability requires:
- Discipline
- Focus
- Maturity
- Responsibility

We have to be honest with ourselves and with people about what each party can handle regarding accountability for the maturity level each of us are at. People mean well and have a mind to change or succeed, but do not always have the heart to change or succeed. Though accountability agreements are made to grow a person into maturity regarding a matter, we must make sure the drive, desire, and conviction is present to really work an accountability plan. Without these three ingredients, the parties involved may not incur the discipline, focus, maturity, and responsibility needed to fulfill that agreement.

People must also understand that when you enter an accountability agreement, you are establishing covenants, oaths, and vows are being made.

> *Deuteronomy 23:21-22 When thou shalt vow a vow unto the LORD thy God, thou shalt not slack to pay it: for the LORD thy God will surely require it of thee; and it would be sin in thee.*

> *James 5:12 But above all things, my brethren, swear not, neither by heaven, neither by the earth, neither by any other oath: but let your yea be yea; and your nay, nay; lest ye fall into condemnation.*

When accountability agreements are broken, we must give an account to God for our actions so that we do not reap the consequences of an unpaid vow. This is the reason it is so important to watch what we commit to, and being slow to agree when we are not sure if we are ready to follow through on the matter at hand. It is okay to take time to examine an agreement before God and make sure you have the drive, desire and conviction to work that plan.

Accountability in Covenant Relationships

Often times we say we are accountable to our covenant relationship, but much of what we call accountability is us getting the other person to agree, conform or accept our ideas and actions. An authentic spiritual relationship involves legitimate accountability where each party is willing and open to carry the burden of that covenant agreement, and is open to receiving truth from one another. Truth is spoken with respect and honor for one another, and sincere concern for the state of one another's soul and walk with God. If there is initial disagreement of what is being spoken, examining what has been shared before God is vital to making sure deception of the enemy is not at work.

The enemy wants to alter and kill your progress, process, covenant relationship, and destiny. If God spoke it then he will confirm it. If you do not receive initial clarity, then allow what has been spoken to remain conscious within you until you are sure it is of God or not of God. This will save you from being deceived if the word was indeed true, and from any seeds that the enemy will try to sow through disagreement; as often times we agree to disagree and think that is resolution. The subject was dropped, but true accountability was not in operation.

Amos 3:3 Can two walk together, except they be agreed?

New Living Bible Can two people walk together without agreeing on the direction?

When we agree to disagree we are actually operating in a false peace and superficial harmony, as our actions present as we are on one accord, but our spirits are divided. Also, the disagreement is lying dormant until the next time there is a challenge or search for truth.

The reason this is important is because accountability means we each take blame and ownership for our actions and because we are in covenant, we are affected by one another's actions. We each are equally responsible as if we have committed the act personally. Each of our actions must be reported one to another, justified, and explained; and through our covenant, we are contending that we answer and are responsible to one another and to God for one another. With that being said, if either of us are engaging in actions that cannot be vouched for, with no regard for the "truth" the other person has spoken, we are violating our covenant of honor one to the other, and unto God. We are in consensus, but not in covenant.

It is important for the body of Christ to mature in this area. We jump from relationship to relationship, and enter covenants with no regard to the spiritual ramifications. We have to learn healthy relationship skills, and study the biblical truths regarding fellowshipping and walking together, so we can grow in relationship with one another. If we contend we are journeying in life with God, then we will never bypass true accountability. It is an essential discipline necessary to maintain covenant with him and to those he puts in our life. Do not allow unresolved relationship issues and irresponsibility thwart your ability to be accountable. Decreeing healing and increased maturity in the things of the Lord is your portion! SHIFT!

WISE PREACHING

Chapter 35

We need wisdom to properly govern the lives and preaching styles of leaders, and the pulpits of our churches and ministries.

> ***Proverbs 4:7-9*** *Wisdom is the principal (chief) thing; therefore get wisdom: and with all thy getting get understanding. Exalt her, and she shall promote thee: she shall bring thee to honour, when thou dost embrace her. She shall give to thine head an ornament of grace: a crown of glory shall she deliver to thee.*

> ***The Amplified Bible*** *The beginning of Wisdom is: get Wisdom (skillful and godly Wisdom)! [For skillful and godly Wisdom is the principal thing.] And with all you have gotten, get understanding (discernment, comprehension, and interpretation). Prize Wisdom highly and exalt her, and she will exalt and promote you; she will bring you to honor when you embrace her. She shall give to your head a wreath of gracefulness; a crown of beauty and glory will she deliver to you.*

> ***James 1:5*** *If any of you lack wisdom, let him ask of God, that giveth to all men liberally, and upbraideth not; and it shall be given him.*

> ***James 3:17*** *But the wisdom that is from above is first pure, then peaceable, gentle, and easy to be intreated, full of mercy and good fruits, without partiality, and without hypocrisy.*

In this day and age where people are anti-church and anti-God, it is important to explore the benefits of wise preaching. Though we should never veer from biblical truth, fail to admonish sin and error, constrain from Godly rebuke, correction, and chastening, we cannot continue to use slave master preaching tactics to fear, manipulate, and whip people into salvation. If we are going to reach people and save souls, we will have to be wise in how we approach sin issues, and present the word of God to people and to the world.

- No we do not want to gimmick people!
- No we do not want to sway from the word!
- No we do not want to water down the gospel!

But we have to recognize that offensive rebukes, murderous jabs, abusive commentary, and death threats wrapped in scripture, is noneffective soul winning and deliverance strategy in this day and age. People have deemed this to be control, manipulation, religious abuse, and hatred. And in some instances they are correct. If a teacher, boss, or parent behaved this way in how they relay information, that is what we would call it - abuse. But because it contains Godly truth and they are the "*anointed of God*" that we fear correcting (touching not the anointed, ***Psalms 105:15***), the church has labeled what would ordinarily be considered abuse under other circumstances, as fearless preaching.

We then contend that people are rebellious and lack the fear of the Lord if they do not receive the abusive chastisement that many leaders are giving them. These preaching tactics have helped to breed rebellion, anti-church, and anti-Christ mentalities, and are continually pushing people further away from the church and God. People are stripping their identity and taking on a new identity, while trying to mold God into an idol to fit their self-made image. God is never going to conform to man's identity, thus many of these people are going to hell, partly by the doings of abusive leaders. We have to take a step back and examine ourselves, and consider everyone in the pews. Not just those who will say *"Amen,"* . We have to acknowledge those who need more than just biblical truth, but a processing to wholeness.

Though as leaders and saints, we cannot apologize for the word of God, we must start admitting and apologizing for how we wound and offend people all *"in the name of the Lord."* We are big on saying *"we are standing for persecution sake,"* but no where does the bible say to blast people with ridicule, condensation, abuse, and mockery, then wrap it in biblical truth. We have to become sufficient examples of the word we are preaching. If we can call out people's sin, but not admit that this is sin, then we are continuing to set ourselves up to be attacked and rejected by those we claim we are trying to reach.

Many leaders have made some people enraged in how they have handled, presented, and represented the gospel. Yet, leaders do not want to take responsibility in acknowledging this truth, bringing deliverance and healing to those we let down and abused. And then changing our methods, so that we present and represent the gospel where people can be reconciled and restored unto Jesus Christ. We want to keep doing the same ole same ole, while reaping worst results than we were in time past. We must recognize the separation of church and state is in jeopardy. Though some of it is the world and the devil wanting to silence the church, some of it is also our own error. We definitely do not want to be censored and should not be silent. The revelation and implementation of wise preaching must come forth if we are going to rectify our wrong doings, present a healthy gospel to the world, and be a demonstration of the word we preach, where people will want the God we live for.

There are times where chastening and rebuke, while speaking truth, has been released through the well of abuse. There is also a pride and haughtiness, and even at times a split personality that is presented with this type of preaching. The leader is one way in the pulpit and another way when outside of the pulpit. The leader is like an entirely different person up close. To this point in the body of Christ, we have contended that this is the anointing, especially since the people tend to be afraid of the leader. We have deemed this respect, honor, and anointing. But it is not because of the anointing or reverence, it is because the people do not know how the leader is going to present, and what he or she may speak. Therefore, the people are guarded. Though there should be a reverence and an honor, there should not be a guard or a fear. This is the reason many leaders feel justified in their abrasive actions. They will even state, *"but I love the people."* That is the same thing the abuser says after he has beat up his victim. He is nice, and contend he did it out of love. And then he demonstrates that love until the next time he decides that person needs another beating. Now think about the harsh preaching of some leaders as you consider the abuser mentality? Sigh!!!! Change us Jesus!

Moreover, the body of Christ has to take into consideration that what is being preached is not being demonstrated in the daily lives of many saints, especially leaders. Many are slinging one word from the pulpit and living another in our lifestyles. Many leaders have profited off the sins of others, then preach "*holiness or hell*" from the pulpit. Where believers used to remain silent in how they have been pimped and taken advantage of by leaders, they are now attacking in the same abusive manner that was done to them when under years of religious abuse, manipulation and control. They are willing to die and go to hell, then to return to the bondage of religion that they feel betrayed them by not changing their lives, yet holds them to a standard of righteous living they feel they will never attain.

It is important to recognize that some of these preaching styles were passed down from slavery. They are rooted in slave mentalities, where the master used control and abuse to whip his servant into submission. The slave was to show praise, gratitude, honor, and loyalty to the master for being chastised, and dehumanized. Often for no reason at all. Simply because the master was in a position of power. Slave masters would also use the bible to justify their actions towards slaves. They would contend it was their Godly right to be served and to buy, sale, and own slaves. This is the reason many of the church dynamics and preaching tactics mimic master and slave mentalities. I address this because though such preaching possesses biblical truth, the style and undertones, are abusive, offensive, and wounding. Those preaching styles and concepts came from the slave age. When you add a scripture to them, they appear as Godly principles that we dare not defy. It is utilized with the intent to fear people into getting right with God, or whip people into getting right with God. This does not work with the present generation, and even though it had some impact in previous generations, it is really abuse.

Dictionary.com defines *abuse* as:
1. to use wrongly or improperly; misuse
2. to treat in a harmful, injurious, or offensive way
3. to speak insultingly, harshly, and unjustly to or about; revile; malign
4. to commit sexual assault upon; rape or sexual assault, abuse oneself, to masturbate
5. *Obsolete.* to deceive or mislead
6. wrong or improper use; misuse
7. harshly or coarsely insulting language
8. bad or improper treatment; maltreatment
9. a corrupt or improper practice or custom

Our focus must be speaking the word in the character and nature of God, and letting his anointing and word in our lives go into people, climates, communities, regions and nations, and root out, pull down, destroy, throw down, build, and plant (*Jeremiah 1:10*). The anointing is not mean, insulting, abusive, controlling, and offensive. The anointing is revealing, convicting, precise, keen, delivering, empowering, and liberating. We do not have to abuse, control, or manipulate people to win their souls. We have to discern the dispensation we are in and ask God to give us wisdom in how to operate in the anointing on our lives, such that we overthrow darkness, reach people, and impart a drawing that makes them want to be saved.

John 12:32 And I, if I be lifted up from the earth, will draw all men unto me.

2Corinthians 10:4-6 For the weapons of our warfare are not physical [weapons of flesh and blood], but they are mighty before God for the overthrow and destruction of strongholds, [Inasmuch as we] refute arguments and theories and reasonings and every proud and lofty thing that sets itself up against the [true] knowledge of God; and we lead every thought and purpose away captive into the obedience of Christ (the Messiah, the Anointed One), Being in readiness to punish every [insubordinate for his] disobedience, when your own submission and obedience [as a church] are fully secured and complete.

Luke 4:18-19 The Spirit of the Lord [is] upon Me, because He has anointed Me [the Anointed One, the Messiah] to preach the good news (the Gospel) to the poor; He has sent Me to announce release to the captives and recovery of sight to the blind, to send forth as delivered those who are oppressed [who are downtrodden, bruised, crushed, and broken down by calamity], To proclaim the accepted and acceptable year of the Lord [the day when salvation and the free favors of God profusely abound].

Wisdom Keys for Wise Preaching:

Preach Fearless with Godly Character: There is no way around preaching truth, repentance, and conviction. The gospel of Jesus Christ is built on these foundations and rooted in the holiness and righteousness of God. People cannot be saved if they are not willing to accept these truths and have a converted heart that love the truth, repentance, conviction, holiness, and righteousness of God. Though we never should veer from preaching through these wells, we must know how to operate in bold fearless preaching that does not belittle, ridicule, or slander people. Being fearless means speaking the truth of God's word that draws them to repentance and conviction. This can be done without being abusive as you preach through the character, nature, and heart of God. Sometimes fearless preaching can be matter of fact, display a tone of urgency, fierce, and appear angry. Fearless preaching may even expose sin and appear as judgment as God is revealing the issues and challenges of the people and his desire to deliver, heal, and save them. But even in this, people should hear the heart and hearkening of God. They should feel his redemption through their conviction. If people become upset, reject the word, and even become abusive towards you, it should be because they did not want to hear the truth, not because you belittled, degraded, and abused them.

Jeremiah 1:7-8 But the Lord said unto me, Say not, I am a child: for thou shalt go to all that I shall send thee, and whatsoever I command thee thou shalt speak. Be not afraid of their faces: for I am with thee to deliver thee, saith the Lord

Philippians 2:3 *Let nothing be done through strife or vainglory; but in lowliness of mind let each esteem other better than themselves.*

Acts 13:45-49 New International Bible *When the Jews saw the crowds, they were filled with jealousy. They began to contradict what Paul was saying and heaped abuse on him. Then Paul and Barnabas answered them boldly: "We had to speak the word of God to you first. Since you reject it and do not consider yourselves worthy of eternal life, we now turn to the Gentiles. For this is what the Lord has commanded us: "'I have made you a light for the Gentiles,*
that you may bring salvation to the ends of the earth.'" When the Gentiles heard this, they were glad and honored the word of the Lord; and all who were appointed for eternal life believed. The word of the Lord spread through the whole region

Zeal for Souls: Focus on saving souls and advancing the kingdom of God. Ask God to give you a compassionate heart for souls, and continual revelation of how to draw the people to salvation. Seek him for this every time you prepare to teach and preach and even in your daily life. Look for souls. Look to set the captives free.

Proverbs 11:30 *The fruit of the righteous is a tree of life; and he that wins souls is wise.*

John 18:5 *This is to my Father's glory, that you bear much fruit, showing yourselves to be my disciples.*

Evangelize & Building Quality Believers: Focus on the quality of ministry that builds healthy Godly people, not the quantity of people you have in the pews. Be cognizant to evangelize daily, while spreading the gospel of Jesus Christ and saving souls for his glory, and preach through the well of evangelizing souls. God wants people to be drawn to him so they can live for and through him. Align people with destiny and provide avenues for them to walk in their calling so they can be empowered in their salvation and relationship with the Lord.

Romans 1:16 New International Bible *For I am not ashamed of the gospel, because it is the power of God that brings salvation to everyone who believes: first to the Jew, then to the Gentile. For in the gospel the righteousness of God is revealed – a righteousness that is by faith from first to last, just as it is written: "The righteous will live by faith."*

Ephesians 4:11-14 *And he gave the apostles, the prophets, the evangelists, the shepherds and teachers, to equip the saints for the work of ministry, for building up the body of Christ, until we all attain to the unity of the faith and of the knowledge of the Son of God, to mature manhood to the measure of the stature of the fullness of Christ, so that we may no longer be children, tossed to and fro by the waves and carried about by every wind of doctrine, by human cunning, by craftiness in deceitful schemes.*

Walk People to Wholeness: Know when to be meek, while walking people through a process of wholeness.

> *James 3:13* Who is a wise man and endued with knowledge among you? let him shew out of a good conversation his works with meekness of wisdom.

Be A Living Example: Be the gospel before people. Live as a living example of God's word.

> *Titus 2:7-8* And show your own self in all respects to be a pattern and a model of good deeds and works, teaching what is unadulterated, showing gravity [having the strictest regard for truth and purity of motive], with dignity and seriousness. And let your instruction be sound and fit and wise and wholesome, vigorous and irrefutable and above censure, so that the opponent may be put to shame, finding nothing discrediting or evil to say about us.

Avoid Unnecessary Warfare: Know the difference between persecution that comes for the gospel sake and persecution that comes from error and foolishness. Be wise and discerning in your words and actions, and how you judge and expose sin and character flaws in people's lives. Understand that standing in biblical truth does not mean you can say whatever you want to people, whenever you want, and however you want. Trust the anointing and character of God on your life, and allow it to lead you in breaking yokes off people's lives. Do not get puffed up with pride where you make careless mistakes and inappropriate remarks that causes slander upon you, your ministry, and God. Do not put yourself in situations that cause unnecessary warfare.

> *Proverbs 17:28* Even a fool, when he holdeth his peace, is counted wise: and he that shutteth his lips is esteemed a man of understanding.

Teach People the Application of the Word: Instead of slinging scriptures, religious cliches, and offensive rhetoric at people, teach them how to apply the bible to their daily lives. When they see the word work in and for their lives, they will pursue more deliverance and healing, and a deeper relationship with God, while pursuing and maturing in a destiny lifestyle.

> *Colossians 3:16* Let the word [spoken by] Christ (the Messiah) have its home [in your hearts and minds] and dwell in you in [all its] richness, as you teach and admonish and train one another in all insight and intelligence and wisdom [in spiritual things, and as you sing] psalms and hymns and spiritual songs, making melody to God with [His] grace in your hearts.

> *2Timothy 3:16-17* Every Scripture is God-breathed (given by His inspiration) and profitable for instruction, for reproof and conviction of sin, for correction of error and discipline in obedience, [and] for training in righteousness (in holy living, in conformity

to God's will in thought, purpose, and action), So that the man of God may be complete and proficient, well fitted and thoroughly equipped for every good work.

Teach People Relationship with God: Teach people how to have a personal relationship with the Lord and the Holy Spirit. When people know God and his presence for themselves, they are empowered in their purpose and destiny, and in their ability to live out his word in their daily lives.

>*John 14:26 But the Comforter, which is the Holy Ghost, whom the Father will send in my name, he shall teach you all things, and bring all things to your remembrance, whatsoever I have said unto you.*

Demonstrate With Signs & Wonders: Preach Jesus then follow the word with demonstration. When people see deliverance and healing manifest, they will want to be saved and set free.

>*1Corinthians 2:4 And my speech and my preaching was not with enticing words of man's wisdom, but in demonstration of the Spirit and of power.*

Build Relationship: Fellowship and build relationship with those in your church, Move beyond the four walls of the church. Engage in fellowship and develop relationship with people, the community, businesses and organizations, where people recognize that the church cares about the entire life of people.

>*Hebrews 10:24-25 And let us consider how to stimulate one another to love and good deeds, not forsaking our own assembling together, as is the habit of some, but encouraging one another; and all the more as you see the day drawing near.*

Know Your Remnant: Know your purpose and calling and the remnant you are to minister to. Your remnant will know God's voice in you and will respond, and draw to his word in you. Much of your remnant will be spiritual sons and daughters, and mentees who you are to impart into and raise up to deliver the world and next generation, and help carry the vision God has placed on your life.

>*Romans 12:3-8 For I say, through the grace given unto me, to every man that is among you, not to think of himself more highly than he ought to think; but to think soberly, according as God hath dealt to every man the measure of faith. For as we have many members in one body, and all members have not the same office: So we, being many, are one body in Christ, and every one members one of another. Having then gifts differing according to the grace that is given to us, whether prophecy, let us prophesy according to the proportion of faith; Or ministry, let us wait on our ministering: or he that teacheth, on teaching; Or he that exhorteth, on exhortation: he that giveth, let him do it with simplicity; he that ruleth, with diligence; he that sheweth mercy, with cheerfulness.*

Ephesians 4:16 From him the whole body, joined and held together by every supporting ligament, grows and builds itself up in love, as each part does its work.

Lead with Vision: Seek God for clear vision for the people you are leading, your community, and region, rather than just implementing traditional church structure and doctrine. What do the people you are leading and the community and region you minister in need for God's kingdom to shine, be established, and to successfully advance with signs following.

Proverbs 29:18 *Where there is no vision, the people perish: but he that keepeth the law, happy is he.*

Wisdom with Sharing God's Warnings & Strategies: As leaders God will always give you prophetic words, knowledge, warnings, judgments, and insight into the lives you oversee, and the congregation as a whole. I get a lot of warnings and insight regarding the devils tactics, and what he is up to. The Lord will tell me what the devil is trying to do, or I will just see into his camp. Or I will have dreams and visions that reveal warnings and wisdom keys on how to address these situations. Even though sometimes these words are blatant and straightforward, and some are warnings of death and hardship, I am responsible for what I do with what God reveals to me, and how I present it to the people. Often times, God is showing me so I can pray and stand in the gap with that person or on that matter. Or I will seek him for strategy on how to help that person counter attack that word so that destruction is not their demise. God is redemptive. He is all about reconciling, restoring, and life. His judgment is real and the consequences to our actions are real, but God is all about us living in eternal life with him. Therefore, if the word is of him then there is often a strategy that goes along with that word. Many preachers do not seek God for the strategy. We say we have compassion for people and do not want to see them perish, do we really? Abraham bargained with God for Sodom and Gomorrah (***Genesis 18:16-23***). He was seeking the heart of God for compassion to spare people, even though they were in sin. Many leaders tend to sling the word at people, rather than seeing ourselves as gatekeepers of their lives, and how we can work with God and them to spare redemption. God may not even want the people to know what he said. But many are quick to share dreams and visions, and insight, without considering the entire matter. God may want the people:

- To have the wisdom keys
- To be interceded for in prayer
- To be given a vision plan or strategy for breakthrough, while you walk out the process with them

It is important to ask God so the leader can know what the will of the father is. This is important because many people tend to reject warnings or words with a death sentence because of the misappropriation of grace. It is just the era we live in. We therefore, must use wisdom in being able to reach this generation.

Wisdom with Media Outlets: We have to be wise in what we stream across social media. There are some sermon messages that are for the our personal congregation, and some for the world. Though we have nothing to hide, there are some messages that our congregation would understand that the world at large would find challenging and would not be able to comprehend. This is because we tend to minister to our congregation based on where the members are personally, and where the congregation is as a whole. The world however, may not be ready for that level of intimacy, relationship, and mature meat of the word that you will share with your congregation or ministry. We keep trying to give the world gulps of God that they cannot handle or digest, and it is and will continue to backfire on us. Now that we have these free media world changing platforms, we must use wisdom in when to stream and what to stream, such that we do not bring reproach on ourselves and upon God.

I sense God strongly warning us in this area. I keep having a vision of the government watching our videos and using them to justify the censorships they want to place on what we speak, what we believe, on 501c3's, and stifle other ways there is a separation of church and state. Without wisdom, we will become our own sabotager's in this area. We are so excited and elated with having world wide platforms, until we are not discerning to use those platforms to present God's word in a favorable light that will really transform lives. We are just posting any and everything, and then we are being laughed at and slandered when it is misunderstood or taken out of context.

> **1Corinthians 2:14** *But the natural man receiveth not the things of the Spirit of God: for they are foolishness unto him: neither can he know them, because they are spiritually discerned.*

Awareness Cyber & Media Bullying: Despite there being a law of free speech, cyber and media bullying is used to strip the person of their right to speak their opinion, belief, and to be different. Once the person is the current trending topic, then the cyber and media bullies come to help destroy that person's life. These pathways are used to put the person in an unfavorable light where those who once supported them, and even those who are just now learning who the person is, will give divided opinion, shun, slander, betray, vilify, and ostracize, that person; thus causing a catastrophe and reproach to the person's name, character, career, opportunities, life, and ultimately their destiny. Cyber and media bullying is a controlling spirit seeking to kill the person's purpose and calling.

Cyber bullying has been occurring for years, mostly among youth. Many people, especially youth, have killed themselves due to the trauma of cyber bullying. With the rise of live stream video, and main stream media attempting to sway and control our ideologies, values, and standards, cyber and media bullying has become widespread commonplace. The concept of tolerance, unity, and inclusion is a delusion because change is forced out of trend, fad, fear and abuse, rather that truly respecting one another's differences. We therefore, live in the fantasy of free speech and not the reality of the law. This is only going to get worse with the changing of the presidency, the increase of live stream platforms, and with media outlets having to compete with livestream platforms for the latest hot story.

Cyber and media bullying is really just justified retaliation, revenge, abuse and hatred. Most who engage in it feel it is okay because they have decided the person deserves it or brought it upon themselves. Even as I have encouraged Christians to use wisdom when engaging in live streaming and social media platforms, we must also understand that these avenues are real realms. These are spiritual airways that require responsibility and rule just like our earthly realm. We need to be governing these realms in warfare and intercession, lest we leave ourselves exposed to the devices of the enemy. We must be wise in what we post and live stream, and we must be led of God in how we use the social media platforms for his glory. That way it can stand against any persecution that will come, while not yielding ourselves to unnecessary hardship.

> ***Ephesians 6:12*** *For our struggle is not against flesh and blood, but against the rulers, against the authorities, against the powers of this dark world and against the spiritual forces of evil in the heavenly realms.*

THE LEADER'S REMNANT! VISION OF SPIRITUAL CHILDREN
Chapter 36

A spiritual child is released to the parent by God in an ordained covenant relationship. Spiritual parents are birthed out by God as generational coverings and leaders to oversee and raise up a specific remnant in the earth. Many leaders have a remnant that has been assigned to the anointing and destiny on their lives. These are spiritual children who they are to birth in the spirit, and cover and guide them in their destiny lifestyle.

> *Isaiah 43:6* I will say to the north, 'Give them up!' And to the south, 'Do not keep them back!' Bring My sons from afar, And My daughters from the ends of the earth.

God gives the parent a vision and prototype of the spiritual children he has called them to birth out in the earth. The parent is ordained and anointed to identify and snatch back God's chosen remnant from the enemy, the world, and religion, and walk in covenant relationship with them, so they can be raised up in God's kingdom, blessings, revelation, identity, and destiny for their lives. The covenant relationship between a parent and child is ordained and guided by God.

Children should be seeking God for who their spiritual parent/s are, but the child does not choose their own parent. And parents only identify, claim, and birth out children that God reveal as a part of their remnant. Spiritual parents do not conform to fit the vision of a child, for it is inordinate for a child to birth a parent. God chooses the children and the parent; for them to choose one another is an ordinate man made relationship rather than a God designed relationship that can alter the purpose of that child's destiny and position in the earth.

> *Hebrews 12:7-8 7* If ye endure chastening, God dealeth with you as with sons; for what son is he whom the father chasteneth not? 8 But if ye be without chastisement, whereof all are partakers, then are ye bastards, and not sons.

The spiritual parent aides in birthing, shaping, and molding that child into true sonship with Jesus Christ through chastening.

<u>Chastening is *paideia* in the Greek and means:</u>
1. tutorage, i.e. education or training; by implication, disciplinary correction: — chastening, chastisement, instruction, nurture
2. the whole training and education of children (which relates to the cultivation of mind and morals, and employs for this purpose now commands and admonitions, now reproof and punishment)

3. It also includes the training and care of the body, whatever in adults also cultivates the soul, esp. by correcting mistakes and curbing passions
4. instruction which aims at increasing virtue chastisement
5. chastening, (of the evils with which God visits men for their amendment

Chastening is not just about correcting. It is about instructing, training, educating, nurturing, caring, restoring, enlightening, cultivating, empowering, and bringing discipline and sustaining consistency to a child's journey of sonship with the Lord. God knows what type of chastening a child needs and what parent can effectively nurture and chasten that child.

Children must be willing to embrace and submit under the authority of parenting that God has chosen for them, and parents must accept and properly govern the children God has ordained for them. A true spiritual child will want the truth and authenticity of God. A true spiritual parent will only want the children that have their DNA, are their offspring, that they birthed and labored in the spirit for.

> *Isaiah 61:9* *Then their offspring will be known among the nations, And their descendants in the midst of the peoples. All who see them will recognize them Because they are the offspring whom the LORD has blessed.*

> *Psalms 127:3-5* *Behold, children are a gift of the LORD, The fruit of the womb is a reward. Like arrows in the hand of a warrior, So are the children of one's youth. How blessed is the man whose quiver is full of them; They will not be ashamed When they speak with their enemies in the gate.*

True sons and daughters are revealed by God, then birthed through all manner of prayer and intercession. Once the child and parent come into covenant relationship, the child is continually birthed out in their destiny and cultivated in the likeness and image of sonship unto the Lord. The child is not a clone of their spiritual parent, but will possess their parents' DNA, while maintaining his or her own identity and uniqueness of the Lord Jesus Christ.

> *Galatians 4:19* *My little children, of whom I travail in birth (labor in pain) again until Christ be formed in you.*

The child may have many mentors and teachers, and could very well have another spiritual parent if their parent is unable to birth a part of their destiny, or if birthing in other areas of your walk are needed. Having another parent is rare and is usually (but not always the case), when that ordained parent has altered their course of life in some fashion. If an ordained parent is in alignment with the Lord, then that child should not be looking for, expecting, and never should they choose another parent. Remember the choosing should be God led, for God knows what you have need of. Even as mentors and teachers are revealed, covenant parent/child relationships should not be broken unless, they become idolatrous, inordinate, unhealthy, or detrimental. And in healthy spiritual parent child relationships, the parent should have a voice in who parents into the child.

> **1Corinthians 4:15-17** *For though ye have ten thousand instructors in Christ, yet have ye not many fathers: for in Christ Jesus I have begotten you through the gospel. Wherefore I beseech you, be ye followers of me. For this cause have I sent unto you Timotheus, who is my beloved son, and faithful in the Lord, who shall bring you into remembrance of my ways which be in Christ, as I teach every where in every church.*

Paul was sending Timotheus to teach and oversee as he went abroad to do the work of the Lord. But this did not make Timotheus the father of the Corinthians. Paul was still their father and they were instructed to remain in covenant with him. Paul provided trusting leadership over the Corinthians to which he knew would be able to effectively equip and impart into their lives with pure chastening. This is important as many children will receive chastening from mentors, teachers, prophets, leaders, etc., without consulting their spiritual parent. They will do this out of zeal, hype, etc., and the spiritual parent then ends up having to deliver them from impurities that came with that impartation. That is the reason Paul told the Corinthians that he had to "BIRTH THEM OUT AGAIN!"

> **Galatians 4:15-20 The Amplified Bible** *What has become of that blessed enjoyment and satisfaction and self-congratulation that once was yours [in what I taught you and in your regard for me]? For I bear you witness that you would have torn out your own eyes and have given them to me [to replace mine], if that were possible.*
>
> *Have I then become your enemy by telling the truth to you and dealing sincerely with you?*
> *These men [the Judaizing teachers] are zealously trying to dazzle you [paying court to you, making much of you], but their purpose is not honorable or worthy or for any good. What they want to do is to isolate you [from us who oppose them], so that they may win you over to their side and get you to court their favor.*
>
> *It is always a fine thing [of course] to be zealously sought after [as you are, provided that it is] for a good purpose and done by reason of purity of heart and life, and not just when I am present with you! My little children, for whom I am again suffering birth pangs until Christ is completely and permanently formed (molded) within you, Would that I were with you now and could coax you vocally, for I am fearful and perplexed about you!*

The Corinthians were resistant in receiving truth and being dealt with in a sincere fashion. They waned in their passion for God, and what he was doing and imparting into them, the process he was taking them through, and they began to dishonor and disregard their covenant relationship with Paul. This opened a door to them becoming zealous, dazzled, and drawn away by chastisers who did not properly govern their identity and calling with purity. So they were receiving a tainted gospel whereby they had to be rebirthed in purity through prayer and intercession.

Zealous can be a good thing if it is after God's own heart. It can be a bad thing if it is not governed by God and is focused on man, spiritual acts, personality and charisma, fame, etc. in this case it is idolatrous and dangerous.

<u>Zealous</u> in the Hebrew is z<u>ēloō</u> and means:
1. to have warmth of feeling for or against: — affect, covet (earnestly), (have) desire, (move with) envy, be jealous over, (be) zealous(-ly affect)
2. to burn with zeal
3. to be heated or to boil with envy, hatred, anger
4. in a good sense, to be zealous in the pursuit of good
5. to desire earnestly, pursue, to desire one earnestly, to strive after, busy one's self about him, to exert one's self for one

Really zeal is a burning lust that drives your passion and motives. It is good if it is after God, it is bad if it is not God led, God designed, God ordained.

We are seeing this all over the body of Christ:
- Children being dazzled away from their God ordained parents.
- Parents being dazzled away into a tainted gospel that defiles children.
- Children receiving from teachers, preachers, leaders, mentors, idolatrous or inordinate parents, that are not a part of their God ordained plan, or without being able to adequately separate the fruit from the filth.
- Parents who do not have status and position, but have been ordained by God to oversee that child, being negated for those who do.
- Children resisting truth and sincere chastising for hype, charisma and a puffed up gospel that does not have the character, nature, and purity of the Lord; the devil can counterfeit power, but he cannot counterfeit God's character, nature and purity.
- Parents who are having to rebirth children because they have become zealous and try to become their own parents, and birthed by leading themselves and doing what is right in their own eyes, without resting and journeying in the process and chastising of their spiritual parent/s.

Many believe their zeal - burning drive after spiritual things is of God. But it has no guidance, no purpose, no true submission to God, or to those God has given. And often times ordained spiritual parents are resistant to speaking truth because they are then seen as jealous and controlling. Yet even in the face of reproach and rejection, ordained spiritual parents must be like Paul and speak truth and yield sincere chastisement in love. Even if the child breaks covenant and leaves the relationship, we must understand that sometimes we must allow children to stray, while we stand in proxy and war for their souls and destinies until the prodigals return. But we must not silence truth and true chastening, such that the child thinks his or her inordinate zeal is of the Lord.

***1Timothy 1:18-20 The Message Bible** I'm passing this work on to you, my son Timothy. The prophetic word that was directed to you prepared us for this. All those prayers are coming together now so you will do this well, fearless in your struggle, keeping a firm grip on your faith and on yourself. After all, this is a fight we're in. There are some, you know, who by relaxing their grip and thinking anything goes have made a thorough mess of their faith. Hymenaeus and Alexander are two of them. I let them wander off to Satan to be taught a lesson or two about not blaspheming.*

Spiritual children need a clear revelation of the DNA that their parents possess so they can know what they have in them, and the reason they are aligned for a strategic purpose and well of sonship.

I will admit that I personally, yet ignorantly have tried to adopt potential. Due to having the eyes of God, I see potential in everyone, and I see the potential Kingdom Shifter in many that have crossed my path. Potential however, does not equal reality and does not mean covenant. I also will admit that the apostolic counselor in me wants to save this generation. But I have learned that I must have a clear revelation of my spiritual DNA and who has it. I must know who are the Kingdom Shifters I am ordained to raise up for God's glory and kingdom advancement.

Many will appear to have my DNA due to their peculiarity and bold rebel like anointing. The key for me is whether they are committed to walking in covenant with me and submitted to learning and growing in Godly relationship with me. They will not rebel or be resistant, but will embrace our covenant and the process it entails. Many want covenant and want destiny but not process. Process is key to me raising up Kingdom Shifters that can sustain in destiny and produce fruit that remains until JESUS returns. As a spiritual parent you have to find your key to unlock the discernment needed to identify your remnant.

My spiritual sons and daughters have my DNA. They are Kingdom Shifters that live a lifestyle of stability and maturity in the Lord and flow through the wells of all manner of prayer, warfare, deliverance, healing, miracles, signs and wonders, and worship. They have an unquenchable love for prayer and the word, as these are an enjoyable hobby that they tend to choose over anything else in life. My spiritual children have a relentless drive to live "in Christ." They are sold out to their calling, and are grounded and focused in sustaining a lifestyle relationship of intimacy, truth, and sonship "in Christ;" abiding in him and letting everything flow in their identity in him.

A true spiritual son and daughter of mine:

1. Knows their identity and will not waver in what God has said for their life.
2. Are destiny driven and everything they do aligns with the destiny God has ordained for their lives.
3. Lover and pursuer of personal deliverance, healing and wellness.

4. Visionaries; have vision for their lives, generations, ministries, relationships; they think big and dream big.
5. Full of God, constantly in pursuit of God, full of faith, full of glory and power; glory carriers and glory cultivators and producers.
6. Naturally smart and intelligent.
7. Possess the counsel, knowledge, revelation, and wisdom of God beyond their years.
8. Possess strict standards that enable them to sustain in destiny.
9. Live a lifestyle of fasting and consecration; fast and consecrate without being directed.
10. Possess a spirit and lifestyle of excellence.
11. Love purity, virtue, righteousness, holiness and Godly truth; are role models of these characteristics.
12. Love the unlovable; are passionate and compassionate.
13. Have and continually cultivate the character and nature of God on their lives.
14. Meek and temperate; not easily angered and offended; forgiving; some will have to grow into this due to combating unresolved and stuffed anger.
15. Quick to apologize and accept responsibility for their actions.
16. Have a repenting heart and welcome the conviction and chastisement of the Holy Spirit; embrace constructive criticism.
17. Humble but a bit cocky; will have to remain submitted to God so they won't yield to pride.
18. Long suffering; can weather times and seasons and not quit or despise God, their calling, or the work he has granted to their hands.
19. Battering rams; values the process and contending for God's will and plan concerning a matter.
20. Effective communicators, and live a life of transparency despite being difficult to understand due to the complexity of the anointing of their lives.
21. Are worshippers and praisers; will never build a high place regarding spiritual experiences, but always seeking to go deeper and higher in worship, praise and encountering God.
22. Live from heavenly realms; can appear peculiar and weird; have wild and weird encounters with God and demons that others will not understand; will have to be cautious with not giving into flightiness and witchcraft due to the ability to journey in the spirit realm; will use this information to bring heaven to earth, deliver people, ministries, communities, regions and nations.
23. Move by the spirit, timing and seasons of God; Not afraid to transition into greater things and operate in the momentum and movement of God.
24. Are Kingdom Shifters; their very presence shifts atmospheres, climates, environments and regions; they impact all they are a part of simply by being present.
25. Are curse breakers; some are Kingdom Heirs to their generation; they have been called to restore the kingdom and blessing of God back into their family line.
26. Are blessers and givers; not stingy, not self absorbed; self-sacrificing.
27. A rising remnant called to SHIFT this world into the kingdom of God.

28. Spiritually and naturally beautiful, while possessing distinct qualities physically and spiritually that cause them to stand out among crowds and peers; they do not fit in, do not try to fit in, and are okay with not fitting into the status quo; uniquely stylish.
29. Discerners of darkness and light: can see, sense, hear, smell, feel darkness and light; can hear, sense and see God all around them; know when Devils are present.
30. Has prophetic and revelatory dreams and visions.
31. Spiritual surgeons in the area of prayer; able to strategically bring deliverance, healing, and breakthrough via prayer.
32. Are valiantly skilled, strategic warriors and demon busters; they hate devils and are always looking to beat a devil down; they are fearless, fierce, bold, confident, and pursue continual knowledge and skill in spiritual warfare, intercession and walking in their authority over all powers of darkness; judge principalities and powers.
33. Fight witches and warlocks; convert them and judge them as necessary.
34. Keenly walk in their spiritual gifts and/or fivefold ministry calling; able to impart gifts into others and to equip others in their calling and destiny.
35. Spiritual and natural producers, reproducers and multipliers.
36. Are teachable, life long learners, and eager to be trained and equipped in their gifts, callings and on the destiny call on their lives.
37. Scribes; long winded; love to journal; receives in-depth revelation from the scriptures, their personal studies, and time with the Lord.
38. Have a heart for the regions and nations God has called them to; some may be gatekeepers of regions and nations depending on their calling.
39. Have a heart for their current generation, generation next, and future generations; are committed to building their family lineage, generation, and the ministry with a future mandate that can sustain until Jesus returns.
40. Kingdom minded; hate religion; They possess a righteous indignation for it and rebel against it.
41. Love what God loves, hate what God hates.
42. Risk takers, walk in faith; will step out even if they are afraid.
43. Love all people; not racist, not prejudice; possess the eyes of God where they can see people like he sees them.
44. Love to laugh; love to have fun, may be quick witted; will have to guard their tongue due to being quick witted.
45. Love time alone and time with God; prefers this at times over fellowship with people.
46. Hate to see people in bondage; look to perform miracles, bring healing, salvation, and encouragement.
47. Empowering and refreshing to all those they encounter.
48. Understand who they are as a son or daughter.
49. Protective of the ministry, and their relationship with me.

50. They are honoring of their natural family and parents, and understand that though I may restore and impart certain things in this area, I can never replace or usurp their natural family and parents.
51. Covenant keepers; honoring; they will not dishonor me or replace covenant with me over seasonal mentoring and training; they are be accountable to covenant while embracing other covenant and mentoring relationships that are necessary for their personal growth and development.
52. Will not pimp the ministry or pimp me.
53. Recognize that they have something to pour into me; prays for me; balanced in giving and receiving in our relationship.
54. Embracing of their other spiritual siblings; open to cultivating covenant relationships with them.
55. Resist coveting and jealousy while recognizing and valuing who they are to me and who their siblings are to me.

Not Necessarily the Case:
- Impartation does not equal a spiritual parent and child relationship.
- Teaching, training, mentoring does not equal a spiritual parent and child relationship.
- Being ordained and licensed by someone does not equate to a spiritual parent and child relationship.
- Being pastored by someone or attending a church does not equate to a spiritual parent and child relationship.
- Operating in gifts and works does not equate to a spiritual parent and child relationship.

God Made Versus Man Made Covenant Relationship:
- Did God ordain it; is God the beginning, center, head, and governor of it?
- Did God design it; is it personal and tailor made to your identity and calling?
- Did God reveal it; did you decide what you needed and went after it, or did you seek God about what you needed and he guided you to it?
- Did God confirm it; is God's seal of approval on it; is he pleased with the relationship; did you ask him; even if he said you were to learn and be trained, did he confirm it as a parent/child covenant relationship or you just assumed that?
- Is your character and nature being challenged and shaped into God's image; does your character match your calling; can your character sustain your destiny?
- Does your the leader/parent tell you to have good character while theirs is flawed, mixed, wavering, and/or ungodly; do as I say not as I do? Remember they can say the right things, but you are receiving impartations of what they SAY AND DO.
- Does it align with your gifts, calling and destiny; Does it provide clear vision and a clear processing to your gifts, calling and destiny; are you working on a clear vision plan that unveils and releases your destiny, or are you just participating in

man's works while confused or blinded in what your purpose is; while your destiny is shelved; while you fear aligning with destiny?
- Does it empower your gifts, calling and destiny; are you growing, are you submitted to process and training so you can grow; are you being empowered in your identity and destiny, and provided training and avenues to be who God called you to be?
- Is it pure; is there not only power, miracles, signs and wonders, but the pure character, nature, holiness, and virtue of God? The devil mimics power but despises purity.
- Are you being nurtured; nurturing is intimate. It cannot be done from a pulpit, a video or cd of your favorite speaker, a gathering, social media stalking I mean fellowshipping, etc.; nurturing involves personal rearing, upbringing, training, educating, equipping, support encouragement, cultivation; personal feeding and protection where one is actually nourishing off the bossom (spirit) of another; you are receiving nutrients that can only come from intimate one to one interaction with that person; are you being nurtured?
- Are you doing life with this person? Mentorship tends to be seasonal; impartation and training is fleeting and intermediate; me seeing you on Sunday when you preach, or on Wednesday during bible study is not us doing life together; do you promote and embrace doing life together; Jesus spent quality time pouring himself into his disciples.
- Empowered identity; Is there a genuine concern for who you are personally or are you just a seduced number - notch in the belt? Is there a strategic plan for your personal welfare, deliverance, and healing, or a general formula for everyone to follow?
- Fruitful impartation; can you remain stable and grounded with a firm grip in the faith, through what is being imparted into you? Are you faithful and fearless despite struggle? Or are you tossed to and fro by life challenges, your desires, emotions?
- Zeal or DNA; are you dazzled by fame, giftings, charisma, peculiarity, potential, what you wish you were or fear you will never achieve or do they have your DNA?
- Do you have unfulfilled momma and daddy issues? This is important to know as this needs to be put in proper place so you can adequately discern who your parents are. If you are driven by unhealed and unfulfilled parenting voids, you are subject to be seduced into relationships that are not God ordained, idolatrous, inordinate, unhealthy, dangerous and detrimental.
- Do you have child issues, sheep issues, numbers issues? As if so, you will prey on people to fill your void for children, void for folks to oversee, and void to fill the pews.

Exploration:
1. What is the DNA of your spiritual children?
2. Share your DNA revelation with the spiritual children you are sure have it. Ask them to journal and share their thoughts regarding what was revealed.
3. Are you in any relationships with children that do not have your DNA? What do those relationships entail? Ask God for direction on how to address these relationships.
4. If you are a spiritual child, do you know and have your spiritual parent's DNA?
5. What is the purpose of your covenant relationship?
6. What needs to improve to make your covenant relationship with each spiritual child more healthy, Godly, and destiny focused? If you are a spiritual child answer this question as well.

UNDERSTANDING PLATFORMS

Chapter 37
(Written By: Nina Cook)

With the release of social media platforms and the rise of market place ministry, the self-establishing of platforms has become a new fad and move in the body of Christ. This is not only a new move and fad, but there is a hidden agenda driven by the spirits of pride, haughtiness, dishonor, and idolatry, that are striving to enmesh themselves in the current and upcoming generation, while perverting their true callings, purposes, and identities. These spirits want to embed themselves in our identities, and in our callings, and desensitize the word, will, and plan of God for our lives. The deceiving success, achievement, and drawing of an audience that comes from the self-made platforms will be seen as God's favor and blessing, and become the example of what walking in destiny and calling looks like. It will be the display and picture of success, but it will surely be untrue. People will begin to view this as an example of reaching the masses, and how they should walk in the fullness of God's calling and ordination for their lives. This is, and will be detrimental to an entire generation of those who were originally appointed as God's leaders, remnant rising, and kingdom shifters, but sold the truth of God for a lie, yet, still believe that they are in God's will.

- There will be an abundance of ministry and opportunities, but not a lot of God's ministry and Godly opportunities.
- There will be a an abundance of platforms, but not a lot of God's platforms.
- There will be a whole lot of voices and word proclaimed, but not a lot of God's voice and word being released in the earth.

It is pressing that we become aware of the deceit of self-made platforms, so that idolatry does not find place in our lives, ministries, and churches. As we become aware, we can stay in a alignment with God's will and process of maturity and growing in destiny, such that we live and thrive on God's ordained platform for our lives.

We must understand that we were not designed to create our own platforms. That is God's job.

> ***Isaiah 64:8*** *But now, O LORD, thou art our father; we are the clay, and thou our potter; and we all are the work of thy hand.*

> ***New Living Bible*** *And yet, O LORD, you are our Father. We are the clay, and you are the potter. We all are formed by your hand.*

He is the potter and we are the clay. In creating our own platforms, we become our own potter. We form ourselves in what we want, see, desire and aspire after, and/or what we think is God. It is like the clay saying to the potter *"make me this,"* when truly only the potter can decide what the creation is to be. We are the work of his hands and not of our own. Although you could be very well be fit and successful on the platform that you create, since it was not by God's positioning and design, it is not God's platform. It also could be your time to be elevated and platformed, but if God does not do it and you took matters into your own hands, you have thwarted and aborted what he had for you. You chose to be your potter, thus deeming it better than what God had.

The scripture says *"we all are formed by your hand."* In creating your own platform you:
- Remove yourself from the hand of God and position yourself in your own hand.
- Are no longer in the form (design, fashion, and embodiment) of God for your life.
- Although you present yourself as being in God, you are in your own form, which is idolatry, as a new image has been created.
- You and your platform become your own graven image.
- You become the clay and also the potter, which is a distortion of the order of God.

Jesus did not create his own platform and he is God. God sent him and created the platform for him.

> ***John 3:17*** *For God sent not his Son into the world to condemn the world; but that the world through him might be saved.*

Jesus was sent by God, given an assignment, and placed on a world wide platform to to fulfill this ordained purpose. You cannot establish yourself on your own platform, as the purpose of a platform is to fulfill a specific assignment. So since God is the only one who has the power to provide an assignment on our lives, he also is the only one who can position us on the platform to fulfill it. If you create your own platform, please know that your assignment is also self-created. Many believe that they are doing the work of the Lord, but the true work of the Lord can only be completed by the leading and the assigning of the Lord.

When Jesus was on the cross he cried out to God *"why hast thou forsaken me,"* which lets us know that for the sake of us obtaining salvation (the assignment), God placed Jesus upon the cross (the platform). In this instance, he was speaking to God as he endured the weight of the assignment on the platform. So this lets us know that God platformed Jesus.

> ***Matthew 27:46*** *And about the ninth hour Jesus cried with a loud voice, saying, Eli, Eli, lama sabachthani? that is to say, My God, my God, why hast thou forsaken me?*

We also read about Jesus in the garden of Gethsemane asking for God to take his cup from him. He was speaking of the cross. He then continues on to say *"not my will but your will be done Lord,"* Jesus understood that the platform was created by God, it was the will of God.

> *Luke 22:42 Saying, Father, if thou be willing, remove this cup from me: nevertheless not my will, but thine, be done.*

In creating our own platforms we are in our own will and not the will of God. The platform must be the will of God for your life. Jesus submitted to God's will, so that he could complete his assignment and glorify the father. He drank the cup that was presented before him, and that cup was representative of his God given assignment.

<u>Cup</u> in the Strong's in this scripture means:
1. a lot, or fate
2. one's lot or experience, whether joyous or adverse, divine appointments, whether favourable or unfavourable, are likened to a cup which God presents one to drink: so of prosperity and adversity

God's platform will place a cup before you that will present to you your lot, fate, and portion, in both its prosperities and it adversities. Drinking the cup of your experiences and divine appointments in the will of God is like digesting the sacrifice of letting go of your will and desires, for the fulfilling of God's will and plan for your life. It is like drinking the cost of all that pertains to your platform. Jesus' platform cost him his life. What does your platform cost you? Though we sacrifice true identity and destiny, as we create our own platforms, they cost us nothing naturally, but spiritually they cost us everything. God's platform will cause us to drink our portion in both its prosperities and adversities, both the good and the bad. But on self-made platforms only the good, blessings, favor, increases, glamour, and etc. are displayed; which then gives a false perception that it truly is of God, when God has not orchestrated or approved it.

Platforms Are Not of Our Own Accord
Jesus continually said that he was not here on earth on his own accord, but he was here on his Father's accord. When we create our own platform we are there on our own accord.

> *John 12:49 For I have not spoken of myself; but the Father which sent me, he gave me a commandment, what I should say, and what I should speak.*

On God's platform for our lives he tells us what to say, and do, and he teaches us how to live, act, process, progress, maintain, and sustain. All things have holy, pure, and righteous standards since everything is being done on God's accord and through his will. As we create our own platforms, on our own accord, there tends to be no clear set of standards of purity, and of what is holy. We do not have God or anyone leading and guiding us in the governing of the platform. This is why we see so many ungodly things being done and said on these platforms, and this is also why the standards of purity and holiness are dwindling, while becoming mixed with things of the flesh and world. As we become the platform creators, we make up our own standards by replacing what God has already established. We in turn, lead all of those who are following us and receiving from our platform astray or into mixture.

Those following you begin to come into alignment and agreement with you. And you begin to produce after your own kind, rather than producing after the likeness of God. So those who are following the ministry are then filled with this same spirit of idolatry and self-focus. This effects and infects our followers, and leads them away from their authentic destiny and calling, into ungodly standards and worldly mixture. We draw people away from God, which results into thwarted and aborted destinies.

As I thought about this concept I realized that no one in the bible created their own platform by God's design. There have been people in the bible who have tried to, but death and destruction became there demise, and even the destruction of their generations and lineage. Saul tried it, Jezebel tried it, Athaliah tried it, and God killed them all. Saul before he became the Apostle Paul also tried it. He thought he was in the will of God, killing people for God's sake. He had his own platform of killing God's people and he felt strong and justified in it. But God knocked him off of his high horse and blinded him *(Acts 9)*. He was killed spiritually, then resurrected with a new vision. He became accountable to the leadership God placed over him, the other apostles, received deliverance and clarity about his purpose, and then he was platformed.

Apostle Paul:

Acts 8:3 As for Saul, he made havock of the church, entering into every house, and haling men and women committed them to prison.

Acts 9:3-18 And as he journeyed, he came near Damascus: and suddenly there shined round about him a light from heaven: And he fell to the earth, and heard a voice saying unto him, Saul, Saul, why persecutest thou me? And he said, Who art thou, Lord? And the Lord said, I am Jesus whom thou persecutest: it is hard for thee to kick against the pricks. And he trembling and astonished said, Lord, what wilt thou have me to do? And the Lord said unto him, Arise, and go into the city, and it shall be told thee what thou must do. And the men which journeyed with him stood speechless, hearing a voice, but seeing no man. And Saul arose from the earth; and when his eyes were opened, he saw no man: but they led him by the hand, and brought him into Damascus. And he was three days without sight, and neither did eat nor drink.

And there was a certain disciple at Damascus, named Ananias; and to him said the Lord in a vision, Ananias. And he said, Behold, I am here, Lord. And the Lord said unto him, Arise, and go into the street which is called Straight, and enquire in the house of Judas for one called Saul, of Tarsus: for, behold, he prayeth, And hath seen in a vision a man named Ananias coming in, and putting his hand on him, that he might receive his sight. Then Ananias answered, Lord, I have heard by many of this man, how much evil he hath done to thy saints at Jerusalem: And here he hath authority from the chief priests to bind all that call on thy name. But the Lord said unto him, Go thy way: for he is a chosen vessel unto me, to bear my name before the Gentiles, and kings, and the children of Israel: For I will shew him how great things he must suffer for my name's sake. And Ananias went his way, and entered into the house; and putting his hands on him said, Brother Saul, the Lord, even Jesus, that appeared unto thee in the way as thou camest, hath sent me, that thou mightest receive thy sight, and be filled with the Holy Ghost. And immediately there fell from his eyes as it had been scales: and he received sight forthwith, and arose, and was baptized.

Acts 9:26-27 *And when Saul was come to Jerusalem, he assayed to join himself to the disciples: but they were all afraid of him, and believed not that he was a disciple. But Barnabas took him, and brought him to the apostles, and declared unto them how he had seen the Lord in the way, and that he had spoken to him, and how he had preached boldly at Damascus in the name of Jesus.*

Saul who is also Paul, was on the platform of killing many all while persecuting Jesus. God stopped him in his tracks and gave him a new vision to fulfill his true will in the earth.

King Saul:

1 Samuel 15:2-3 *Thus saith the LORD of hosts, I remember that which Amalek did to Israel, how he laid wait for him in the way, when he came up from Egypt. Now go and smite Amalek, and utterly destroy all that they have, and spare them not; but slay both man and woman, infant and suckling, ox and sheep, camel and ass.*

1 Samuel 15:7-9 *And Saul smote the Amalekites from Havilah until thou comest to Shur, that is over against Egypt. And he took Agag the king of the Amalekites alive, and utterly destroyed all the people with the edge of the sword. But Saul and the people spared Agag, and the best of the sheep, and of the oxen, and of the fatlings, and the lambs, and all that was good, and would not utterly destroy them: but every thing that was vile and refuse, that they destroyed utterly.*

1 Samuel 15:13-22 *And Samuel came to Saul: and Saul said unto him, Blessed be thou of the LORD: I have performed the commandment of the LORD. And Samuel said, What meaneth then this bleating of the sheep in mine ears, and the lowing of the oxen which I hear? And Saul said, They have brought them from the Amalekites: for the people spared the best of the sheep and of the oxen, to sacrifice unto the LORD thy God; and the rest we have utterly destroyed. Then Samuel said unto Saul, Stay, and I will tell thee what the LORD hath said to me this night. And he said unto him, Say on. And Samuel said,*

> *When thou wast little in thine own sight, wast thou not made the head of the tribes of Israel, and the LORD anointed thee king over Israel?*
>
> *And the LORD sent thee on a journey, and said, Go and utterly destroy the sinners the Amalekites, and fight against them until they be consumed. Wherefore then didst thou not obey the voice of the LORD, but didst fly upon the spoil, and didst evil in the sight of the LORD? And Saul said unto Samuel, Yea, I have obeyed the voice of the LORD, and have gone the way which the LORD sent me, and have brought Agag the king of Amalek, and have utterly destroyed the Amalekites. But the people took of the spoil, sheep and oxen, the chief of the things which should have been utterly destroyed, to sacrifice unto the LORD thy God in Gilgal. And Samuel said, Hath the LORD as great delight in burnt offerings and sacrifices, as in obeying the voice of the LORD? Behold, to obey is better than sacrifice, and to hearken than the fat of rams.*

Saul was disobedient to the Lord's commands, and then tried to say that it was to present a sacrifice to the Lord when it was just blatant rebellion. He had created his own platform before the people by following his own directions and not the directions that were given to him by the Lord. This cost him the throne, his kingdom, and his destiny.

Jezebel:

> **1 Kings 21:3-7** *And Naboth said to Ahab, The LORD forbid it me, that I should give the inheritance of my fathers unto thee. And Ahab came into his house heavy and displeased because of the word which Naboth the Jezreelite had spoken to him: for he had said, I will not give thee the inheritance of my fathers. And he laid him down upon his bed, and turned away his face, and would eat no bread. But Jezebel his wife came to him, and said unto him, Why is thy spirit so sad, that thou eatest no bread? And he said unto her, Because I spake unto Naboth the Jezreelite, and said unto him, Give me thy vineyard for money; or else, if it please thee, I will give thee another vineyard for it: and he answered, I will not give thee my vineyard. And Jezebel his wife said unto him, Dost thou now govern the kingdom of Israel? arise, and eat bread, and let thine heart be merry: I will give thee the vineyard of Naboth the Jezreelite.*

Jezebel had her own platform of manipulation, control, and idolatry. She usurped God and her husband, as she used her husband's throne to push her own idolatrous self-willed agenda. As we create our own platforms, we become susceptible to this spirit operating in our lives. We become controlling and manipulative at all cost to gain and receive what we want on these self-made platforms.

Athaliah:

> *2 Kings 11:1-3 And when Athaliah the mother of Ahaziah saw that her son was dead, she arose and destroyed all the seed royal. But Jehosheba, the daughter of king Joram, sister of Ahaziah, took Joash the son of Ahaziah, and stole him from among the king's sons which were slain; and they hid him, even him and his nurse, in the bedchamber from Athaliah, so that he was not slain. And he was with her hid in the house of the LORD six years. And Athaliah did reign over the land.*

> *2 Kings 11:12-16 And he brought forth the king's son, and put the crown upon him, and gave him the testimony; and they made him king, and anointed him; and they clapped their hands, and said, God save the king. And when Athaliah heard the noise of the guard and of the people, she came to the people into the temple of the LORD. And when she looked, behold, the king stood by a pillar, as the manner was, and the princes and the trumpeters by the king, and all the people of the land rejoiced, and blew with trumpets: and Athaliah rent her clothes, and cried, Treason, Treason. But Jehoiada the priest commanded the captains of the hundreds, the officers of the host, and said unto them, Have her forth without the ranges: and him that followeth her kill with the sword. For the priest had said, Let her not be slain in the house of the LORD. And they laid hands on her; and she went by the way by the which the horses came into the king's house: and there was she slain.*

Athaliah killed all of the royal seed, an entire generational line to reign on her own self-made platform. She killed them, thus killing their inherited platform of rulership, so she could rule in their stead. As we create our own platforms, not only does it destroy us, but it will destroy our seed and lineage. It makes the rest of the generation susceptible to the destiny killing spirit and spirit of generational sabotage.

In each of the instances above, the people created their own platforms because of idolatry, and a desire to fulfill their own visions and purposes. It had nothing to do with God. So we have to be careful of creating these platforms and then saying that it is God, as he will kill what he is not a part of.

When the platform is created and we position ourselves on it, there is an expectation for God to fund the platform. We expect God to give us words, direction, and wisdom so that we can be presented as anointed and powerful. Yet, we have exalted ourselves above God, and must operate in talent and gifting, rather than purpose and destiny, to appear that God is in it. Gifts are without repentance and will produce if we work them. But they will not produce purpose without God. If God did not platform you, he will not stand on your platform with you. You will be running on the fumes of your fire, passion, and gifting, rather than being truly positioned, and set a part in your calling and purpose.

I believe in this generation, some of the reason we are creating our own platforms is because of the spirits of rebellion, pride, and entitlement that are ruling and running rampant. There have been many things occurring in our world and society within these last few years that have left many feeling voiceless, angry, and enraged, and so there is a need to get our voices heard, and a sense of entitlement to be heard. But it is about getting our own voices heard and not the voice of God. It is not really about God. It is about being able to finally speak up, and feeling entitled to a soapbox since there has been so much wrongdoing and injustice occurring around the world. It is more about the person, rather than doing the will and work of the Lord. And the platform has become a high place to complete a self-motivated agenda. These ruling spirits of the world and society are taking over those in the body of Christ, and causing many to feel that they are entitled to speak their truth and be heard, rather than truly being about the rule and kingdom of God being established in the earth through their platform.

Sometimes we are creating these platforms because we are being abused, misused, and overlooked in our churches and the anointing, fire, and calling of the Lord is burning upon us, and we are looking for a way to release it and do what we feel the Lord is saying to us. Although we may mean well in wanting to do what God has put on us to do, as we learned about earlier in this chapter there is still a divine order and code of honor where God the potter, creates the platform. If your leaders, spiritual fathers and mothers, are not allowing you to be released and they are not positioning you on the platform that God has ordained for your life, then evaluate if those are the leaders for you, and if they are truly your spiritual mothers or fathers. Not all cases are the same, but if you feel that it is time for you to be elevated in your calling and assignment of the Lord that is on your life, this is something that should be discussed with your leaders, spiritual mothers and fathers, and or those who have rule over you. They can search this out with you, help you receive direction and instruction from the Lord on what this looks like for your life, and how they can cover and help birth you forth. Genuine leaders and spiritual parents will have clear and keen vision for you, and they will be willing and ready to release you as God leads, and as you share with them what God is saying to you.

Many times as a spiritual parent, or leader they will already know and can be a source of confirmation and push into further motion and elevation in fulfilling your calling and purpose. If they are not willing to search who you are in the Lord, what your destiny and calling is, and they have no desire to ever elevate you beyond sitting on a pew and eating from their tree, it would be good to ask the Lord whether or not they are your spiritual parent, leader, or not. If they do not have vision for your life, cannot adequately uplift and empower you in who you are, and have no ability to birth you out spiritually, they cannot be your God ordained spiritual parents. They may be nice and powerfully anointed people, but they do not have the womb for you. Parents have both the seed and the womb that helps to produce you and birth you forth in what the Lord is saying. If they are not doing this and they have never birthed you in anything, this is proof that they are not your true mother, father, or leader. And even with all of this being said, if this is what is happening or has happened to you, this does not justify means for creating your own platform. This however, does justify means of searching with God who your true leader, and spiritual parents are, so that God can align you with them. If you do not seek him for revelation, you will either die where you are under those leaders and parents, or you will die on the platform that you create. As once you get up on your man-made platform you will not be able to birth yourself so eventually you will die. If you have leaders and parents who do not have the vision for you and are not birthing you, it is ok to ask God to position you where you need to be so that you can be birthed, elevated, and platformed in fulfilling his calling and purpose on your life.

Also, if you have leaders or mothers and fathers who are in name only this too is not means for justification in creating your own platform, and then contending that the *in name only leader* is covering you and your ministry. As typically, this is not true for in name only leaders, mothers, and or fathers. In name only coverings are not truly consistently birthing you through prayer and intercession, holding you accountable, correcting and encouraging you, and walking in close relationship with you. They do not have the full vision of who you are. When you get up on the platform and begin to make mistakes and have challenges, that person is not in a true covenant and accountability relationship with you. They will not be able to help steer, direct you, and sustain you in a platform that they have no authority over, as they have no true authority over you in the spirit because they did not birth you. Just like Adam needed a help meet, and every other ordained person in the bible, needed others to cover and walk with them, you need more than God to journey with you in destiny. He orchestrated our lives so we would need covenant relationships to achieve destiny.

> ***Genesis 2:18*** *And the LORD God said, It is not good that the man should be alone; I will make him an help meet for him.*

Adam was in the perfect garden before sin, and God said that it was not good for him to be alone so he provided him a much needed help meet. No matter how good or how perfect things seem to be, God still has designed and ordained people to your life to help you walk in and fulfill his call on your life. There is a leader and a spiritual momma and or daddy for you, who will honor you and do for you what God wants them to so that you can be elevated on the platform God has for you. Resist the temptation to create your own, and take your time in allowing God to lead you to where you need to be in order to be platformed. God's purposes stand, so if God has purposed it, it will happen.

> ***Proverbs 19:21 The Amplified Bible*** *Many plans are in a man's mind, But it is the LORD'S purpose for him that will stand (be carried out).*

Trust God and remain in a place of honoring him and his will for your life, while keeping the fire in your belly pure to do what thus saint the Lord. Resist yielding to an impure fire, impatiently lusting and burning for the platform for one's own sake.

If we allow God to elevate us in our destiny and calling, we will come into the unique, rare, one of a kind, tailor-made platform, that was created for us individually. In this time a lot of people's ministries and platforms are beginning to look the same because we are creating them after our own images and the likenesses of what we see, want and desire. Outside of God, our creative abilities are limited as this is an attribute in our DNA that we only get from God. As we allow God to platform us, we will discover the genuine authenticity of who we were created to be. We will be able to tremendously effect and impact all that we were called to by his power resting on us, as we complete his will and not our own, for HIS glory.

Guard Your Trading Floors

As you infiltrate the world's system, be cognizant of your trading floors. Trading floors are essentially altars. Be aware of what you agree with, sacrifice to, and sow into. When we think of altars, especially demonic altars, we tend to think they are built in a specific location, and you have to actually go to that location to offer up a sacrifice. However, it is important to realize that altars are platforms.

Dictionary.com defines *altar* as:
1. an elevated place or structure, as a mound or platform, at which religious rites are performed or on which sacrifices are offered to gods, ancestors, etc.
2. a table or flat-topped block used as the focus for a religious ritual, especially for making sacrifices or offerings to a deity

Wikipedia defines altars (Hebrew: *mizbe'ah*) *"a place of slaughter or sacrifice."*

Biblestudytools.com states that, particularly in the Old Testament: *"Altars were places where the divine and human worlds interacted. Altars were places of exchange, communication, and influence. God responded actively to altar activity. Altars could be natural objects or man-made constructs. Sacrifices were the primary medium of exchange in altar interactions. Sacrifices was the essential act of external worship. Unlike idol gods, the Yahweh God, did not need sacrifice to survive. The New Testament write of Hebrews 13:10 implies that the ultimate altar is the cross. Here divine and human interchange is consummated. The cross becomes the sanctuary of the believer, providing protection from the penalties of sin."*

Essentially altars are a place of worship, sacrifice, atonement, and redemption. The God of the altar governs your life and offered safety, health, wealth, and happiness in exchange for your worship and sacrifice.

In the New Testament, Jesus became the ultimate sacrifice, therefore the stationary altar became a moving platform, where we can now trade in worship and sacrifice with God through relationship with him.

From this revelation, we discern that an altar aka platform is not just a constructed area. It is any avenue where a person can voice an agenda or expose an agenda for a particular purpose. When these agendas are released, it services as a sacrifice being offered on the altar of that platform. The purpose or origin of that agenda determines what God is being sacrificed upon that altar. A transaction then occurs between the person and that God to which that altar belong. The person thus trade what they sacrifice for what that deity is releasing in their life through that agenda.

Even if you say you serve the true and living God, there no way to agree, sacrifice unto, or sow into, an altar that does not serve his kingdom agenda and still contend you do not serve an idol god. You have just eluded into strange fire and mixture whether you want to admit it or not.

TV, commercials, social media, the internet, ad displays at stores, clothing, your job, your career, etc., are all platforms. They are all altars designed to get our attention and get us to buy into and trade our time, money, morals, beliefs, destiny, life, heritage, etc. for their product. Sadly because these platforms are self-serving altars or demonic altars, if we are not careful, we can open up gateways for idolatry, pornography, perversion and the anti-christ agenda to constantly seep into our lives. And depending on what we take in and give ourselves to, we end up sacrificing unto idol gods, and trading the hedge of God for demonic attacks, strongholds, and influences of the enemy.

Also if we have platforms in these arenas, we must make sure our platform is rooted in God, such that what we promote and release from God's glorifies and offers up sacrifices unto him.

For example:
Your facebook page is a platform. What you like, comment on, share, write, allow on your page, determines what God you are sacrificing unto at the time. Because there is so much being released on facebook, many tend to have a lot of mixture and be desensitized to many videos, statuses, pictures, etc., that do not glorify God. We have to be careful that our likes, shares and comments have not giving way to trading on altars that are not of God. We also have to be careful that we do not yield our page to idolatry, pornography, and perversion.

We do not realize it, but when we are watching things on TV or listening to vile music that are rooted in perversion and idolatry, we are sacrificing our purity, dream realm, sleep realm, unto idolatry. These platforms are meant to confuse us or make use desensitized to sin and demonic infiltration. This gives demons the avenue to fill us with lustful thoughts and desires, sleep with us in our dreams where they are sexually molesting and raping us as we sleep, get us to compromise the word of God and make light of issues that hold us in bondage. A trade is occurring on the altar whether we like it or not, whether we acknowledge it or not, whether we agree to it or not. It is a platform, therefore, it is an altar where transactions are being done between you and that agenda.

Examples of trading in the Bible:
- Adam and Eve traded eternal life for the knowledge of good and evil *Genesis 3:6*
- Essau traded his birthright for food *Genesis 25:29-34*
- Athaliah traded the life and lineage of her grandkids by killing them so she could be heir to the throne *2Kings 11*
- Sampson traded his purity and the secret of his strength for sex and the heart of a woman Judges 16:6
- Judas traded his apostolic calling and relationship with Jesus for money *Matthew 26:27*

Guard where you are trading because you are buying into more than just entertainment or a nice product. You could be trading with an idol god who eventually is going to want more than what the trade was worth. #SHIFT

Shifting with God
One revelation we want to be aware of is that just as there is a SHIFTING of the guards taking place where many major leaders are dying and some are/have fallen, and new leaders are emerging, there is also a SHIFTING in platforms occurring. Many are tired of the same ole same ole, tired of their own sins and challenges, and tired of the sins and challenges of the body of Christ and world at large. This has resulted in a crying out to God for revival, transformation, and to be used for God's glory. Do not ask God to use you if you are not ready for a SHIFT. When God prepares to use us, he SHIFTS us and roots us in his foundation. Anything that is not of him or not beneficial to his new move is sacrificed for the new dimension he is SHIFTING us to. We may think our current platform is sufficient for God's use, but God may think otherwise.

HEALING FOR THE RICH & FAMOUS!

Chapter 38

This chapter is designed to:
- Address wounds in the rich and famous
- Help leaders minister to the rich and famous
- Provide wisdom for those who feel they are called to Hollywood, or to be famous

Please note that when I refer to the world systems in this chapter, I am referring to Hollywood, market place ministry, secular platforms, and even the world at large.

There is an increasing number of famous people falling from their platforms due to
- Sin and soul issues
- Unhealthy cycles, strongholds, and addictions
- Character flaws
- Unresolved present and past issues
- Immaturity in being able to handle fame and fortune
- Lack of organizations, effective counseling centers/ministries, and life vision plans in place to aide people in personal growth and development as they live in the spotlight
- Lack of revelation and understanding regarding the difference with operating in gifts versus purpose

I have heard many famous people who have received negative exposure due to inappropriate behavior, state that they did not ask or claim to be a role model. It is important to understand that having a public platform comes with expectations and responsibilities regardless to whether we want them are not.

The entire reason the person is famous is because of the influence and impact he or she has on people. Even though the person is talented, those that follow their career helped to promote and position them. Fans have expectations and perceptions of that person based on what he or she does even though they do not personally know the person. Moreover, people are going to expect decent morals and values from anyone that is in the spotlight. This is not about putting pressure on that person. This is simply the humanitarian way.

It is important for famous people to understand that anything they do or do not do has the potential to affect:

- Laws
- Trends
- Societal Morals and Values
- Children and Teenagers

- Generations

Because of the famous person's stature, his or her influence reaches beyond their personal life. Their influence also stretch pass their personal desire not to want responsibility for their actions beyond their gifts and talents.

The biggest challenge with Hollywood is that most people are made famous based on their gifts and talents and not based on their maturity and character. Mainly people are required to display healthy maturity and character after they have been made famous and mostly when they have fallen from their platform. And then cover ups are implemented to help the person maintain their famous status and position. There is minimal regard placed on accountability, personal healing and development, and providing the person the tools and skills they need to be a healthy and balanced. This is where famous people must recognize that the posture and dynamics of fame and fortune, of Hollywood, and of the world's system, is that it is designed to care about their gifts and talents, but not about theirs soul or their destiny. These idolatrous systems are rooted in self-exaltation, competition, and wealth. It is designed to sacrifice your gift even at the expense of forfeiting your purpose and destiny. Whether you acknowledge that this is occurring or not, your gift serves as an offering to these idolatrous platforms. The system does not care if you claim to serve another god aside from its platform. They will make money, succeed, and gain prestige off your gift, while letting you declare you serve whatever god you want, as long as you do not try to exalt your God above their platform. As long as you do not try to operate in a purpose contrary to or that ridicule and expose their idolatrous platform. The minute you cross this line, you will learn quickly that you are replaceable, your gift is dispensable, and your destiny has no platform on their altar. This is the reason many Christians who attempt to infiltrate these realms of influence either:

- Conform to the idolatrous ways
- Yield to mixture
- Covenant through toleration
- Do not succeed
- Get put out
- End up leaving

You have to know your identity in God and allow him to lead you if you desire to truly infiltrate Hollywood, and other idolatrous systems without becoming contaminated. And in order to remain clear and pure in your identity, you cannot become unequally yoked with unbelievers.

> ***2Corinthians 6:14-17*** *Be ye not unequally yoked together with unbelievers: for what fellowship hath righteousness with unrighteousness? and what communion hath light with darkness? And what concord hath Christ with Belial? or what part hath he that*

believeth with an infidel? And what agreement hath the temple of God with idols? for ye are the temple of the living God; as God hath said, I will dwell in them, and walk in them; and I will be their God, and they shall be my people. Wherefore come out from among them, and be ye separate, saith the Lord, and touch not the unclean thing; and I will receive you, And will be a Father unto you, and ye shall be my sons and daughters, saith the Lord Almighty.

The Amplified Bible Do not be unequally yoked with unbelievers [do not make mismated alliances with them or come under a different yoke with them, inconsistent with your faith]. For what partnership have right living and right standing with God with iniquity and lawlessness? Or how can light have fellowship with darkness? What harmony can there be between Christ and Belial [the devil]? Or what has a believer in common with an unbeliever? What agreement [can there be between] a temple of God and idols? For we are the temple of the living God; even as God said, I will dwell in and with and among them and will walk in and with and among them, and I will be their God, and they shall be My people. So, come out from among [unbelievers], and separate (sever) yourselves from them, says the Lord, and touch not [any] unclean thing; then I will receive you kindly and treat you with favor, And I will be a Father to you, and you shall be My sons and daughters, says the Lord Almighty.

This is a yoke.

A yoke is fastened around the neck so that you and that person, system, or thing, are bond together for the purposes of working systematically on a common task.

Bonded by a yoke.

Since you are fastened together, you really cannot go anywhere without your partner, and must be in agreement to fulfill your task or assignment. Whatever you are fastened too, may look like you, look like God, may have similar capabilities as you and God, but may not necessarily be like you or like God.

Fastened in agreement.

When we consider this spiritually, an unequal yoke is with one who may resemble you, but is not equal in beliefs with you - is not equal in lifestyle or worship with you. It may have your form or a Godly form, but not the substance or standard. Moreover, a yoke insinuates an agreement, covenant, soultie, and an intimate exchange has and is occurring. I state this because the word *fellowship* in this scripture actually means "*a sharing, participation, communion, intercourse.*" Essentially a yoking is a marriage. When you yoke, you have married that thing. The scripture is not saying we cannot be around, engage, or be acquaintances with those who are not equal in beliefs or identities as we are. But we cannot covenant, sacrifice, or spiritually receive who they are into our identities and lifestyles. We cannot mix or intertwine their values, standards, ideas, acts, workings, and habits with ours.

When you are yoked together, somebody has to lead. And usually it is the believer, because the unbeliever is not trying to submit to a pure God, especially at the expense of fame and fortune. This is the reason Paul was warning the believers of unequal yokes, because he knew the drama and challenges it would incur in trying to be in a relationship where there was a yoke of the soul and the flesh, but no true yoking in the spirit. Many believers do not want to hurt people's feelings or to end the relationship, especially those they have yoked with, so they end up yielding and being followers instead of leaders. They end up being drawn into ungodly systems rather than remaining in the kingdom of the only true and living God.

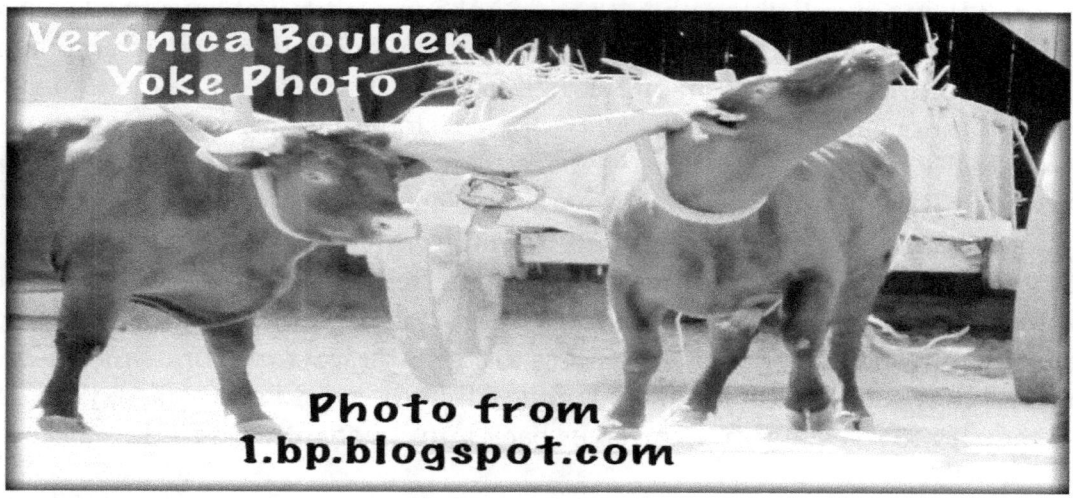

Whose leading the yoke?

The challenge with the world systems is, believers will contend God sent them to be a light and this is true, but they end up feeling obligated and pressured to conform to the world's system. Though the believers contend they are sent by God and are zealous to holding fast to their biblical truths, they are not clear in their identity and purpose, and are not mature and trusting of God enough. They also may not be fully delivered from the world, or even though they are saved, they still have a love for the world. As the world systems leads, the believer contends that the compromises they are having to make are of God's design to win the soul of the unbeliever. Yet the more they yield to compromises, the more they become yoked to the system of the unbeliever. What should have simply been an acquaintanceship becomes a covenanting yoke binding relationship. The world systems are clear that they are serving themselves and are sacrificing and doing whatever is necessary to fulfill themselves. They are also clear that this is the essence of their covenant relationship with the believer. There perception does not change just because the person says they serve Jesus. It cannot change because *"In their case the god of this world has blinded the minds of the unbelievers, to keep them from seeing the light of the gospel of the glory of Christ, who is the image of God (**2Corinthians 4:4 English Standard Bible**)."* But the believer often does not grasp this revelation until, they attempt to lead and operate operate contrary to the the world's systems. The challenge with the ungodly covenant is regardless to how much the believer contends they are serving God, by engaging in an unequal yoke, they have lived and operated in a false reality and false identity. They have claimed to be of God, but have sacrificed and worship at the table of idols – of Belial. The believer and the unbeliever have mistaken the tolerance as covenant. They each have tolerated one another for personal gain, and have even exchanged and partaken of one another's God's. As even the unbeliever will let you encourage them, share scripture with them, and pray with them. We equate them being a decent person as change or accepting of our God. But Godly transformation results in being redeemed in his likeness and his image. Both the believer and unbeliever, feel betrayed the minute the believer tries to stand for righteousness sake in a way that defy's the world's system, thus exposing the truth that though they are yoked together, they do not agree, they just have used each other. The world systems ends up vilifying the believer, defaming them, snatching them off their platforms, and putting them out of their system. The believer has to understand that they cannot be a true example of God for a system that they have compromised to, partaken of, and gained from. Even as you will try to expose or witness to those in that system, they will remind you of your sins. They will remind you of how you have been yoked to, engaged in and succeeded from the crookedness, debauchery, and perversion that you now claim is ungodly. The more the believer attempts to expose the knowledge he or she has gained from the world's systems, the more vilifying they endure. Most believers are not willing to admit their wrong for being unequally yoked and all they sacrificed for personal gain within the world systems, so they become silent as they try to re-establish themselves back into covenant with God.

Unlike the world, God cares about your gifts, your calling, and your soul. God's focus is not about what he can get from you. It is about what he can do through you.

> ***Psalms 37:23 New Living Bible*** *The LORD directs the steps of the godly. He delights in every detail of their lives.*

> ***Jeremiah 29:11 New International Bible*** *For I know the plans I have for you," declares the LORD, "plans to prosper you and not to harm you, plans to give you hope and a future.*

Another challenge with the "***I did not ask to be a role model***" mentality is that God placed gifts and callings in us at creation. We were never designed to live from a place of talents/giftings. We were created to live through the well of our calling - our destiny. So once a person becomes famous, there is more regarding their destiny that should unveil. Many however, remain stuck in operating in their gifting and never SHIFT to living their calling. This is because most do not know what their calling is or they think their talent is their calling.

> ***Proverbs 18:16*** *A man's gift maketh room for him, and bringeth him before great men.*

The gift makes room for you. That means it creates a pathway for destiny to unfold.

> ***The Message Bible*** *A gift gets attention; it buys the attention of eminent people.*

The gift gets you in the door, but destiny keeps you there.

One thing about the gift is that when someone comes along that is better you are replaceable, but with destiny you are irreplaceable. That is is the reason it is important for a person not to rely on the gift, and use it to SHIFT into destiny. A balanced Godly character is what enables a person to SHIFT and operate in destiny after their gift has made room for them. When our gifting makes room for us that is just one realm of destiny. Once you conquer one realm of destiny, you have to make room for the next and the next and the next.

> ***Proverbs* 2:20-21** *So you will walk in the way of the good and keep to the paths of the righteous. For the upright will inhabit the land, and those with integrity will remain in it.*
>
> ***Proverbs* 11:3** *The integrity of the upright shall guide them: but the perverseness of transgressors shall destroy them.*
>
> ***Proverbs* 28:18** *Whoever walks in integrity will be delivered, but he who is crooked in his ways will suddenly fall.*
>
> ***Psalms* 37:34** *Delight thyself also in the LORD; and he shall give thee the desires of thine heart.*
>
> ***Psalms* 41:11-12** *By this I know that thou favourest me, because mine enemy doth not triumph over me. And as for me, thou upholdest me in mine integrity, and settest me before thy face for ever.*
>
> ***Psalm* 101:1-2** *I will sing of mercy and judgment: unto thee, O Lord, will I sing. I will behave myself wisely in a perfect way. O when wilt thou come unto me? I will walk within my house with a perfect heart.*
>
> ***English Standard Bible*** *I will sing of steadfast love and justice; to you, O LORD, I will <u>make music</u>. I will ponder the way that is blameless. Oh when will you come to me? Will walk with integrity of heart within my house;*
>
> ***Isaiah* 26:7** *The way of the just is uprightness: thou, most upright, dost weigh the path of the just.*

A Godly character:
- Possess the character and nature of God.
- Possesses his essence and love for righteousness, holiness, and uprightness.
- Delights in God, such that even if they make a mistake, the heart brings conviction where the person quickly repents, and realigns with the Lord.
- Seeks God's mercy and judgment and instruction for his/her life and destiny.
- Is disciplined in, conducted through, and guided by God's will and plan for his or her life..
- Creates a pathway to reveal and SHIFT the person into their purpose and unfolding destiny.

When you lack character you will:
- Be focused on your gift and how you can continue to be the best.
- Be driven to be the greatest in your gift but not the greatest in your destiny.

- Have a drive to compete but not at peace to be fulfilled in your destiny, while esteeming others in their destiny and calling.
- Choose the world's ways and standards over God's ways and standard
- Contend you are living for God though your actions, but your actions will be that of the world or the devil.
- Engage in non-integral and uncharacteristic acts to get ahead, without considering or caring about the consequences or how they affect others.
- Live one life on Sunday and among your saved friends, and a worldly life among your unbelieving or compromising friends.
- Have glimpse of purpose and destiny, but not consistency. You will sway in and out of purpose and destiny due to compromising and trying to fit in rather than standing out in who God has ordained you to be.
- You will mistake fame, fortune, and big platforms like Hollywood, for destiny. There are an abundance of people who have neither of these, but are very successful in their destiny lifestyle. These can be the fruit and pathways of destiny, but are not the determination of destiny.

There are many leaders and saints who feel they are called to the secular world and/or to Hollywood. It has indeed become a fad to converse about marketplace ministry. Especially since there is such a reproach on the church. Many are trying to distance themselves by contending they are called to the market place. But anyway, I do believe God has a remnant called to infiltrate these realms of influence. Many are going or want to go, but are not able to resist succumbing to the worlds ways.

> ***John 17:16 The Amplified Bible*** *They are not of the world (worldly, belonging to the world), [just] as I am not of the world.*

When you infiltrate you have to know that though you may walk and live in the world, you are not of the world systems. You have infiltrated their systems and yes your gift is being used on their platforms, but you are not of their platforms. YOU ARE NOT YOKED TO THEIR PLATFORMS! You are on God's platform and of his kingdom system, and have been established within the world's realms as a light among darkness. LET ME SAY IT AGAIN! We where never meant to succumb to demonic worldly systems and platforms. We were called to infiltrate these realms, but not yoke to them. God has his own spiritual realm we are to govern from.

> ***Ephesians 2:4-5*** *But God, who is rich in mercy, for his great love wherewith he loved us, Even when we were dead in sins, hath quickened us together with Christ, (by grace ye are saved;) And hath raised us up together, and made us sit together in heavenly places (realms) in Christ Jesus:*

We are seated in heavenly places and therefore, we are called to be lights and standards in dark places.

> *Matthew 5:14-15 The Amplified Bible You are the light of the world. A city set on a hill cannot be hidden. Nor do men light a lamp and put it under a peck measure, but on a lampstand, and it gives light to all in the house. Let your light so shine before men that they may see your moral excellence and your praiseworthy, noble, and good deeds and recognize and honor and praise and glorify your Father Who is in heaven.*

The seat is in heaven, it is a governmental rule. It yields the ability to be an unbidden light that cannot be hidden regardless to where you are. When we infiltrate, we are to go in on our heavenly sphere of influence. We should never leave our realm and serve on the world's systems and platforms. We use these opportunities to establish our kingdom on top of the ungodly kingdom. Many leaders and saints, go into the world's systems serving on their platform, while contending they are seated in heaven. And initially they probably are, but the moment they yoke through compromises and mixture, they have SHIFTED to the world's platform.

Sidebar Exploration: One of my mentors is convinced that the seven mountain theology is unbiblical. As I consider the revelation is this chapter, I would have to say that I agree with him. The seven mountain theology, encourages saints and ministries to enter into the seven worldly arenas of business, government, education, family, arts, religion and media, and assert influence and control on those platforms. There is no way to take over a worldly mountain unless you have jurisdiction there. You can infiltrate, it but you are being unrealistic to think the devil is going to give it to you. There is not enough infiltration to take it over, and truth is God does not want it anyway. God does not want the world's seven idolatrous mountains. He wants to either destroy them or establish his kingdom in their midst so souls can be drawn out of those areas to his light and salvation. I WILL SAY IT AGAIN! God does not want any idolatrous systems. He does not want Hollywood. He does not want the demonic market place. He either wants demolish it or establish his kingdom within it, so he can draw souls to eternal life with him. Truth is, many Christians do not want to demolish Hollywood, because they want fame and fortune. They do not want to admit this truth, but it is the reality of their heart. So instead of seeking to destroy, most, are content with trying to influence it every now and again. But God is not trying to just have influence in the world, his focus is to establish his kingdom. He is not trying to share space with the devil. And until we grasp this mindset, we will keep trying to infiltrate through the world's systems, rather than using our platform to usurp and destroy demonic kingdoms and strongholds.

> ***2Corinthians 3:6*** *For though we walk in the flesh, we do not war after the flesh: (For the weapons of our warfare are not carnal, but mighty through God to the pulling down of strong holds;) Casting down imaginations, and every high thing that exalteth itself against the knowledge of God, and bringing into captivity every thought to the obedience of Christ; And having in a readiness to revenge all disobedience, when your obedience is fulfilled.*

> *Ephesians 6:12 For we wrestle not against flesh and blood, but against principalities, against powers, against the rulers of the darkness of this world, against spiritual wickedness in high places.*

Okay back to the topic. When we are lights we are not yoked to idolatry, but to God and his platform. So though we are infiltrating the enemy's camp, they cannot control or dictate our gift, legislate what we say and stand for, and cannot extinguish our calling and destiny. We are not on their plane. We do not work for them. We work for God.

> *Ephesians 5:7-11 Be not ye therefore partakers with them. For ye were sometimes darkness, but now are ye light in the Lord: walk as children of light: (For the fruit of the Spirit is in all goodness and righteousness and truth;) Proving what is acceptable unto the Lord. And have no fellowship with the unfruitful works of darkness, but rather reprove them.*

We must stop giving unbelievers a little of God, while letting them stay bound to their idol god. And then we take part of their unfruitful works, while holding on to a little of our God. We are not to share space, but to be the light that annihilates darkness. Our light should draw unbelievers out of darkness. We must draw them to our realm, so they can be lights for Jesus.

Christians need their own production companies, recording studios, awards shows, businesses, companies, organizations, etc. A secular system is going to sensor our talents and products, where we can only say and do so much. And when God establishes us in our own, we must resist compromising or patterning after the world. You must be at peace with living and operating through our heavenly system, and through our identity as God's child. Otherwise we will long for, be drawn to, and yoked with the systems of the world.

> **Romans 12:2 encourages this:** *Do not be conformed to this world, but continuously be transformed by the renewing of your minds so that you may be able to determine what God's will is – what is proper, pleasing, and perfect.*

> **The Amplified Bible** *Do not be conformed to this world (this age), [fashioned after and adapted to its external, superficial customs], but be transformed (changed) by the [entire] renewal of your mind [by its new ideals and its new attitude], so that you may prove [for yourselves] what is the good and acceptable and perfect will of God, even the thing which is good and acceptable and perfect [in His sight for you].*

<u>Conformed is *syschēmatizō* in the Greek and means:</u>
1. to fashion alike, i.e. conform to the same pattern (figuratively)
2. conform to, fashion self according to
3. to conform one's self (i.e. one's mind and character) to another's pattern, (fashion one's self according to)

God expects us to maintain our identity, our biblical standards and truths, despite being called to the secular world. The scripture lets us know that a renewing of the mind is essential to remaining grounded in the will, plan, and truth of God.

Transformation in the Greek is *metamorphoō* and means:
1. to transform (literally or figuratively, "metamorphose"): — change, transfigure, transform
2. to change into another form, to transform, to transfigure
3. Christ appearance was changed and was resplendent with divine brightness on the mount of transfiguration

When we go through a metamorphosis, we completely SHIFT into someone totally different than who we where. Therefore, our minds become like God's rather than like the worlds. Our ideas, perceptions, and processings are no longer like the world.
- We think and reason like God.
- We recognize, discern, comprehend and envision like God.
- We evolve in the image and likeness of God.
- We behave and live through the character and nature of God.

Many people infiltrate these secular realms without:
- A renewed mind.
- Godly character.
- Clarity and peace in their identity and calling.
- Clarity in who God is and is not.
- A life vision plan that entails the biblical standards they need to sustain in the destiny calling on their life.
- Having lived a mature lifestyle in God and in the biblical standards he requires for their life.

Instead of transforming the world, the world ends up fashioning them in its likeness.

If called to the secular world, it is important to be clear and pure in your motives.

- ***Proverbs 21:2*** *Every way of a man [is] right in his own eyes: but the LORD pondereth the hearts.*

- ***The Message Bible*** *We justify our actions by appearances; God examines our motives.*

- ***Matthew 6:1*** *Take heed that ye do not your alms before men, to be seen of them: otherwise ye have no reward of your Father which is in heaven.*

- ***Proverbs 30:12*** *There is a generation that are pure in their own eyes, and yet is not washed from their filthiness.*

When our motives are impure:
- We will think God is pleased with things we do that really do not possess his character or nature (**Matthew 7:23** *And then will I profess unto them, I never knew you: depart from me, ye that work iniquity*).
- We will call right wrong and wrong right (**Isaiah 50:20** *The Living Bible They say that what is right is wrong and what is wrong is right; that black is white and white is black; bitter is sweet and sweet is bitter*).
- We will think we are Godly, but be full of filth and debauchery (**Ephesians 5:10-11** *Determine which things please the Lord. Have nothing to do with the useless works that darkness produces. Instead, expose them for what they are*).
- We will be guided by what we see (**1John 2:16** *For everything in the world--the lust of the flesh, the lust of the eyes, and the pride of life--comes not from the Father but from the world*).
- Seek to please people and gain the applause of people instead of God (**Galatians 1:10** *For do I now persuade men, or God? or do I seek to please men? for if I yet pleased men, I should not be the servant of Christ*).

Many of the people God used in the Bible were famous. And many of them were rich. God is not against fame and fortune. It is indeed a heart matter for God. Do you know what is in your heart?

> **John 17:9-11 The Message Bible** *The heart is hopelessly dark and deceitful, a puzzle that no one can figure out. But I, God, search the heart and examine the mind. I get to the heart of the human. I get to the root of things. I treat them as they really are, not as they pretend to be." Like a cowbird that cheats by laying its eggs in another bird's nest Is the person who gets rich by cheating. When the eggs hatch, the deceit is exposed. What a fool he'll look like then!*

God wants us to be all he has called us to be, achieve all he has designed for us, and receive all the riches that are due unto us. He does not want us to sell our identity and our calling for it. We are fooling ourselves if we think we can cheat our destiny without consequences. We will gain what we desire, but in the end it will surely cost us our soul.

> **Mark 8:36** *For what shall it profit a man, if he shall gain the whole world, and lose his own soul?*

Our motives must be pure and our focus must be God focused. God is focused on saving souls.

God wrapped himself in flesh, just so he could restore the soul of man.

> **John 3:16** *For God so loved the world, that he gave his only begotten Son, that whosoever believeth in him should not perish, but have everlasting life. For God sent not his Son into the world to condemn the world; but that the world through him might be saved.*

God made sure we knew that it was wise to save souls
> ***Proverbs 11:30*** *The fruit of the righteous [is] a tree of life; and he that winneth souls [is] wise.*

God mandated that we preach to every person, not just those who knew him or wanted to know him. But all souls.

> ***Mark 16:15*** *And he said unto them, Go ye into all the world, and preach the gospel to every creature.*

God used Apostle Paul to show us that though we will be among different people, and we adjust to win their souls, we never compromise our light, our identity, yield to sin, or carnal ways and behaviors. The focus is not appeasing our flesh. The focus is souls.

> ***1Corinthians 9:19-23*** *For though I be free from all men, yet have I made myself servant unto all, that I might gain the more. And unto the Jews I became as a Jew, that I might gain the Jews; to them that are under the law, as under the law, that I might gain them that are under the law; To them that are without law, as without law, (being not without law to God, but under the law to Christ,) that I might gain them that are without law. To the weak became I as weak, that I might gain the weak: I am made all things to all men, that I might by all means save some. And this I do for the gospel's sake, that I might be partaker thereof with you.*

As you pursue souls, God will allow you to shine in your gifts, while unfolding your purpose. Your destiny and all he has for you, will be revealed and given to you. You will be fulfilled beyond anything the world could give.

> ***Matthew 6:33*** *But seek ye first the kingdom of God, and his righteousness; and all these things shall be added unto you.*

> ***Proverbs 10:22*** *The blessing of the LORD, it makes rich, and he adds no sorrow with it.*

Vision Plan for Healing the Rich and Famous
- What is your calling? (Not your gift but your purpose in life)
- How does your purpose glorify God?
- What is your heart for souls? Ask God to increase your zeal for souls?
- What is the specific remnant your calling is connected to? What characteristics should you look for to discern and connect with them in the earth?
- Do you believe your fame is your doing or God's going?

- If it is God's doing, what reasons do you feel God called you to be rich and famous?
- If it is your doing, do you feel it is something God wants you to continue doing? If so for what purpose? If not, then journal what he says and ask him for a plan to SHIFT you into what your true life purpose is. Implement that plan at his direction.
- Do you have any impure motives regarding fame and fortune? If so what are they? Spend time in prayer repenting and cleansing these motives out of your soul, heart and mind. Ask God to give you healthy motives that are rooted in your destiny. Practice living from this transformed place with God until it becomes a lifestyle.
- What are some challenges and pressures you experience or feel regarding being rich and famous?
- Where do you think these challenges and pressures stem from?
- What skills can you learn and work on to assist you with dealing with these challenges in a healthy manner?
- Journal the present and past unresolved issues that require healing in your life? How are these issues impacting your career? Spend time expressing your thoughts and feelings regarding each situation with God. Forgive where necessary and release all pain and hurts to him. Receive Christian counseling to process through deeply rooted issues. Healing is an essential key to maintaining balance as a famous person.
- What false obligations, false loyalties, or cultural perceptions do you have regarding your past that is hindering you from successfully operating in your present life of success? Spend time in prayer breaking soulties with these negative obligations, loyalties and misperceptions. Break vows you have made to family members that are using you for your money while making you feel guilty about your success and not being the fixer and savior of the family. You may have to relinquish some relationships to fully break these ties. Just saying!
- What Godly standards do you need to to have to sustain as a healthy role model in your career?
- What standards do you need maturing in?
- What disciplines do you need to mature in those areas?
- What personal skills do you need to be maturing in? (Communication, conflict resolution, social skills, healthy boundaries, etc.)
- Acquire a spiritual mentor or counselor that can assist you with growing and maintaining your standards. You may have to change some friends, stop going some places, work on your behaviors and character as you seek to live your standards. Do whatever you need to do where your standards become your lifestyle. Do not settle or compromise your standards for career advancement, opportunities, platforms, people, etc.
- Implement a consistent daily regimen of prayer and communion with God and studying your bible. Begin to filter your entire life through your relationship with him.

Vision Plan for those who are Called to Hollywood or the Secular World
- Is your reason or wanting to infiltrate Hollywood or the secular world God ordain or self ordained? Explain your answer
- What reason do you feel God is sending you to Hollywood or the Secular world?
- Do you have any impure or mixed motives for wanting to go to Hollywood or the Secular world? If so what are they? Spend time in prayer repenting and cleansing these motives out of your soul, heart and mind. Ask God to give you healthy motives that are rooted in your destiny. Practice living from this transformed place with God until it becomes a lifestyle.
- What is your ministry assignment in these arenas?
- What is your heart for souls? Ask God to increase your zeal for souls?
- What is the specific remnant your calling is connected to? What characteristics should you look for to discern and connect with them in the earth?
- Do you have a renewed mind? Explain your answer?
- What is your Godly vision plan for sustaining in destiny? Do you consistently walk in this plan as a lifestyle?
- What character traits you need to improve on to fortify yourself in these arena?
- What are some sin areas you need to rid you life of to ensure success in these arenas?
- Journal the present and past unresolved issues that require healing in your life? How are these issues impacting your career? Spend time expressing your thoughts and feelings regarding each situation with God. Forgive where necessary and release all pain and hurts to him. Receive Christian counseling to process through deeply rooted issues. Healing is an essential key to maintaining balance in secular arenas.
- What false obligations, false loyalties, or cultural perceptions do you have regarding your past that is hindering you from successfully operating in your present life of success? Spend time in prayer breaking soulties with these negative obligations, loyalties and misperceptions. Break vows you have made to family members that are using you for your money while making you feel guilty about your success and not being the fixer and savior of the family. You may have to relinquish some relationships to fully break these ties. Just saying!
- How do you plan to remain focused in your assignment without succumbing to the world's ways?
- Who are you accountable to? Are they able to speak truth to you and provide constructive criticism? Do they provoke you to conviction and to want to change? If not work on acquiring accountability partners that do.
- What Godly standards and skills do you need to have to sustain as a healthy role model in the secular arena?
- What standards do you need maturing in?
- What disciplines do you need to mature in those areas?
- What personal skills do you need to be maturing in? (Communication, conflict resolution, social skills, healthy boundaries, etc.)
- Acquire a spiritual mentor or counselor that can assist you with growing and maintaining your standards. You may have to change some friends, stop going

some places, work on your behaviors and character as you seek to live your standards. Do whatever you need to do where your standards become your lifestyle. Do not settle or compromise your standards for career advancement, opportunities, platforms, people, etc.
- Implement a consistent daily regimen of prayer and communion with God and studying your bible. Begin to filter your entire life through your relationship with him.

Decreeing God opens doors that no man can shut! Decreeing that as you align with him, and you become successful and stable and infiltrating your sphere of influence and living a destiny lifestyles that fulfills you, pleases God, and brings glory to him in the earth. SHIFT!

BOOK REFERENCES

- *Blueletterbible.com*

- *Olivetree.com*

- *Wikipedia*

- *Dictionary.com*

- *Biblestudytools.com*

- *Millstone photo is from http://kingsenglish.info/wp-content/uploads/2011/09/millstone-232x300.jpg*

- *Millstone drowning photo is from http://www.destinywordoftheday.com/wp-content/uploads/2013/03/millstone.jpg*

- *Grow More Food Photo http://foag.org/images/agriculture_large.jpg*

- *Veronica Boulden Yoke Photo http://1.bp.blogspot.com/_uYgE3W5yf1E/TJNdt2_4-pI/AAAAAAAAD6Y/Io3I00vg9NE/s1600/IMG_1579.JPG*

- *I heard A Funny Yoke Picture is from http://www.epicchurch.us/wp-content/uploads/2009/09/yoke.jpg*

- *Serious Faith photo is from http://www.seriousfaith.com/wp-content/uploads/2009/09/Untitled-1.jpg*

- *Cover photo by Latasha Hyatt. Connect with her via Facebook.*

Kingdom Shifters Books & Apparel
Available at Kingdomshifters.com

BOOKS FOR EVERYONE

Healing The Wounded Leader	Kingdom Shifters Decree That Thang
There Is An App For That	Kingdom Watchman Builder On the Wall
Embodiment Of A Kingdom Watchman	Dismantling Homosexuality Handbook
Releasing The Vision	Feasting In His Presence
Kingdom Heirs Decree That Thing	Let There Be Sight

Atmosphere Changers (Weaponry)

BOOKS FOR DANCERS

Dancers! Dancers! Decree That Thang

Dance & The Fivefold

Spirits That Attack Dance Ministers & Ministries

TEE SHIRTS

Kingdom Shifters Tee Shirt	Let The Fruit Speak Tee Shirt
Releasing The Vision Tee Shirt	Kingdom Perspective Tee Shirt
Stand in Position Tee Shirt	No Defense Tee Shirt
My God Rules Like A Boss Tee Shirt	Destiny Blueprint Tee Shirt

CD'S

Decree That Thing CD

Kingdom Heirs Decree That Thing CD

Teachings & Worship CD's

www.ingramcontent.com/pod-product-compliance
Lightning Source LLC
Chambersburg PA
CBHW080546230426
43663CB00015B/2730